The Practice
of Psychoanalytic
Criticism

The Practice
of Psychoanalytic
Criticism

edited by
Leonard Tennenhouse
Wayne State University

Wayne State University Press
Detroit 1976

Library of Congress Cataloging in Publication Data
Main entry under title:

The Practice of psychoanalytic criticism.

   Includes bibliographical references and index.
   1. Criticism. 2. Psychoanalysis and literature.
3. English literature—History and criticism—
Addresses, essays, lectures. 4. American literature—
History and criticism—Addresses, essays, lectures.
I. Tennenhouse, Leonard, 1942–
PN98.P75P67   801.95   76-26079
ISBN 0-8143-1562-3
ISBN 0-8143-1563-1 pbk.

Permission to Reprint

"Romances, Novels, and Psychoanalysis," by Patrick Brantlinger from *Criticism*, 17 (1975), 15–40. "More's *Utopia*: Confessional Modes," by David Bleich from *American Imago*, 28 (1971), 24–52. "The Personal History of David Copperfield," by Leonard Manheim from *American Imago*, 9 (1952), 21–43. "Kafka and Dickens: The Country Sweetheart," by Mark Spilka from *American Imago*, 16 (1959), 367–378. "David Copperfield Dreams of Drowning," by E. Pearlman from *American Imago*, 28 (1971), 391–403. "Raskolnikov's Motives: Love and Murder," by Edward Wasiolek from *American Imago*, 31 (1974), 252–269. "The Creative Surrender," by Anton Ehrenzweig from *American Imago*, 14 (1957), 193–210. "Yeats's 'Second Coming': What Rough Beast?" by Richard P. Wheeler from *American Imago*, 31 (1974), 233–251. "LeRoi Jones's *Dutchman*: Inter-racial Ritual of Sexual Violence," by Dianne Weisgram from *American Imago*, 29 (1972), 215–232. "At Play in the Garden of Ambivalence: Andrew Marvell and the Green World," by Jim Swan from *Criticism*, 17 (1975), 295–307. "Leontes' Jealousy in *The Winter's Tale*," by Murray M. Schwartz from *American Imago*, 30 (1973), 250–273. "Melville's Lost Self: *Bartleby*," by Christopher Bollas from *American Imago*, 31 (1974), 401–411. "Myth and Mystery in Steinbeck's 'The Snake': A Jungian View," by Charles E. May from *Criticism*, 15 (1973), 322–335. "Reichianism in *Henderson the Rain King*," by Eusebio L. Rodrigues from *Criticism*, 15 (1973), 212–233.

Contents

Introduction

The psychoanalytic essays in this volume were selected from *American Imago* and *Criticism*, two journals published by Wayne State University Press. Readers unfamiliar with the new directions in which psychoanalytic criticism has moved in recent years will be surprised at the range of concerns displayed here and the variety of critical approaches employed. Unlike cruder studies confined solely to the revelation of oedipal material and the hunt for sexual symbolism, the essays in this volume offer intelligent and complex examinations of literature. The practice of this more sophisticated psychoanalytic criticism has slowly become possible as scholars and critics, well trained in critical methodologies, have made a conscientious effort to study psychoanalytic theory in a systematic and disciplined manner. Psychoanalysis has, of course, continued to develop since Freud. This development has been marked by revisions in the model, by greater elaboration of the theory of drives, by detailed study of the mechanisms of defense, and by the rise of ego psychology and object-relations theory. With the growth of psychoanalysis has come not only a greater understanding of the theory but also the slow discovery of possibilities for its finer and more intelligent application to the study of literature.

Because psychoanalytic criticism is based on a model of the mind rather than on an aesthetic theory, we should really speak of psychoanalysis in relation to literature as a perspective or a mode of thought rather than as a distinct school of extrinsic literary criticism. Almost any standard critical approach can be used by a psychoanalytic critic, as the essays in this volume demonstrate. While most of the essays are psychoanalytic in perspective, they vary greatly in method. Patrick Brantlinger, for instance, is concerned with a problem of generic criticism, Leonard Manheim works with biographical criticism, Richard Wheeler and E. Pearlman use New Critical methods, and Diane Weisgram employs a kind of sociological criticism.

Working either explicitly or implicitly with psychoanalytic theory, the authors of these essays seek a satisfactory account of the meaning of an order of words. As many of the essays in this volume demonstrate, the psychoanalytic perspective is concerned with both latent and manifest meaning, and the way in which the ego manages transformations of fantasy material. One finds in these essays a recognition of the mechanisms of defense, concern with pregenital motifs, the application of object-relations theory, and, most important, a consideration of the reader and the reader's emotional as well as intellectual responses. In addition to their psychoanalytic sophistication, the authors of the essays collected here reveal a rigorous attention to intrinsic literary concerns.

For several reasons critics find the psychoanalytic perspective useful. In the first place, many studies of literature involve assumptions of a psychological nature. As readers we ask questions about plot, structure, language, character, and—whether we admit it or not—intention.[1] Implicit in the answers such questions must elicit are assumptions about the way in which the mind works. These questions concern how the text was made, how it was perceived by the author, how it may have been read by its original audience, and how it is read by a particular reader. Most formalist methodologies, however, refuse to recognize the assumptions about mental processes implicit in the acts of both creating and reading a text, because of the desire to examine the text in isolation from contexts, from author, and from reader. A pure formalism assumes that we can study literature as if it had no origins and needed no audience. It operates on the pretence that there is little or no connection between a literary work, an individual artist's creative processes, and a reader's creative reception.[2] While New Criticism has provided us with very useful tools for attending to the details of the text, it has forced several generations of readers into an untenable theoretical relationship to a text. For try as we may, we cannot pretend that literature really exists in its own self-enclosed space.[3] Literature is a product of a complex process, and it is encountered through an equally com-

---

[1] See E. D. Hirsch, Jr., *Validity in Interpretation* (New Haven and London: Yale University Press, 1967), pp. 1–23.

[2] For extensive exploration of the reader's creative reception, the psychodynamics of the reading process, and how personality affects interpretation, see Norman N. Holland, *5 Readers Reading* (New Haven: Yale University Press, 1975) and the companion volume *Poems in Persons: An Introduction to the Psychoanalysis of Literature* (New York: W. W. Norton and Co., 1973).

[3] Murray Schwartz, "Where is Literature," *College English*, 36 (March 1975), 756–765.

plex process. Quite simply, psychoanalytic theory offers the most comprehensive model and the most precise vocabulary for understanding the psychodynamics of these processes.

We have methodologies which address matters of genre, genesis, style, history of ideas, sources, and archetypes. We have as well a variety of critical methods which locate a text within the author's canon, within a literary period, and within an historical context. There is, however, a tendency on the part of some scholars using such methodologies either to imply that all decisions about the making of a work of art were conscious and deliberate or to posit that the form and content of the text were determined solely by the autonomous authority of a literary convention, an intellectual tradition, or an historical occasion. The range of aesthetic judgments and intellectual choices any artist can make is, of course, culturally limited by time and place. Moreover, it is perfectly true that there is deliberation and conscious choice in the making of a work of art. Nonetheless, underlying all that is deliberate and planned in a work of art is the psychodynamic of the artist. The history of psychoanalytic criticism reveals a constant concern with the unconscious life of the artist, but over the years the focus of this concern has shifted. The first generation of psychoanalytic critics used literary texts to verify psychoanalytic insights. Subsequently, psychoanalytic critics concentrated almost exclusively on the psychic life of the artist as revealed in the text. At the present time, however, developments in psychoanalytic theory and the increased skill of psychoanalytic critics have made possible the study of the literary work in far greater complexity—that is, as an interaction between the artist, the text, its multiple contexts, and the reader.

Obviously not everyone using psychoanalytic theory and literary criticism has achieved this level of critical sophistication. A number of psychoanalytic essays still being published tend to a reductive and mechanical simplification of a text.[4] Yet as a general statement of literary principle, we should insist that the complex interplay between the signs, the words, the elements of the text,

---

[4] A number of critics voice this objection. A polemical essay to this effect by a sympathetic critic is Frederick Crews, "Reductionism and its Discontents," *Critical Inquiry,* 1 (March 1975), 543–558.

and the way in which we perceive them are of primary importance.[5] In the hands of an unskilled critic, a psychoanalytic insight can become a sterile observation. An adept critic, however, is able to delineate the psychic processes shaping both the text and the reader's response to it, that is, the dynamic interplay within the artist and reader between the fantasy material and the strategies the ego employs in managing this material. It goes without saying that any good psychoanalytic reading should deal quite thoroughly with the formal elements of the text. By the same token, care and skill are required to recognize the historical and cultural contexts of the text and not to perceive them simply as the product of an individual pathology. Just as psychoanalysis is concerned with the interplay between latent and manifest meaning, so too the practice of psychoanalytic criticism must be careful not to destroy the significant relations between the text and its cultural and historical reality.[6] Many essays in this volume reflect an awareness of this problem and attend to it not only in order to preserve the cultural location of the text but also as a necessary aspect of the psychoanalytic reading.[7]

The use of a psychoanalytic approach to the study of genre begins with an attempt to understand the way in which each genre controls fantasy material. Within the conventions of a given genre, the reader and the author are able to enjoy the fantasy through forms of healthy regression. Patrick Brantlinger considers the difference between the opportunities for this regression offered by the romance and by the realistic novel. Concerned primarily with the characters in the two genres, Brantlinger suggests that in the realistic novel the characters strive for self-awareness and adulthood. The experience of that struggle from infantile to adult modes of perception also takes place within the reader as part of the process of reading. The realistic novel em-

---

[5] Paul Ricoeur, *Freud and Philosophy: An Essay on Interpretation*, tr. Denis Savage (New Haven and London: Yale University Press, 1970), pp. 163–177.

[6] Jim Swan, "Giving New Depth to the Surface: Psychoanalysis, Literature and Society," *Psychoanalytic Review*, 62 (1975), 5–28.

[7] Psychoanalytic theory applied to sociology, anthropology, and history offers valuable insight to the literary critic who is concerned with the cultural setting of a text. A most important book for literary critics is George Devereux, *From Anxiety to Method in the Behavioral Sciences* (The Hague and Paris: Mouton and Co., 1967). See also Fred Weinstein and Gerald M. Platt, *Psychoanalytic Sociology: An Essay on the Interpretation of Historical Data and the Phenomena of Collective Behavior* (Baltimore and London: The Johns Hopkins University Press, 1973).

ploys stern punishment for those characters who resist adult socialization. The romance, on the other hand, by its very nature openly allows a regression so extreme that the character's ego-boundaries are threatened with dissolution. Through identification the reader can enjoy such regression as well, while the feelings of guilt and anxiety are carefully controlled by the form itself.

David Bleich's examination of the genre of More's *Utopia* places that work within the context of More's private and public life. Bleich holds that the *Utopia* was More's vehicle for expressing wishes for power and authority while the form he employed allowed him to renounce those wishes and the sometimes murderous fantasies through, among other things, the guise of a humble speaker. Bleich's use of Norman Holland's very important thesis that form is a defense goes a long way toward explaining the function of form in the *Utopia*.[8] At the same time the essay is firmly rooted in a tradition of biographical and historical criticism.

Character analysis and biographical study are two areas usually associated with psychoanalysis, and Leonard Manheim, Edward Wasiolek, Murray Schwartz, and Christopher Bollas, among others in this collection, undertake a psychoanalytic interpretation of character. Of the four, Manheim most clearly links the character to the author's life and produces a work of biographical criticism from a psychoanalytic perspective in his study of *David Copperfield*. Two other essays on *David Copperfield* included in this book demonstrate the variety of concerns to which psychoanalytic theory can be applied in illuminating a text. Mark Spilka employs a source study approach to describe Kafka's debt to Dickens and to highlight their respective narrative concerns.[9] Spilka points to the childish fantasy of regressed sexuality in *David Copperfield* and the theme of economic subservience as two elements which Kafka perceived in the Dickens novel and drew upon in writing *Amerika*. Kafka's reading of Marx and Freud accounts in part for some of the conscious exploitation of thematic material which Dickens supplied unconsciously. As Spilka shows, however, the fantasies of

---

[8] *The Dynamics of Literary Response* (New York: Oxford University Press, 1968), pp. 104–33.

[9] See his book-length study *Dickens and Kafka: A Mutual Interpretation* (Bloomington: Indiana University Press, 1963).

Dickens played upon Kafka's unconscious in subtle ways that can only be understood psychoanalytically. Pearlman's treatment of the novel focuses on David's fantasies in relation to major concerns in the novel. By examining David's dream of drowning, Pearlman reveals a structural pattern within the novel reflected in the relationship between David, Steerforth, and Heep.

The attitude toward character is frequently a distinguishing feature between various critical theories. New Criticism, for instance, assumes that a character in a literary text must never be separated from the text, for a literary character is not a human being with an history, an origin or a separate life outside of the text. Aristotelian criticism assumes a character is that which reveals moral purpose (*Poetics* VI. 17). As a moral agent which makes choices, it encounters other moral forces in the process of working out an action.[10] Structuralism, by contrast, argues that the very concept of character is a myth. At best character is a space in which forces meet, and we may recognize that space as a construct of traits.[11] And yet, while on one level we might perceive the character in terms of an agent, an order of words, a collection of traits, an idea, or as a sign, on another level as readers we *experience* characters as human beings. Norman Holland has suggested that our experience is due to the process of identification.[12] In essence we create characters based on what we see in the text and what we know from our public and private experiences. Although a character is more than simply an autobiographical projection, and is a highly wrought formal element of the literary text, nonetheless a character takes on for the author, as for the reader, an independent personality.[13] This is to say simply that a character is always a product of life and art, the creation of an artist and the recreation of a reader, and therefore we should study character both formally and psychoanalytically.

[10] See, for example, Francis Fergusson, *Idea of a Theater* (Garden City, N.J.: Doubleday, 1949).
[11] Jonathan Culler, *Structuralist Poetics: Structuralism, Linguistics, and the Study of Literature* (Ithaca, N.Y.: Cornell University Press, 1975), pp. 230–238.
[12] *The Dynamics of Literary Response*, pp. 262–289. In *5 Readers Reading*, Holland writes, "Identification as such . . . takes place not because of external likenesses, but because of an internal matching of adaptation and defense within a total dynamic of response," p. 205.
[13] W.W. Meissner, "Some Notes on the Psychology of the Literary Character: A Psychoanalytic Perspective," *Seminars in Psychiatry*, 5 (1973), 261–274.

A sophisticated psychoanalytic approach cannot afford to study character in isolation. It is important therefore to understand the nature of the external world which the character encounters and the kinds of demands that the external world makes as the character struggles to deal with the range of his or her needs. Edward Wasiolek in his study of Raskolnikov demonstrates the virtues of such careful attention to the drives of the character in the context of his world.[14] In a slightly different vein and taking into account his own responses, Murray Schwartz seeks to uncover the unconscious strategies of Leontes' jealousy. Although the jealousy breaks out suddenly, there is a complex relationship of motives that lie behind Leontes' paranoia. Schwartz draws on a different area of psychoanalytic theory than does Wasiolek and shows that Leontes' crisis is to be understood at the deepest level of oral anxieties where the infant, " . . . craves love as nourishment and dreads maternal malevolence." We can thus understand the logic of that extreme irrationality while seeing its coherence in terms of the structure and language of the play.[15] Schwartz and Wasiolek, like other authors in this volume, deal with a wide variety of formal elements in their texts. The formal elements point in turn to the kinds of fantasies that are defended in *The Winter's Tale* and *Crime and Punishment* and the variety of mechanisms and strategies that manage the fantasies. It is precisely the desire and ability to account for and integrate into a complex reading of the text those illogical, uncomfortable and "messy" details that would ordinarily be ignored or glossed over by other critics that lends particular value to sophisticated psychoanalytic interpretations.

Richard Wheeler and Dianne Weisgram are two good cases in point. They begin with their own responses to texts. In the case of Jones's *Dutchman,* it is not enough merely to attribute the feelings generated by that play to its political and social themes. Dianne Weisgram attends to these themes, but she locates the particularity of their power in Jones's dramatic language that, in its imagery, reveals deeply buried conflicts of oral loss, boundary dissolu-

[14] Edward Wasiolek's comments on psychoanalytic criticism can be found in "The Future of Psychoanalytic Criticism," *The Frontiers of Literary Criticism,* ed. David H. Malone (Los Angeles: Hennessey and Ingalls, 1974), pp. 149–168.
[15] For the extension of Schwartz's comments see his *"The Winter's Tale:* Loss and Transformation," *American Imago,* 32 (1975), 145–199.

tion, and phallic violence. Jones's achievement rests on his ability
to summon up these images in the service of his art while consciously concentrating on the social and political elements of the
drama. By the same token, Richard Wheeler discovers that the
sense of power both he and many other readers have experienced
in Yeats's "Second Coming" builds upon the repressed experience
of infantile helplessness countered by a fantasy of omnipotent and
destructive rage. Like Dianne Weisgram, Wheeler is careful to
include those elements of secondary process thinking we all note
and discuss readily. To them he adds the private uses and psychological strategies of Yeat's own unconscious which manage the
more public material of history, politics, and sociology in the service of the poet's art.

The way in which the creative process operates is the subject
of the essay by Anton Ehrenzweig. This essay is one of several
which preceded Ehrenzweig's major study *The Hidden Order of
Art.*[16] In his work, Ehrenzweig draws on the object-relations theory of the British analysts. He is less concerned with id and superego conflicts, instinctual drives, or the question of meaning as he
turns to the role of the ego in the creation and perception of art.
The unconscious ego, he says, scans a field with the same kind of
undifferentiated perception that an infant uses in perceiving its
environment. The oceanic feeling that accompanies this unconscious scanning is like that of the nursing infant, and the artist's
relation to the work of art—in this case to a painting—as it takes
shape is like an infant's relation to a mother. Most people have
what Ehrenzweig calls a horizontal split between the layers of the
ego. In the artist, however, there is a vertical split which allows the
ego to swing from the perceptions of reality that the mature ego
provides to the most primitive or infantile perceptions of a world
undifferentiated in itself and from the ego. The ability of the
artist to relax a rigid perception of reality, with its demand for an
organized surface Gestalt, and to allow an ego rhythm which
moves between the ego's unconscious and conscious organizing
power, brings about a dissolution of ego boundaries. At the lowest

---

[16] *The Hidden Order of Art: A Study in the Psychology of Artistic Imagination*
(Berkeley and Los Angeles: University of California Press, 1971). A valuable re-
view of Ehrenzweig's publications is Paul Kuntz, "The Hidden Order of Anton
Ehrenzweig," *Journal of Aesthetics and Art Criticism,* 27 (1969), 349–360.

level of unconscious perception the momentary experience of self-destruction (hence the dying god associations that some artists speak of as accompanying the creative process) brings with it the feeling of omnipotence in which the ego of the artist, like that of the infant, literally creates an entire universe. Although the process Ehrenzweig outlines is more complicated in the creation of literature than in painting because the medium is verbal and patterns are not spatial, the significance of his contribution cannot be stressed too heavily. Not only does he offer an explanation for the importance of the ego in the creative process, but he also suggests its importance in the experiencing process of the audience. A creative participation by readers in a work of literature would require that they relax their perceptions to a certain degree in order to tolerate primitive ego experiences by which they exercise their own abilities for unconscious scanning. A good reader thus does not look prematurely for an organizing principle in the surface Gestalt based, for instance, on categories of imagery. Such a reader thus avoids one of the worst tendencies of New Criticism.

The articles by Jim Swan and Christopher Bollas are also clearly indebted to object-relations theory. Swan applies D. W. Winnicott's concept of the mirror relationship between mother and infant to a well studied problem in Marvell criticism. Swan's subtle reading of the crucial stanzas of "The Garden" depends on his contextualization of the poem within a tradition of readings, his placing it in relation to other poems by Marvell, and his familiarity with the conventions of the genre. The psychoanalytic concepts Swan draws on, like those of Ehrenzweig, are a model for the communication system established between the artist and the work of art, for a painting or a text function in terms of what Winnicott calls a transitional object. A transitional object for an infant may be a toy, a blanket, the mother, or the infant's own body, which the infant uses to make the transition from being merged with the mother to experiencing the mother as something outside of and separate from the infant. As Winnicott says, "Transitional objects and transitional phenomena belong to the realm of illusion which is at the basis of initiation of experience." Winnicott stresses the importance of this illusion: "This intermediate area of experience, unchallenged in respect of its belonging to inner or external reality, constitutes the greater part of the infant's experience, and throughout life is retained in the intense experiencing that belongs to the arts and to religion and to imaginative living, and to creative scientific work."[17]

The space between infant and mother is the matrix wherein the differentiation between self and other, subject and object, infant and mother takes place. This is the primary context in which the individual receives culture, where cultural experiences first take place, and where as well identity first takes shape for the individual. It is here where the earliest levels of ego formations and the most serious psychotic disorders have their origins. In his essay on Bartleby, Christopher Bollas illustrates several concerns of contemporary psychoanalytic theory which deal with the character faults that form in this space. Bollas is thus able to offer an explanation of the complex relationship between Bartleby and the narrator while at the same time he places *Bartleby* psychoanalytically within the context of Melville's fiction.

The last two essays in this collection provide an illustration of the use of a different kind of model and offer an example of psychological theory used as ideational content. Charles May's Jungian reading of Steinbeck's "The Snake" points to the possibilities of a Jungian approach. It suggests as well why a psychoanalytic reading that draws on early Freud and seeks out oedipal patterns is unsuccessful with this story. May's use of a Jungian myth system serves to turn our attention to the pregenital fears and aggressive drives that run through the story, and invites in turn the possibility of a psychoanalytic reading that deals with pregenital elements in the story. The essay on *Henderson the Rain King* provides a useful lesson for a critic who would undertake a psychoanalytic reading of a modern text. Eusebio Rodrigues discusses Bellow's debt in *Henderson* to Wilhelm Reich's theories. The appearance in literature of concepts and conventions drawn from the work of Freud or Jung or Adler or Reich indicates the extent to which psychological writings have become part of the intellectual context for modern literature. Moreover, it means that a critic must employ as much skill in recognizing these ideas when used in a literary text as would be required for recognizing any other body of ideas. The use of psychology by modern authors, and it is difficult

[17] D.W. Winnicott, *Playing and Reality* (New York: Basic Books, 1971), p. 14.

to find an author unaffected by modern psychological theory, should not mislead a critic into thinking that the author's exploitation of this material is by itself a code to the unconscious springs of the literary work. The text must be seen in its cultural and historical contexts, and its interpretation must deal with the full interplay between conscious and unconscious elements.

Psychoanalytic criticism, like psychoanalysis itself, accepts the principle of multiple function.[18] Simply put, this principle states that many different needs are accommodated by the mediation of the ego. These needs, which come from the sexual and aggressive drives, the unconscious prohibitions against them, the repetition of certain behavior, and the demands of external reality, are constantly satisfied even as they are being tested by the agency of the ego. Since the ego satisfies these different needs simultaneously, the choices the ego makes are "overdetermined." If dreams and conscious behavior are overdetermined, art is even more so. The forces at work which affect the choices an artist makes are complex and many. The pattern of the choices is what we recognize in the style or "character" of a work or an author. At the same time, depending on the reader's style or character, which affects the aspects of the text emphasized and the focus of the reader's attention, many different interpretations of a given work are possible. There is no pretending that at any time we have the whole text, just as Freud admitted the impossibility of understanding the whole dream. The danger for literary criticism, as for psychoanalysis, is the lure of a simplistic and mechanistic interpretation. The essays in this volume amply demonstrate that psychoanalytic criticism, still in its formative stages, requires, like any good literary criticism and like psychoanalysis at its very best, artful application.

Leonard Tennenhouse

[18] Robert Waelder, "The Principle of Multiple Function," *Psychoanalytic Quarterly*, 5 (1936), 45–62.

Romances, Novels, and Psychoanalysis

Patrick Brantlinger

The old distinction between "novels" and "romances" is not merely, as Henry James contended in "The Art of Fiction," either nonexistent or else a matter of good versus sloppy technique. Rather, the distinction between them is rooted in two opposed functions of literature, and ultimately in two opposed functions of fantasy. The fact that James himself often reverted to this distinction in his later criticism (for instance, in the preface to *The American*) is a partial proof of its authenticity. "Romance" implies wish-fulfillment and is bound up with dreams and illusions. The chivalric romances which Cervantes attacks are full of "enchantments, knightly encounters, battles, challenges, wounds, with tales of love and its torments, and all sorts of impossible things" which turn Don Quixote's head. And later romances—those of Anne Radcliffe and of Hawthorne, for example—combine the "real" with the "marvelous" in "a neutral territory," like the moonlit parlor where Hawthorne conceived *The Scarlet Letter,* "somewhere between the real world and fairy-land, where the Actual and the Imaginary may meet, and each imbue itself with the nature of the other."

This "neutral territory" is a region in which the symbols of fiction approximate the symbols of dreams. If we add that dreams are often unpleasant, then F.L. Lucas's definition of romanticism as "the Sleeping Beauty dreaming of the Fairy Prince" applies to the whole range of romantic fiction. Many of Poe's tales—"The Fall of the House of Usher" and "Ligeia," for instance—may be viewed either as nightmares or as the products of delirium. So, too, *Wuthering Heights* begins with Lockwood's bad dreams, and James Hogg's great *Confessions of a Justified Sinner* is satire disguised as a nightmare of lunacy and demonic possession. The association of dreams with the romance form is even more apparent in the most primitive and naive examples, as *Dracula* and its folklore antecedents show. And the locus of the most thrilling episodes at the Castle of Udolpho is the heroine's bedroom, for several not wholly mysterious reasons.[1]

"Realism" suggests the opposite of the ideas of wish-fulfillment, illusion, and dreams. The best and most characteristic works of literary realism from *Don Quixote* down to the present have taken disillusionment as a theme. On a rudimentary level, realism functions like psychoanalysis, unmasking the infantile and irrational bases of illusion in its characters. In its ethical bearings, a novel like *Middlemarch* is often quite close to the values expressed in Freud's work. Of course I do not mean that *The Interpretation of Dreams* owes something to *Middlemarch*, or for that matter to the psychologies of George Lewes and Herbert Spencer. But Eliot, Lewes, Spencer, and Freud all shared a scientific, late nineteenth-century worldview, and their attitudes and conclusions about human nature are often comparable. George Eliot is not only like Lydgate but also like Freud in her desire "to pierce the obscurity of those minute processes which prepare human misery and joy, those invisible thoroughfares which are the first lurking-places of anguish, mania, and crime, that delicate poise and transition which determine the growth of happy or unhappy consciousness." She is like Freud in her sense of character as "a process and an unfolding," in her acute perception of the blindness of most of us to the real forces which shape our lives, and in her awareness of the distortions of egoistic illusions. She is like him in her rejection of theism as an illusion. Furthermore, her attitude towards the imagination is similar to Freud's idea of literature and dreams as expressions of unacknowledged wishful thinking. As

[1] I have focused upon nineteenth-century romances because that is what I know best, but regressive and dream-like qualities are clearly present in medieval and Renaissance romances as well, as *Don Quixote* and Prospero show. And it is also easy to find modern equivalents of nineteenth-century romances. Fictions based on dreams, such as *Finnegan's Wake* and Kafka's *The Trial*, are sometimes too ironic or too nihilistic to be romances, but writers like Shirley Jackson and Faulkner make use of romance conventions. See Richard Chase, *The American Novel and Its Tradition* (New York: Doubleday, 1957), especially on Faulkner. A great comic novel which employs romance conventions for satiric purposes is Mikhail Bulgakov's *The Master and Margarita*. And there are modern Gothic thrillers and occult fantasies that carry on the romance tradition much as it was practiced by Mrs. Radcliffe and LeFanu—works like Tryon's *The Other*, Levin's *Rosemary's Baby*, and Blatty's *The Exorcist*.

The quotation from F.L. Lucas is from *The Decline and Fall of the Romantic Ideal* (Cambridge: Cambridge University Press, 1963), p. 42.

I am grateful to Lee Sterrenburg of Indiana University for his help and advice.

she says in reference to Peter Featherstone, "We are all of us imaginative in some form or other, for images are the brood of desire. . . . " And a central theme throughout *Middlemarch* is the difficult time we all have in freeing ourselves from the trammels of infancy, in achieving moral adulthood: "We are all of us born in moral stupidity, taking the world as an udder to feed our supreme selves. . . . " All these attitudes are conscious themes in *Middlemarch,* as they are in one form or another in most of the greatest realistic fiction. Realistic novels are shaped by struggles for rational self-awareness in ways impossible in dreams, even though these struggles may be weak or may fail; but romances reject the rational and tend to imitate dreams.[2]

This does not mean, however, that literary realism contains no elements of wish fulfillment or of uncontrolled fantasy. All art is analogous to magic—illusory attempts to control or to order reality through the manipulation of symbols. Insofar as the literary realist makes the greatest claim to a serious, rational dissection of reality, he may in fact be the most irrational sort of artist because the most deluded. As Richard Sterba writes:

> The imitation of reality in itself represents a primitive kind of mastery of reality which is made possible by an exchange of psychic for actual reality. Frazer has called this, "mistaking an ideal connection for a real one," and the technique of such mastery, magic. The foundation of this magical technique resides in the pleasure principle; it originates in a very early phase of psychic development at which the individual looks upon himself as omnipotent because wishes are experienced at this period as if their fulfillment in reality were achieved by the mere act of wishing. We call this the stage of "omnipotence of thought."[3]

It may be that the objectivity claimed by the great realists is related to the stage of the "omnipotence of thought," an illusion of the mastery of reality based on its verbal reproduction. In any case, in *Fiction and the Unconscious,* Simon Lesser points out that "the desire to conciliate a sensed fear of fantasy . . . is one of the

---

[2] The quotations from George Eliot are from *Middlemarch* (Boston: Houghton Mifflin [Riverside Edition], 1957), pp. 122, 111, 237, and 156.

[3] Richard Sterba, "The Problem of Art in Freud's Writings," *Psychoanalytic Quarterly,* IX (1940), 265.

perennial motives for 'realism,'" and also that "the theme of failure may conceal wishful elements and perverse satisfactions."[4]

A problem arises here which psychological approaches to literature have not yet resolved. *Middlemarch* may seem to express attitudes and values close to Freud's, but the more it does so the more George Eliot may be failing to distinguish between fantasy and reality. It is possible to see her realism as an elaborate defense mechanism which, the more insistent and complex it becomes, the further it removes her from the primary sources and significance of her act. Psychoanalytic criticism tends to identify the genesis of works of art with their significance; the more obscure and distant the genesis seems—the more elaborate the defense mechanisms which shape the art work—the further its surface structure is from the "truth." Romantic fiction, on the other hand, by its willing expression of wish fulfillments and by its likeness to dreams, seems actually to come closer to capturing psychological truth than does realism. According to this logic, *The Mysteries of Udolpho* may tell us more about our hidden psychic lives than *Northanger Abbey*. As Lionel Stevenson says, "In departing from realism Mrs. Radcliffe stumbled upon the whole realm of the unconscious,"[5] although her discovery was no discovery at all because it was so entirely accidental. But in the hands of more conscious and controlled writers—Hawthorne, Melville, Poe, James Hogg, the Brontës—the romance form may prove to be epistemologically superior to the novel form. Such a result would contradict the long tradition in realism in which novelists have belittled the romance form: Don Quixote, Catherine Morland, Emma Bovary, and Tom Sawyer are just a few of the characters in realistic fiction whose heads have been stuffed with romantic twaddle. In any case, in an essay on Robert Louis Stevenson, Mark Kanzer claims a great measure of both analytic and therapeutic value for his tales and poems:

There are few instances in literature in which an author shows so much sensitivity to and awareness of the unconsci-

[4] Simon O. Lesser, *Fiction and the Unconscious* (Boston: Beacon Press, 1957), pp. 7 and 99. See also Hanns Sachs, *The Creative Unconscious* (Cambridge, Mass.: Sci-Art Publishers, 1942), p. 40: "The most effective method of disarming the resistance against the introduction of the repressed contents is the downright opposite of the happy end."

[5] Lionel Stevenson, *The English Novel: A Panorama* (Boston: Houghton Mifflin, 1960), p. 165.

ous processes underlying his creative activities, as with
Stevenson. . . . It is not too much to say that the tales of this
writer were, in essence, a self-analysis; and . . . he evolved a
theory about the unconsciously creative processes within the
mind that shows unmistakable parallels to Freud's own later
discoveries.[6]

This is to claim for "Dr Jekyll and Mr. Hyde" and *Kidnapped* a far
greater degree of insight than most literary critics have claimed
for them. But Kanzer could not have made a similar claim for any
writer of realistic fiction, because realism involves the control of
and, apparently, the repression and distortion of unconscious impulses.

It is well known that psychoanalysis has encouraged the fantastic more than the realistic in art and literature. Although it is
possible to see the moral realism of George Eliot as in several ways
comparable to psychoanalysis, Freud himself tended to view all art
as daydream and to reject its claims to cognitive seriousness. As
Phillip Rieff puts it,

Because the therapist appraises action by its adequacy to
reality, we might expect some transfer to art of criteria, such
as fidelity of reproduction and adherence to probability, that
would link Freudian norms to the literary norms of realism.
Actually, Freud's writings bear anti-realistic implications.
The clinical naturalism with which he treated art—separat-
ing it sharply from reality—saved him from realism. Art was
judged not by the reality principle but by the pleasure principle, as conation rather than recognition.[7]

Rieff goes on to point out that rather than the realistic criteria of
"verisimilitude and consistency, Freud erected the aesthetic category of complication." Here psychoanalysis would seem to join
with the New Criticism in praise of ambiguity.

From a psychoanalytic viewpoint, the fantastic, the grotesque,
the irrational are closer to the true sources of art than is realism,

[6] Mark Kanzer, "The Self-Analytic Literature of Robert Louis Stevenson," in
Psychoanalysis and Culture, ed. George Wilbur and Warner Muensterberger (New
York: International Universities Press, 1951), p. 426.
[7] Philip Rieff, *Freud: The Mind of the Moralist* (New York: Anchor Books,
1961), pp. 154–155.

and are therefore at the very least interesting if not actually "better." According to Freud, all forms of literature are analogous to dreams, which are disguises of the truth rather than expressions of it. In his early essay "On the Relation of the Poet to Daydreaming" (1908), Freud argues that literary productions, like dreams, are based upon patterns of wish fulfillment, and that "His Majesty the Ego" is "the hero of all daydreams and all novels." Freud says "*all* novels," even though he excludes from his examination "those writers who are most highly esteemed by critics," including poets, which limits the scope and coherence of his argument.[8] Also, his later elaborations of the reality principle and of the death instinct altered his views of art in several ways, although after these qualifications it remains true that, for Freud, all dreams and all art works are substitute gratifications. From a Freudian viewpoint, neither the novel form nor the romance form is to be trusted to mean what it says, and therefore it is just as well if the writer makes no claim to cognitive seriousness.

On the other hand, from a Jungian viewpoint, while all forms of literature are still analogous to dreams, both literature and dreams are seen more as expressions of truth than as disguises of it. "Truth to tell," says Jung, "I have a very high opinion of fantasy."[9] In his famous chapter on "Psychology and Literature," Jung distinguishes between "the psychological and the visionary modes of artistic creation," categories which are directly related to those of novel and romance. According to Jung, there is a sort of art which deals with the conscious surface of experience, and there is a different sort of art which deals with "primordial experience," or with the archetypes of the collective unconscious. It is the latter which fascinates Jung more; we might expect him to affirm, with Mark Kanzer, the type of literature which imitates dreams, rather than the type which deflates them. But while Jung claims a large measure of cognitive value for "the visionary mode of artistic expression," he runs afoul of a contradiction by asserting that psychological novels are uninteresting to psychologists not because they are distant from the truth, but because the novelists have already performed the necessary work of analysis.

[8] Sigmund Freud, *On Creativity and the Unconscious,* ed. Benjamin Nelson (New York: Harper Torchbooks, 1958), pp. 44–54.

[9] C. G. Jung, *Modern Man in Search of a Soul* (New York: Harvest Books, n. d.), p. 66.

... the so-called "psychological novel" is by no means as rewarding for the psychologist as the literary-minded suppose. Considered as a whole, such a novel explains itself. It has done its own work of psychological interpretation, and the psychologist can at most criticize or enlarge upon this.[10]

So Jung postulates a romanticism which soars apocalyptically through the depths and heights of the soul at the same time that he postulates a realism which also has access to psychic truth and which "explains itself." He claims too much for all forms of literature, while Freud claims perhaps too little.

Jung believes that *both* the realist and the romancer have easy access to the unconscious, a position which, as Edward Glover has argued, blurs the distinction between the unconscious and the conscious so far as to render it meaningless. "It will be seen that once cleared of the transcendental spinach with which they are coated, Jung's theories contribute nothing to the understanding of art."[11] From a Freudian perspective, on the other hand, neither type of artist has a direct access to the unconscious, although it is part of the traditions of both romanticists and realists to claim that they do. Nevertheless, all art works express the unconscious— unconsciously. The romantic-surrealistic idea that the artist can *deliberately* express the unconscious does not create an art which bridges the gap between manifest and latent contents. From a Freudian perspective, that gap is unbridgeable; it is impossible for an art work to express the unconscious without mediation by secondary mental processes. The art work "must not only represent the kernel phantasies giving rise to conflict in the mind of the artist, but also the expiation or negation of these same phantasies."[12]

An art which "liberates the unconscious" and an art which is "self-analyzing" (Jung's visionary and psychological types) are neither of them real possibilities, because the unconscious remains inaccessible. The Freudian discovery of the unconscious would

[10] *Ibid.*, pp. 152–172.
[11] Edward Glover, *Freud or Jung* (London: George Allen and Unwin, 1950), p. 173.
[12] *Ibid.*, p. 184.

seem thus to have led to countless false alarms by artists bent on expressing it: all they are really capable of expressing are dream-work structures at a remove from their unconscious roots. (Dreams themselves, of course, are not unconscious, although they express, as in a glass darkly, unconscious impulses.) There-fore, neither the romance form nor the novel form may be said to express or to analyze the unconscious better than the other, because both of them express it automatically and unwittingly. What is possible to say is that the romance form always shadows forth a regressive journey inward and backward, through child-like states of mind, threatening the dissolution of the adult ego, while the novel form resists and punishes such dissolution, and also invokes higher principles of socialization and adult moral growth. To say this, moreover, is to use psychoanalysis to charac-terize the psychologizing tendencies in art works, and this is a very different procedure from attempting to arrive at the uncon-scious sources of individual art works. The first is an esthetic mode of criticism; the second is biographical, and involves viewing the art work as a symptom or as a confession in a case-history of the artist.

II

To describe the romance form as regressive is neither to deny to it a cognitive function nor to claim that that function lies in the establishment of direct access to the unconscious. It is rather to suggest that romances shadow forth and, at their best, examine "primordial" or childlike mental processes. Joseph Addison un-derstood the childlike quality of romances when he wrote that they "raise a pleasing kind of Horrour in the Mind of the Reader. . . . They bring up into our Memory the Stories we have heard in our Childhood, and favour those secret Terrors and Apprehen-sions to which the Mind of Man is naturally subject."[13]

Wuthering Heights, in these terms, is clearly a romance: it gains much of its strength from the primitive, infantile quality of

[13] Joseph Addison, *Spectator Papers,* No. 419.

the rebellions which it depicts.[14] Catherine and Heathcliff are not only portrayed as rebellious children at the start of Nelly Dean's story, they behave in exactly the same way as adults, and it is largely this fact which makes them so fascinating: they do what we as adults cannot do—they indulge their unrepressed, infantile desires through rebellious acts which are essentially denials of the rational, the socialized, and the mature. *Wuthering Heights* has the quality of a temper tantrum rendered into poetry, and the parental figures in it (Nelly Dean, Joseph, the elder Earnshaws, Hindley, and Edgar Linton) are unable to cope with such rage. But this is not to deny the justice of the rebellions which *Wuthering Heights* depicts. The story is a powerful expression of the fact that the "mature" and the "socialized" can also be repressive and life-denying, in which case the unleashing of infantile energies becomes the necessary path to freedom—the false strictures of Urizen call forth the wrath of Orc. In any case, from the very outset of *Wuthering Heights,* with Lockwood's nightmare of the *infant* ghost of Catherine wailing to be rescued from the storm, we are in the realm of the regressive motifs of dreams.

> As it spoke, I discerned, obscurely, a child's face looking through the window—Terror made me cruel; and, finding it useless to attempt shaking the creature off, I pulled its wrist on to the broken pane, and rubbed it to and fro till the blood ran down and soaked the bed-clothes. . . .

And after Lockwood has freed himself from this child-ghost, he still hears it moaning in the snowstorm outside: "It's twenty years . . . twenty years, I've been a waif for twenty years!" Later we understand that Catherine dies a grown woman; there seems to be no logical explanation for the childishness of her ghost, and yet nothing could be more appropriate.

The regressive nature of *Wuthering Heights* might be demonstrated in a number of ways, perhaps most obviously through a recollection of its biographical genesis.

[14] See Dorthy van Ghent, *The English Novel: Form and Function* (New York: Harper Torchbooks, 1961), pp. 158–159; Ellen Moers on "Female Gothic" in *New York Review of Books* (March 24, 1974), 24–28, and (April 4, 1974), 35–39; and Lowry Nelson, Jr. "Night Thoughts on the Gothic Novel," in *Pastoral and Romance: Modern Essays in Criticism,* ed. Eleanor Lincoln (Englewood Cliffs, New Jersey: Prentice Hall, 1961), pp. 259–267.

The details of this genesis are too well known to repeat; all we need to recall here is that the romances of the Brontës grew out of the childhood fantasy worlds of Angria and Gondal. The psychic energies of chldhood were carried over in a very direct manner into the fantasies of womanhood, and as a result what is most powerful about *Wuthering Heights* and *Jane Eyre* tends also to be what is most primitive and infantile. The opening paragraphs of *Jane Eyre* offer a striking example of the link between romantic fiction and childhood daydreaming. Outcast from the circle of Mrs. Reed and her "contented, happy little children," Jane nourishes her discontent and self-pity by a retreat into fantasy:

> A small breakfast-room adjoined the drawing-room. I slipped in there. It contained a bookcase: I soon possessed myself of a volume, taking care that it should be one stored with pictures. I mounted into the window-seat: gathering up my feet, I sat cross-legged like a Turk; and, having drawn the red moreen curtain nearly close, I was shrined in double retirement. . . .

Her chosen book, Bewick's *History of British Birds,* leads her into dreams of storm-beaten, arctic landscapes: "Of these death-white realms I formed an idea of my own: shadowy, like all the half-comprehended notions that float dim through children's brains, but strangely impressive." So resentment of parental authority and a retreat into childhood daydreams stand at the threshold of Charlotte Brontë's tale of loneliness, passionate love, and rebellion against social conventions.

Similarly, the stories which Stevenson wrote for adults are in most respects not very different from those which he wrote for children. As Leslie Stephen says, "Stevenson's boyishness was not only conspicuous, but was the very mainspring of his best work. That quality cannot be shown in a mathematical dissertation or a historical narrative, but it is invaluable for a writer of romances."[15] The narrators of *Treasure Island* and *Kidnapped* are boys, as opposed to the adult narrators, MacKellar and Francis Burke, of *The Master of Ballantrae,* but otherwise the three stories share many traits. Thus, all three deal with piracy, and in all three

[15] Leslie Stephen, "Introduction" to *The Works of Robert Louis Stevenson* (New York: [The Vailima Edition] P.F. Collier and Son, 1912), vol. I, p. iii.

it is seen as a distinctly *childish* form of outlawry. In *The Master of Ballantrae*, the chief pirate, Teach, "was a horrible villain," fearful not so much for his murderousness as for another reason: "There was something about him like a wicked child or a half-witted person, that daunted me beyond expression." And throughout *The Master of Ballantrae*, a tale of sibling rivalry carried over into adulthood, villainy is associated with backsliding into childish modes of behavior. The good brother Henry is driven to a state of drunken degeneracy by the evil brother, "the Master." In this state, Henry acquires an eerie habit of singing in a kind of "high, carolling utterance, which was truly neither speech nor song. Something not unlike is to be heard upon the lips of children, ere they learn shame. . . . "

In his essays, Stevenson rejects realism as a literary mode. He thinks of literature, whether written for children or for grown-ups, as an extension of the daydreaming process:

> . . . The great creative writer shows us the realization and the apotheosis of the day-dreams of common men. His stories may be nourished with the realities of life, but their true mark is to satisfy the nameless longings for the reader, and to obey the ideal laws of the day-dream.

And he will have nothing to do with the notion of literature as a means for the difficult winning of rational consciousness. "It is one thing to remark and to dissect, with the most cutting logic, the complications of life, and of the human spirit; it is quite another to give them body and blood in the story of Ajax or Hamlet."[16] In defining literature as "the apotheosis of the day-dreams of common men," Stevenson does indeed come close to Freud's views, as Mark Kanzer claims he does. The main difference between them is that Stevenson sees nothing wrong with literary day-dreaming— he is more tolerant of the irrational than is Freud.

In *The Progress of Romance*, Clara Reeve said that "The Romance in lofty and elevated language, describes what never happened nor is likely to happen."[17] One cannot apply the terms

---

[16] Robert Louis Stevenson, "A Gossip on Romance," *Works*, vol. V, pp. 127–128.
[17] Clara Reeve quoted by Miriam Allott, *Novelists on the Novel* (New York: Columbia University Press, 1966), p. 47.

"lofty and elevated" to the style of *The Old English Baron* or of *The Monk* any more than to *Barchester Towers*. But Clara Reeve meant that the style of romances is based on the sublime, and terms like "vague, obscure, mysterious, and redundant" might have served as well as "lofty and elevated." Now the sublime, according to its eighteenth-century formulators like Burke, is the attribute of any landscape or art work which arouses in the mind of the beholder the emotion of "terror," or religious awe. As Burke puts it: "Indeed, terror is in all cases whatsoever . . . the ruling principle of the sublime." Samuel Monk summarizes Burke's categorization of sublime ideas:

> They are obscurity, where darkness and uncertainty arouse dread and terror . . . ; power, where the mind is impelled to fear because of superior force . . . ; privations, such as darkness, vacuity, and silence, which are great because they are terrible . . . ; vastness, whether in length, height, or depth, the last being the most powerful source of the sublime . . . ; infinity . . . ; difficulty—that is, any object that seems to owe its existence to a vast expenditure of labor and effort . . . ; and magnificence. . . . [18]

These ideas are all variations upon the qualities of immensity and of darkness or obscurity. The clarity and precison of detail that are associated with realism are not important to sublimity, and may even interfere with it. Hawthorne means something like this when he says that the novel "is presumed to aim at a very minute fidelity, not merely to the possible, but to the probable and ordinary course of man's experience," while the romance is more flexible, less tied to probability. It is easy enough to recognize a connection between the darkness and immensity of the sublime and the terror that is often inspired by dreams. The theory of the sublime is central to the literature of dreams, from Edward Young's *Night Thoughts* through DeQuincey, Nerval, Hoffmann, and Poe. What is more difficult to understand is the connection between the terrific as it occurs in dreams and the idea of religious awe. Gothic romances like *The Monk* offer bizarre, apparently contradictory mixtures of sensational events and religiosity. Tales of headless ghosts in

[18] Samuel Monk, *The Sublime* (Ann Arbor: University of Michigan Press, 1960), p. 93.

bloody winding-sheets combine the language of mysticism with
the language of broadside journalism. And even great romances
—*The Scarlet Letter* and *Confessions of a Justified Sinner,* for example
—are similarly contradictory. Both Hawthorne and Hogg are concerned to criticize religious zealotry, and yet both employ the
mysterious, transcendental style common to all romances. Nor do
they use this style ironically, as Hardy uses religious symbolism for
anti-religious purposes in *Jude the Obscure.*

The peculiar combination of spirituality with terror in the
sublime, which serves as the basis for style in the romance form,
approximates the symbolism of dreams. The romance form is
not concerned to present actual events or to "explain itself," as
Jung says the "psychological novel" explains itself. It is rather
concerned to "shadow forth" its meaning, simultaneously expressing and disguising a latent content, much as dreams do.
Furthermore, the category of the sublime which underlies everything from the shoddiest tale of Gothic horror to *Moby Dick* and
Wuthering Heights is related to what Freud has called the *"unheim-
lich"* or the "uncanny."

The "uncanny," Freud maintains, "is that class of the terrifying which leads back to something long known to us, once very
familiar." These "familiar" things have become "unfamiliar" and
terrifying because they have undergone estrangement and distortion through repression. The two chief kinds of things which may
become "uncanny" when lured out of repression into symbolic
expression are materials from infantile complexes and materials
from primitive religious beliefs.[19] "An uncanny experience occurs
either when repressed infantile complexes have been revived by
some impression, or when the primitive beliefs we have sur-
mounted seem once more to be confirmed." "Infantile complexes"
and "primitive beliefs" may seem quite different, but Freud
argues that "primitive beliefs are most intimately connected with
infantile complexes, and are, in fact, based upon them." Animism
and magic, for instance, are both results of narcissistic assumptions
about nature. The mixture of the spiritual with the terrific, of

[19] Ernest Jones, *On the Nightmare* (New York: Grove Press, 1959), limits the
materials of nightmares and the medieval superstitions based on them even farther
to incestuous wishes. He also points out that "In the various stories of the Devil we
find many details strongly suggestive of the mental processes characteristic of
dreams" (p. 184), and the same is true of stories based on other superstitions as well.
Sigmund Freud, "The Uncanny," in *On Creativity and the Unconscious,* pp. 122–161.

religiosity with the crudely sensational that characterizes the romance form is thus comprehensible. So, too, is the need for vague-
ness or obscurity which occurs in all accounts of the sublime. Romances like dreams allow us to regress to infantile stages of development, or to "shadow forth" infantile impulses; the obscurity of
the sublime is one way of disguising and expressing simultaneously.

While realism often seeks to reduce the metaphoric content
of language to a minimiun, the romance form exploits it. Flaubert
told Louise Colet that he fought hard against the swarms of metaphors that beset him as he was writing *Madame Bovary,* although
fortunately it was a losing battle. The language of realistic fiction,
as Ian Watt has shown, is related to philosophical empiricism; the
language of romantic fiction, on the other hand, tends toward
idealism.[20] A landscape in Jane Austen is likely to read like a
travelogue or an essay on the picturesque, and is unlikely to point
beyond itself. A landscape in James Hogg or in Emily Brontë will
read like transcendental poetry, even though Hogg is satirizing
religious fanaticism and Emily Brontë seems to reject other-
worldly religion in favor of a "natural mysticism":

> The grass and the flowers were loaden with dew . . . he per-
> ceived that the black glossy fur of which his chaperon was
> wrought was all covered with a tissue of the most delicate
> silver—a fairy web. . . .
>
> As he approached the swire at the head of the dell . . . he
> beheld, to his astonishment, a bright halo in the cloud of haze,
> that rose in a semicircle over his head like a pale rainbow. He
> was struck motionless at the view of the lovely vision. . . .
>
> (Hogg, *Confessions of a Justified Sinner*)

In the realm of "Kubla Khan" or of "La Belle Dame Sans Merci"
every term seems to point beyond itself to some deeper, visionary
level of meaning, hidden from the scrutiny of mere reason. This
deeper level of meaning, however, is not so definitely religious
and external as it is psychological and internal. So in James Hogg
the symbolic style describes phenomena that are perhaps entirely

[20] Ian Watt, *The Rise of the Novel* (Berkeley and Los Angeles: University of
California Press, 1959), p. 28: " . . . it is interesting to note that although some of
the 'abuses of language' which Locke specifies, such as figurative language, had
been a regular feature of the romances, they are much rarer in the prose of Defoe
and Richardson. . . . "

subjective—the nightmare world of Robert Wringhim's madness. Throughout the tale, Hogg employs the traditional association of lunacy with demonic possession. And at the end, the apparently sane editor has no explanation for the events in the story leading to Wringhim's suicide except to say that they must all be "either dreaming or madness."

The narrative structure of Hogg's romance, furthermore, may be described as one which internalizes events. Like numerous other romances, it is a story with a complex narrative frame; we are invited to compare events as described by the editor and his sources with the same events as described by Robert Wringhim, religious zealot turned homicidal maniac. Early in his "confession," Wringhim tells us how, as a youth, he was "particularly prone to lying," and so came to find himself "constantly involved in a labyrinth of deceit." The structure of Hogg's tale might itself be described as "a labyrinth of deceit"—or, better still, as a maelstrom of insanity in which the boundaries and properties of physical reality are destroyed through the gradual disintegration of Wringhim's mind. After his "election," which is really his damnation, Wringhim tells us that his mind "had all the while been kept in a state of agitation resembling the motion of a whirlpool. . . . " And toward the end of his "confession," a plucky old servant, Samuel Scrape, tells Wringhim the tale of the town of Auchtermuchty, whose rigidly righteous citizens were duped by Satan. The tale is ancient, and was told to Scrape by an old crone, Luckie Shaw, who had it in turn from earlier sources. Scrape tells it to Wringhim, who records it in his "confession," which is then transmitted to us by the editor. The tale of Auchtermuchty is thus like the deepest point of the gyre or maelstrom, surrounded by a vertiginous series of narrative frames, or tales-within-tales.

Other romances with narrative or editorial frames include *Wuthering Heights, The Narrative of A. Gordon Pym, The Scarlet Letter, The Turn of the Screw,* and *Heart of Darkness.* As in Conrad's great elaboration of romance conventions, the frame-tale structure suggests a journey within, into the "heart of darkness" of us all. And multiple narrators, as in *The Moonstone* and *The Woman in White,* suggest psychic decomposition or fragmentation, although Willkie Collins was too solid and sensible a Victorian to lose sight of physical reality, even in imagination. In *Confessions of a Justified*

Sinner, we are led to understand that Robert Wringhim is possessed by the devil, who acts as a "second self" or "double."
Wringhim's description of the height of his madness is a terrifying
account of psychic disintegration in terms of demonic possession
and the existence of a second self leading to a complete, dizzying
loss of identity:

> ... I was seized with a strong distemper. ... I generally
> conceived myself to be two people. When I lay in bed, I
> deemed that there were two of us in it; when I sat up I
> always beheld another person, and always in the same posi-
> tion from the place where I sat or stood. ... The most per-
> verse part of it was that I rarely conceived *myself* to be any of
> the two persons.

The theme of the "double" or the "divided self" is present in
countless romances. Freud and Otto Rank have explained it as the
product of repressed narcissistic impulses, and later writers
agree.[21] One of its effects is to suggest that two or more characters
are parts of a single self, the process of whose disintegration the
tale shadows forth. The events which these fractional selves act
out seem often to represent some dim, mysterious conflict within
one mind. Architecture, as in "The Fall of the House of Usher,"
becomes skeletal or skullish:

> ... I reined my horse to the precipitous brink of a black and
> lurid tarn that lay in unruffled lustre by the dwelling, and
> gazed down ... upon the remodelled and inverted images of
> the gray sedge, and the ghastly tree-stems, and the vacant
> and eye-like windows.

The simultaneous destruction of the house and the family of
Usher suggests the final dissolution of a single demented mind,
that which must peer mournfully out from "the vacant and eye-
like windows" as the narrator approaches. It is a commonplace of
psychoanalytic criticism that writers "split up their ego by self-
observation into many component-egos, and in this way ... per-
sonify the conflicting trends in their own mental life in many

---

[21] See Robert Rogers, *The Double in Literature* (Detroit: Wayne State University
Press, 1970). Ernest Jones, *On the Nightmare,* p. 159, points out the etymological
associations of "devil" with "deuce," "double," "two," and cognate terms in Indo-
European languages.

heroes."[22] Furthermore, psychic splitting is present in realistic fiction as well as in romances. But characters in great realistic novels do not exist merely or mainly as symbolic projections of aspects of their creators; they provide us with at least the illusion of a wholeness and independence which characters in romances lack. An interpretation of the characters in a realistic novel solely in terms of psychic splitting, therefore, is bound to seem inadequate or incomplete. In the subjective world of romances, however, the fractional characters seem to stand for different mental attributes or psychic forces, and the effect is often close to allegory.[23] The good angel of the conscience or superego battles against the devil of impulse or id, and the ego, whether directly embodied in a character or not, is torn apart by the process.

In any case, the frame-tale structure of romances reinforces the subjective nature of their central stories. Like dreams, romances express the demonic within the framework of physical reality, or the framework of the apparently waking, common-sense minds of narrator and reader.

But the narrators or editors of romances whose voices frame the central stories do not function in the same way as the authorial voices of realistic works. A tendency of literary realism has always been to express a scientific worldview, and realistic writers sometimes present themselves as scientists—witness Balzac and Zola. Occasionally the narrator or editor of a romance will also present himself as a scientist, as in the case of LeFanu's Dr. Hesselius of the tales in *Through a Glass Darkly*, but when this happens it seems to be only to lend credibility to the incredible. The narrator of *Middlemarch* has the duty of "raveling and unraveling certain human lots" to show their necessary social interdependence, and in doing so she analyzes the egoistic blindnesses which keep the individual characters from recognizing their interdependence. But the narrators of romances do not often provide detailed accounts of the social relations between characters, and frequently give us quite unreliable analyses of the central events. In LeFanu's "Green Tea," Dr. Hesselius offers a quack diagnosis of the madness of the Rev. Mr. Jennings which, we understand, explains nothing satisfacto-

---

[22] Sigmund Freud, *On Creativity and the Unconscious*, p. 51.
[23] Harry Levin finds one of the origins of the American romance in religious allegory. See *The Power of Blackness* (New York: Alfred Knopf, 1958), p. 20.

rily, but only establishes an ironic counterpoint to the mysterious events leading to Jennings's suicide. Hesselius believes that "green tea" has broken down the thin mental partition between reality and the demonic for Jennings. His "scientific" analysis rather affirms the demonic than denies it, and it is powerless to save Jennings. After Jennings has cut his throat, Dr. Hesselius tries to rationalize his failure to effect a cure; he resorts to the shabby argument that Jennings had not officially become his patient yet. Confident and omniscient, the authorial voice in *Middlemarch* shows us rational awareness in control of events. Verging on quackery, Dr. Hesselius shows us the inadequacy of reason to deal with the demonic; he is a scientist who demonstrates the impotence of science to deal with some aspects of experience.

Like rational control during dreams, the voice of reason in romances is portrayed as weak or dormant. The two narrators of *Wuthering Heights*, Lockwood and Nelly Dean, no doubt represent common sense, normality, the voices of reason and of society, but Lockwood is an outsider, and the two central characters are much too strong for Nelly, who is, after all, merely a servant. The pattern of frame-tale narration in romances, perhaps, does not so much enclose irrational events as it excludes rationality, shoving to the periphery of the editorial framework the voices of moral judgment and conscious control. The structure of a romance thus creates a kind of charmed circle within which the demonic, the outlawed, the infantile can be conjured up.

Starting from the theory that romances function regressively, it is thus possible to explain their traits. It is more difficult to explain why such regressive fantasy activity is necessary—why we read and write romances, or why we find it enjoyable to experience the "uncanny" in literature. A solution to this problem may lie in what Lionel Trilling postulates about tragedy, a genre "which must always puzzle us because it seems to propose to the self a gratification in regarding its own extinction."[24] Trilling re-

---

[24] Lionel Trilling, *Freud and the Crisis of our Culture* (Boston: Beacon Press, 1955), p. 25. Harry Levin says of the archetypal conflict between blackness and whiteness in romances that it "take us back to the very beginning of things, the primal darkness, the void that God shaped by creating light and dividng night from day." (*The Power of Blackness*, p. 29.) It isn't difficult to translate this religious language of *Genesis* into psychological language, and to find in it a regressive search for origins.

solves this paradox by referring to Freud's hypothesis of the death instinct. The processes of education and ego-development are painful and difficult, requiring the repression of much that at early stages seems to us desirable. Like dreams, the romance form symbolically carries us backwards down the path of this painful process of maturation, promising us a temporary reprieve from inhibition and repression. It traces the dissolution of the ego, and in so doing mimics death—it is thus at once both pleasing and horrifying, enjoyable and guilt-ridden. Trilling's formulation also offers us an explanation for the generic similarity of the romance form and tragedy. According to Northrop Frye, the conventions of the novel are related to those of the comedy of manners, while the conventions of the romance are related to those of tragedy.[25] This similarity between romance and tragedy suggests that tragedy—traditionally the most dignified of literary genres—is also regressive in its nature. There is nothing contradictory in this. If by "infantile" we mean "elemental," then tragedy takes us close to our roots, to what we feel is most universal and basic within ourselves.

III

The narrative frame that is frequently used in romances creates a boundary between the solid common sense of the reader and the regressive disintegration of the self which lies at the center of the tale. The structure of romances, like the structure of dreams, is thus discontinuous with physical reality. The structure of realistic novels, on the other hand, seems to flow out of the real world and back into it again without interruption. Like the physical world, moreover, a realistic novel is usually built up of countless atomic particles—details of physical objects such as Moll Flander's bills of loot, or the flies drowning in cider in *Madame Bovary,* or the ironic, nearly invisible hairs curling inside the beauty spot on the right side of Jeanne's chin in Maupassant's *Une Vie.*

Although it would be too simple to say that the romance form is subjective and the novel form objective, the first fundamental of realism is the assumption of the existence of a physical realm external to self. According to Fernand Desnoyers, "Realism is the

---

[25] Northrop Frye, *Anatomy of Criticism* (New York: Atheneum, 1966), p. 304.

true depiction of objects."[26] The self is felt to be a discrete, unified entity in a world made up of such entities. The plot of a realistic novel normally turns upon the relations between the separate and indivisible being of one or several main characters and external reality in the form of "society"—that is, of all the other separate and individisible beings in the story or suggested by the story. Part of the language of a realistic novel is devoted to describing the central character or characters, and another part to describing external reality. In post-Jamesian fiction, all of the language may emanate from the viewpoint of one of the characters rather than from an omniscient authorial voice, but the division between central characters and external reality usually remains clear. If the work is truly realistic, the interaction between central characters and external reality cannot lead to the complete conquest or to the destruction of external reality. It must lead instead either to some sort of compromise between central characters and external reality, which is preeminently so in *Middlemarch,* or to the destruction of the central characters, which is often the case in works labeled "naturalistic," such as Zola's *L'Assommoir* and Hardy's *Jude the Obscure.* One might say that with simple realism there is still a measure of geniality, still room for some of the desires of self to be gratified. In naturalism, this liberating room shrinks or disappears. As types of fiction in which the destrucion of the self is shadowed forth, the romance and the naturalistic novel may therefore seem similar. But the regressive disintegration of the self in romances comes from internal forces; like tragedy, the romance form suggests a paradoxical triumph over external circumstances in the midst of chaos, madness, and death. The destruction of the self in naturalism, on the other hand, is due to its weakness in confronting the pressues of external reality.

Both romanticism and naturalism in fiction involve expressions of extreme states of mind and often of violent and melodramatic occurrences which may be less "mature" than the ordinary and probable domain of realism. But it is far more difficult to find elements of moral inspiration or of positive human values in Zola or in Gissing than in Melville or in Emily Brontë. The spirit of romance is regressive, but not nihilistic. If the dreary aims of

[26] Fernand Desnoyers, "On Realism," in *Documents of Modern Literary Realism,* ed. George Becker (Princeton: Princeton University Press, 1963), p. 80.

naturalistic realism as described by Harold Biffen in *New Grub Street* are more mature or more clear-sighted than the aims of Stevenson, they are so only insofar as maturity and clear-sighted-ness can be identified with a negation of human aspirations. Biffen tells Reardon that he aims at " 'an absolute realism in the sphere of the ignobly decent.' " This realism will be even too dull and humdrum to be like Zola's fiction. " 'Zola writes deliberate tragedies,' " says Biffen; he wants nothing to do with the heroic or the dramatic. And later in *New Grub Street,* Biffen describes the novel that he has projected to deal with " 'the ignobly decent' " and with the victims of " 'paltry circumstance.' " It will be called *Mr. Bailey, Grocer.*

> " . . . Mr. Bailey is a grocer in a little street by here. . . . He's fond of talking about the struggle he had in his first year of business. He had no money of his own, but he married a woman who had saved forty-five pounds out of a cat's-meat business. You should see that woman! A big, coarse, squint-ing creature. . . . Now I'm going to tell the true story of Mr. Bailey's marriage and of his progress as a grocer. It'll be a great book—a great book!"[27]

"The sphere of the ignobly decent," one supposes, is itself a sort of literary version of the cat's-meat business—neither very profitable nor very unprofitable, but merely dismal.

Behind literary realism lies the impulse to reject the heroic and the ideal along with the marvelous. Although realists claim that their work is maturely disillusioned, they are not necessarily on more solid ground than the romancers who wander apologeti-cally off into dreams. Consider Taine's characterization of Balzac's work:

> He has depicted with infinite detail and a sort of poetic en-thusiasm the execrable vermin who swarm and teem in the Parisian mud, the Cibots, the Rémonencqs, the Mme. Nourissons, the Fraisiers, poisonous creatures of the dark depths who, enlarged by the concentrated light of his micro-

---

[27] George Gissing, *New Grub Street* (Boston: Houghton Mifflin [Riverside Edi-tions], 1962), pp. 119 and 174–175.

scope, exhibit the multiple arsenal of their weapons and the diabolic brilliance of their corruption.[28]

The pretensions to scientific objectivity of the realist (Balzac's "microscope"), resulting in the disillusioned or even cynical reduction of people to "vermin," might just as well be characterized as a form of literary description based on sadistic impulses. The sado-masochistic basis of realism is even clearer in Flaubert and Zola; as Flaubert told Louise Colet, his novel was going to make "dreary reading; it will contain atrocious things of misery and sordidness."[29] There is an enthusiasm for pain in Flaubert's remark that goes beyond the mere dismalness of Harold Biffin. And while it is true that reality is painful and that the novelist should not gloss over "atrocious things of misery and sordidness," it may also be impossible to isolate the adultness of realism from a more primitive and uncontrolled desire to inflict pain.

Certainly there is no guarantee in the forms and labels of realism of an escape from the infantile. For one thing, again, *all* mental activity has unconscious roots. Beyond this fact, however, the claims to maturity, objectivity, and rationality of realistic writers are no more to be accepted at face value than are the opposite claims of romancers and surrealists to be expressing unconscious contents without the mediation of secondary processes. To accept such claims would involve positing an art form based on the reality principle rather than the pleasure principle, or a type of fantasy whose main result would be the maturation through disillusionment of the reader. The central question which underlies all formulations of literary realism is, How is it possible to achieve disillusionment through the creation of illusions? Maupassant understood this when he declared that "the higher order of Realists should rather call themselves illusionists." And he added that "All the great artists are those who can make other men see their own particular illusions."[30] But if art has no pur-

---

[28] Hippolyte Taine, "The World of Balzac," in *Documents of Modern Literary Realism*, p. 109.

[29] Flaubert to Louise Colet, in *Documents of Modern Literary Realism*, p. 91. Baudelaire noted Flaubert's enthusiasm for pain: "quant á l'ardeur avec laquelle il travaille souvent dans l'horrible. . . . " See Mario Praz, *The Romantic Agony* (Oxford: Oxford University Press, 1951), pp. 161–162.

[30] Guy de Maupassant, "Essay on the Novel," in *The Portable Maupassant*, ed. Lewis Galantiere (New York: Viking Press, 1947), pp. 670–671.

pose beyond the creation of illusions—if it is entirely at the beck of the pleasure principle and has no higher "scientific" or "adult" role like those assigned to it by Zola and George Eliot—why do we take it seriously? Does literature have *any* cognitive function that would allow us to look upon the analogies between *Middlemarch* and psychoanalysis as more than analogies?

According to Freud, literature does not have such a cognitive function. This is true even though Freud himself enjoyed literature and had the highest respect for great writers. He avoided the problem posed by "serious literature" either by ignoring it altogether or by treating the psychological insights contained in it as chance findings based on intuition. Not just romances, but all literature is like dreams from his perspective, and is to be fully understood only by following the same procedures which work for dream analysis. Realism might thus be explained not as a literary mode which produces genuine disillusionment, but rather as one which creates elaborate disguises for its illusory nature.

From this viewpoint, the element of conscious rationality in literary realism is reduced to the status of what Freud calls "secondary elaboration" in the formation of dreams. Freud defines "secondary elaboration" as normal thought processes which intrude into the dream materials in order to give them the appearance of logical cohesion:

> Thus, dreams occur which may, upon superficial examination, seem faultlessly logical and correct; they start from a possible situation, continue it by means of consistent changes, and bring it—although this is rare—to a not unnatural conclusion. These dreams have been subjected to the most searching elaboration by a psychic function similar to our waking thought; they seem to have meaning, but this meaning is very far removed from the real meaning of the dream.

The dream materials have been given a rational significance which is not their true significance; although the initial impulse seems to be towards clarification, the result is rather to further distance and obscure the dream's meaning.

> . . . the psychic agency which approaches the dream-content with the demand that it must be intelligible, which subjects it

to a first interpretation, and in doing so leads to the complete misunderstanding of it, is none other than our normal thought. In our interpretation the rule will be, in every case, to disregard the apparent coherence of the dream as being of suspicious origin and, whether the elements are confused or clear, to follow the same regressive path to the dream-material.[31]

If secondary elaboration creates an illusion of coherence in dreams, then by analogy the far greater coherence of works of literature must be even more devious and misleading. On the other hand, it is obviously possible, albeit difficult, to arrive at interpretations of dreams—at least, it is possible for psychoanalysts to arrive at them. There seems to be no clear reason, moreover, why such reliable interpretation—or, more simply, rational understanding—cannot be produced in works of literature. Both Flaubert and Freud are unravelers of dreams and illusions. If it is true that Flaubert simultaneously indulges in dreams just by being a writer, it is equally true that Freud was not free from unconscious motivations in his more scientific work. That is, it is possible to say of every art work that it has an unconscious base, but it is also possible to say this of psychoanalysis or of any other mental activity. That does not invalidate psychoanalysis, and it does not invalidate the claims to psychological insight of literary realists either. It is true that *Middlemarch* is far removed from its unconscious roots in George Eliot's childhood, but its significance is only partly bound up with its genesis. The fact that an intellectual activity is the result of sublimated libido forces has no bearing on the importance, the authenticity, or the truth of that activity, whether it be the creation of an art work or the creation of a system of scientific analysis. Not only is it possible to have literary works which function both as elaborate defense mechanisms *and* as agents of mature moral discovery, nothing else *can* be possible when the literary works are of high calibre, and this means simply that it is possible to have literary works which are both illusory and true.

The relationship between secondary elaboration in dreams and rationality in literary realism, moreover, applies equally well

[31] Sigmund Freud, *The Interpretation of Dreams*, in *Basic Writings*, ed. A.A. Brill (New York: Modern Library, 1938), pp. 456 and 463.

to romances. Their significance, too, is only partly bound up with their unconscious geneses. Certainly their esthetic value is not in direct ratio to the liberty with which they seem to express unconscious contents. The fact that *Dracula* is more chaotic and more explicitly erotic does not make it a better work of fiction than *Wuthering Heights* or *Jane Eyre*. Its explicitness is a measure of its crude superficiality. What *Wuthering Heights* offers is a profound examination of the destructive and creative capacities of the erotic within a framework which demonstrates the limitations of the adult and the conventional. When Nelly Dean tries to convert Heathcliff and offers to send for a minister, we are forced to recognize the inadequacy both of her common sense point of view and of orthodox religion to encompass Heathcliff. In the crudest Gothic thrillers, on the other hand, nothing is examined—religion, for instance, crops up both in the shape of the mysterious and demonic and in the shape of conventional pious clichés to be mouthed beside graves and over coffins, without any sense of contradiction. But *Wuthering Heights* takes powerful and unsparing account of the failures of conventional piety and morality as well as of the human and social costs of the regressive passion of Heathcliff and Catherine. The element of conflict in all romances is similar to the usually more fully conceived social and moral forces in realistic fiction which haul "His Majesty the Ego" off his pedestal. As Arnold Kettle has shown, it is false to say that *Wuthering Heights* is an asocial fiction. It is really about society— and also about that which society fails to encompass and control. Society in *Wuthering Heights*, as represented by Nelly Dean, Lockwood, and the Lintons, is obviously not the social organism of Middlemarch or of Dicken's London, but that is partly the point. It is much too rudimentary and weak to govern the love and rage of Heathcliff and Catherine, while in *Middlemarch* exactly the opposite is the case—George Eliot's characters are forced to compromise with external circumstances, "for there is no creature whose inward being is so strong that it is not greatly determined by what lies outside it."

In any case, the quality of a romance and the quality of a novel will both depend largely on the truth and subtlety of the rational understanding which their authors bring to them. The analogy between rational understanding in fiction and secondary

elaboration in dreams opens up the possibility of works of literature whose conscious contents contradict rather than explain their
unconscious sources. But it is not clear that such contradiction has
a direct bearing on esthetic quality. The conscious surface of an
art work may deal successfully and powerfully with themes which
simultaneously disguise their sources in the unconscious life of the
author, and perhaps this is always the case. But such conscious
elaboration in art cannot be summarily dismissed as can secondary
elaboration in dreams, since it is there that much of the significance of the art work resides. So far as I am aware, psychoanalysis
has not yet provided an adequate solution to this problem; neither
Freud's habit of moving everything into the categories of the unconscious and irrational nor Jung's habit of moving everything
towards the opposite categories is finally satisfactory.

The regressive nature of the romance form triggers feelings
of guilt which have led to the devaluation of the form itself. In the
preface to *The Yemassee,* Simms says that "The Romance is of
loftier origin than the Novel," but this traditional idea is often
contradicted in practice. As a critic of the romance form,
Cervantes is the archetypal realist. And with his excessive modesty
in his prefaces, in which he calls his tales *mere* romances,
Hawthorne is the archetypal writer of romances. A result of its
lowly status is that the romance form seems to appeal to hack
writers. In dealing with the marvelous and with wish fulfillments,
it is related to melodrama and to modern mass culture forms like
science fiction, and it slides over easily into the shabbiest categories of literary production. The sense of inferiority of the romance form derives partly from the fact that in it defenses are
deliberately relaxed, and often enough this means a relaxation for
the writer as well as for his characters. In *The Mysteries of Udolpho,*
for example, there is both a loosening of inhibitions in the events
of the tale and in the way it is told. That is, Mrs. Radcliffe not
only allows herself a freer expression of unconscious contents
than is permissible in realistic fiction, but she also allows herself to
be relatively unaware of this—she is far less in rational control of
her story than Jane Austen is in *Northanger Abbey.* At the outset of
The Mysteries of Udolpho, Emily's father lectures her about restrain-
ing her excessive sensibility: "I have endeavoured to teach you,
from your earliest youth, the duty of self-command. . . . I would

not annihilate your feelings, my child, I would only teach you to command them. . . . " His voice of rational control, however, is quickly overridden; Emily jumps off the deep end into a delicious wallow in adolescent dreams and thrills. Mrs. Radcliffe identifies closely with this plunge into "feelings"; in terms of literary form and style, the result is the absence of ironic distance and of anything like an adequate awareness of design or structure. There is instead a ramshackle series of events, like the strange shapelessness of events in dreams. But the romance writer doesn't have to relinquish conscious control, and the greatest writers of romances —Hawthorne, Hogg, Poe, Melville, Emily Brontë—are as much in control of their work as the greatest realists. James understood this when he insisted that writers of romances have to be as aware of what they are doing as novelists: "I can think of no obligation to which the 'romancer' would not be held equally with the novelist; the standard of execution is equally high for each."

There is, then, no way of asserting the superiority of one form over the other. George Lukács may be on unassailable philosophical ground when he maintains that "the basis for any correct cognition of reality . . . is the recognition of the objectivity of the external world, that is, its existence independent of human consciousness."[32] When he extends his argument to literature, however, he is mistaken. If he were correct, then realism might seem to take precedence over romanticism as the superior mode; the regressive subjectivity of the romance form might prove to be exactly what the great realists have declared it to be, an indulgence in childish illusions. But a quite different conclusion might be reached by starting from Lukács's materialistic premise, which is that all literature is fantasy and that it is preferable to acknowledge that fact than to seek to disguise it. Such an attitude is implicit, at least, in Freud's equally materialistic explorations of fantasy. One may still value the sense of social responsibility that is paramount in much realism, and devalue the apparently asocial structure of romances. But there is no guarantee that the social values expressed in realistic works will not be of the most conservative and retrograde kind, any more than there is that realistic works are less illusory than romances

[32] George Lukács, *Writer and Critic* (New York: Grosset and Dunlap, 1970), p. 25.

because they seem disillusioned and disillusioning. Besides, measured or controlled regression seems to be as necessary to sanity as the straightforward processes of maturation. As Frederick Crews puts it, "By sanctioning certain regressions a culture enables its members to *reculer pour mieux sauter*," and art—even "realistic" art—is just such a system of beneficial regressions.[33] It is not only that all work and no play makes Jack dull, but also that without the release and freedom of the fantasy activity of art we are apt to lose track of our unconscious life—to cease to indulge it *and* to cease to be aware of it. And it is worth remembering that, for Don Quixote, the hero of the greatest realistic novel, the moment of death and the moment of complete disillusionment are the same.

> Though he'd lived a crazy man,
> When he died he was sane once more.

It seems to be necessary to live partly in the world of illusions—of dreams and of regressive fantasies—if we are also to live in the real world.

[33] Frederick Crews, "Anaesthetic Criticism," *Psychoanalysis and Literary Process* (Cambridge, Massachusetts: Winthrop Publishers, 1970), p. 13.

More's *Utopia*: Confessional Modes

David Bleich

More's *Utopia* is not generally known as a confessional work. Most scholars believe that whatever values derive from the work, they must be humanistic in some basic sense—social, philosophical, historical, or religious values. Conceiving of *Utopia* as a confessional, however, promises to enlarge this orientation to include psychological considerations. New motivations for the work's creation might be suggested, as well as different views of Christian humanism and of the generic utopian fantasy.

Two particular contributions to More studies lend credibility to this approach. Professor David Bevington has argued some years ago that because the overall frame of the work is in the form of a dialogue, it makes sense to treat it as a " dialogue of the mind with itself," with More and Raphael representing the " two polarities of More's own mind." [1] This view is valid, since psychology has taught that characters in a work are usually representations of different facets of the author's personality. Professor J. H. Hexter, meanwhile, has offered biographical evidence for viewing the dialogue as a confession of personal feeling. He points out that Book II was written first in the Netherlands, and that the offer of a job in Court by Henry and Wolsey prompted More to add the dialogue of Book I (when he returned to England) before considering the work complete. [2] This fact suggests that either the dialogue, or perhaps the whole work, became for More an occasion to express and justify his feelings about the state, about power, and most of all, about his capacity to contribute to the public weal. In an immediate sense, at least part of the *Utopia* is a confession of his dilemma whether or not to serve the king.

This essay proposes that considerably more is being confessed. In particular, beneath this tale of social felicity, More

---

[1] David Bevington, "The Dialogue in *Utopia*: Two Sides to the Question," *Studies in Philology*, LVIII (July 1961), 496, 497.

[2] Edward Surtz, S.J., and J.H. Hexter, eds., *The Complete Works of Thomas More*, Vol. 4 (New Haven and London, 1965), p. xxxvi. Hereinafter cited as "Surtz and Hexter."

reveals palpable wishes for power and authority, hostile and sometimes murderous feelings of indignation, all concealed by the confessional humility of the *persona* More, and by the journalistic objectivity of Raphael Hythlodaeus. I would suggest that both the wishes and More's many methods of concealing them are part of a life-long pattern of aspiration and frustration, present in the earliest years and the last days of his life. The *Utopia* represents the most passionate confession of his aspirations and the most artful concealment of his frustrations. An index of the intensity of feeling More attached to this work is the multiplicity of generic forms his writing takes. Each of these forms embodies a different kind of confession, but more importantly, each form is a different type of disguise, particularly suited to the feelings expressed, and can perhaps be correlated with particular infantile modalities.

The use of infantile modalities to describe aspects of the adult world—particularly the detailed aspects of artistic form—could at first seem mechanical or reductive. The reason it is not—and most psychoanalytic theoreticians will agree—is that these early phases represent the first formulations of adult *values.* Erikson, in his work on the correlation of life history and case history, as well as Leon Edel's frontier biographical work on Henry James, document fairly fully that infantile modalities do in fact govern adult behavior. Of course, each adult does seem different from every other adult; individuals *are* individuals because there are unique contributions to personality in each human being. However, looking at people psychologically has led personality theorists to believe that the phasic operation of personality, as defined by Freud and later Erikson, is a reality of human behavior, and that the infantile modalities define the lawfulness in the behavior just as the later contributions define uniqueness. This essay will try to distinguish just what is unique and what is not. Hence, the use of modes to describe the categories of artistic form simply represents the description of the features common in these forms with the general modes of human cultural value.

When we say then that a poetic defense is "anal," it does not mean that More had feces on his mind when writing the poem. Rather, the term " anal " is an allusion to a common poetic penchant for order, neatness, and symmetry, qualities which have been documented as part of this phase of infantile development, and which appear in other aspects of the poet's life-style. Likewise, the term " oral " does not mean that More was secretly wishing for his bottle, but that we are describing a form which is largely undifferentiated, just as the " oral " infant does not distinguish between himself and the source of his nourishment. Finally, to say that a dramatic mode is " phallic " or " oedipal " is not to say that there was a lascivious drool that motivated More, but that the term is an allusion to all infants' first efforts, during the "oedipal " phase, to understand the relationship between two or more people, at least one of which is of the other sex. Erikson patently associates *value* with infantile modalities: hope and trust with orality, order and autonomy with anality, and initiative and purpose with phallicism. To me, the obvious gain in describing adult values in this way is that it names the rationality behind their development, and that while it remains true that there is at least in part an *ad hoc* element in the formation of values, there are parts just as great—if not greater—that are, in a general way, lawfully or systematically determined.

The logic of this system with regard to art has already been studied in some depth in Norman Holland's *The Dynamics of Literary Response* (1968) whose formulation " form is a defense" is deceptive in its simplicity.[3] Strictly or clinically speaking, form *is* a defense, though more commonly speaking, it is a disguise, or a *distracting system* on which we focus our conscious attention (our adult thought systems) , while the more infantile, repressed, unconscious parts of us are stimulated by the implicit emotional ballast of the work. The term " defense " explains why a disguise exists in the artistic situation. The disguise is there to protect us from our own emotions, i. e., to defend us. The emotions that art stimulates, Aristotle noted, are violent, and we are able to enjoy them without being responsible for them. The reason for this condition is that there is this defense or disguise in art that tells our conscious minds that murder is what " Hamlet " wishes, though our unconscious minds apprehend their own wishes to murder. Certainly it makes sense that we need a way to defend ourselves from discovering our murderous wishes.

[3] N. N. Holland, The *Dynamics of Literary Response* (New York, 1968), ch. 4.

The various literary forms in More's *Utopia* successfully hide such unsavory emotions not only from the reader, but from More himself. I will therefore first examine aspects of More's biography that seem contributory, in a psychological way, to the making of *Utopia* and then to its commonly perceived artistic—defense-disguise—structure.

Two poems written in youth and a vision reported to Erasmus just at the completion of the *Utopia* provide an inroad into the nature of More's life-aspirations. The first poem, Professor E. M. G. Routh reports, was written when More was about sixteen.[4] There are nine verses which accompany nine painted "pageants" that More designed for his father's house. The pageants depict, in order, Childhood, Manhood, Venus and Cupid, Age, Death, Fame, Time, Eternity, and The Poet.[4] Each phase of life is shown to triumph over the previous phase, which, in three of the pageants, is characterized as being particularly proud: Venus and Cupid berate Manhood for his " great pryde "; Death tells Age, " Therefore sage father greatly magnifyed,/ Discende from your chayre, set a part your pryde "; and Eternity says that Time " for all thy pride and bostynge " shall be brought to naught. The ultimate conqueror is the Poet, who triumphs over Eternity by stepping out of the game, so to speak, and exhorting the spectator that these fine " figures of invention " [5] mean nothing without the love of God, who is the source of eternal life. In his role of the Poet, More is acting as an intermediary between his audience and his work, but also between Man and God. Within the context of the art, he is an ultimate force, but when he steps out, he reassesses his work in the light of divine permanence and power.

Meanwhile, we might provisionally relate the fall of Manhood's and the " sage father's " pride, respectively, to two biographical facts. We are told by Professor Routh that More had just had his first love experience which was apparently thwarted by " unkind parents." [6] We also know that at this time More's stay at Oxford was curtailed by his father's sending him to

---

[4] E. M. G. Routh, *Sir Thomas More and His Friends* (New York, 1934), p. 12.

[5] The Latin poem was kindly translated for me by Professor David Nordloh and Mrs. Shirley Guthrie. This particular term is Professor Nordloh's.

[6] Routh, *op. cit.*, p. 12. We are not told just whose parents intervened, though it would be interesting to know.

study law. Respectively, the two passages might refer, first, to
his love experience, and, second, might be reminding his father,
through artistic disguise, that he will have to descend sometime
from his "chayre" of his present authority over him. Finally
the Poet, in the picture, is shown "sitting in a chayre" and
the language of the poem is Latin (where the other verses are
English), one of the languages More was learning at Oxford—
and the language of his best known work—*Utopia*. At an early
age, the Latin language assumes an especially private function
which asserts the supremacy, the piety, and, in a sense, the
moral singularity of this particular poet. Indeed, Latin and art
are the symbolic means through which the young More "un-
seats" his own father, and himself moves into the position of
the highest authority he can imagine.

The second poem of interest is a ballad written, Professor
A. W. Reed suggests, as a jocund invocation of welcome to the
Sergeants' Feast at which More's father was made Sergeant-at-
Law in 1503.[7] (Professor Reed indicates that "the Sergeant
of the poem was not a lawyer, but the jest would nevertheless
pass.") The poem is about a sergeant who tries, by posing as
a friar, to collect a debt from a prodigal spender. The sergeant
fails, as the women protecting the spender throw the sergeant
out. The moral of the tale is, stick to your own calling, or, as
the poem puts it, "When a hatter/ Will go smatter/ In phi-
losophy// Or a pedlar/ Wax a meddler/ In theology// All that
ensue/ Such craftes new/ They drive so far a cast// That ever
more/ They do therefore/ Beshrew themselves at last."[8] This
poem might also relate to More's vocational development and
his father's role in it. In the years just previous to this, More
had been seriously considering becoming a friar. While he was
reading law, he lived the life of a Carthusian monk, but without taking vows. Here again his father intervened and pre-
vailed upon him to pursue a law career. We might say then
that in More's imagination, the new "sergeant" became allied
with the peddlar and the hatter when he meddled in More's
philosophical and theological studies. Like the earlier poem's
warning to the "sage father," the fate of this sergeant—whose

   [7] *The English Works of Sir Thomas More*, Vol. 1, ed. W. E. Campbell and A. W.
Reed (New York: The Dial Press, 1931), p. 15.
   [8] *Ibid.*, p. 327.

" harte for pryde/ Lepte in his syde/ To see how well he freered " [9]—is a warning to those with temporal power not to meddle in affairs of learning and faith. Just as the earlier poem might have rendered More a kind of " poet laureate " in his father's house, here too he is acting as a court poet in an official role, and his behavior is similar to the Fool's in *King Lear,* where great " foolish " wit seeks to enlighten the highest temporal power. (See note 22.)

Within the boundaries of art, More reveals a pretense to power. Outside his art, he accepts certain limitations—from God, or from his father's actual authority. We need more explicit evidence, however, of an actual wish for supreme power.

The most explicit evidence I have found in More's writings is the dream vision he confides to Erasmus in December, 1516.

You have no idea how I jump for joy, how tall I have grown, how I hold up my head, when a vision comes before my eyes, that my Utopians have made me their perpetual sovereign. I seem already to be marching along, crowned with a diadem of wheat, conspicuous in a Grey-friar's cloak, and carrying for a sceptre a few ears of corn, surrounded by a noble company of Amaurotians; and with this numerous attendance meeting the ambassadors and princes of other nations,—poor creatures in comparison with us, inasmuch as they pride themselves on coming out, loaded with puerile ornaments and womanish finery, bound with chains of that hateful gold, and ridiculous with purple and gems and other bubbly trifles. But I would not have either you or Tunstall form an estimate of me from the character of others, whose behavior changes with their fortune. Even though it has pleased Heaven to raise our humility to that sublime elevation, with which no kingdom can in my judgment be compared, you shall never find me unmindful of that old familiarity, which has subsisted between us while I have been in a private station; and if you take the trouble to make so small a journey as to visit me in Utopia, I will effectually provide that all the mortals who are subject to our clemency, shall show you that honour, which they owe to those whom they know to be dearest to their sovereign. I was proceeding further with this most delightful dream, when the break of day dispersed the vision, deposing poor me from my sovereignty, and recalling me to prison, that is, to my legal work. Nevertheless I console myself with the reflection, that real kingdoms are not much more lasting.[10]

In a non-psychological context, this is, at most, an interesting and amusing passage. Professor H. W. Donner, for example, in discussing this passage, assures us that " More had no illusions as to its being more than a dream." [11] But in the present context, this fantasy has much relevance. Specifically, it suggests that at some important depth of his personality, More would have liked to be king. Professor Hexter writes:

With every due allowance for the fanciful element in the letter, something about More's yearnings emerges from the usually distinct dream or vision. For to the heart's desire of a man what better guide can there be than his dreams? When More let his imagination range freely it did not reveal ascetic flight from the world or a purely contemplative immersion in scholarship to be the ultimate desire of the heart; More saw himself most completely fulfilled as a ruler or prince.[12]

Professor Hexter then adds that More would be a benevolent ruler, but this observation justifies the vision and removes it from deeper psychological discussion. Although More may have been a good king, he wishes all the same to be a king in perpetuity. Furthermore, if a peddlar or a hatter had this fantasy, we might not have to take it as seriously. More was always close to the counsels of the King. While he knew he could never really be king, when one is close to power it is often true that one can actually wield it, even though he does not hold the office *per se*. For our purpose then, the main point is that More, in some important phase of his personality, did wish to be a king.

[10] F. M. Nichols, trans., *The Epistles of Erasmus*, Vol. 2 (London, 1904), p. 443.
[11] H. W. Donner, *Introduction to Utopia* (London, 1945), p. 1.
[12] Surtz and Hexter, *op. cit.*, p. lxxix.

By considering this vision in conjunction with the two poems, we have the implicit judgment that More's wish to be a king belongs in the same psychological category as his playful warnings to his father. Putting the two pieces of information together, we can say, with somewhat more credibility, that More harbored a wish for ultimate paternalistic authority and that this wish plays a definite role in the creation of the *Utopia.* Let us now look at some further biographical data which will help define the wish more fully.

One of the great successes of More's life was his capacity for making and being friends with certain kinds of people. Erasmus writes that " He seems born and made for friendship, and is a more faithful and enduring friend." [13] We know little of his experience at St. Anthony's, but in the home of Archbishop Morton, More got his first real success in personal popularity and public recognition. Part of this success came through the domain of dramatic art. Roper reports that More " stepped in " to certain Christmas pageants there,[14] and Professor R. W. Chambers adds that such ritualized spontaneity may have been a dramatic convention into which More fit.[15] Augmenting these more formal dramas was the drama of conversation in Morton's house, which may have been the prototypical experience for the framework of *Utopia.* Many of More's other writings are earmarked by the reproduction of whole conversations. More did not actually participate in these conversations, but it seems likely that they became associated with Morton's benevolence and spirituality. This pleasant syndrome—Morton, conversation, and the dramatic limelight—became a more active value for More when Morton sent him on to Oxford.

The idea here is that this set of values is the foundation for More's humanistic leanings. As a student, More took the dramatic limelight. Professor Routh reports that Colet called him, at age 23, " England's one genius." [16] Between the ages of 16

---

[13] Nichols, *op. cit.,* Vol. 3, p. 387.

[14] Mildred Campbell, ed., *"The Utopia" of Sir Thomas More* . . . (New York: W. J. Black, 1947), p. 210.

[15] R. W. Chambers, *Thomas More* (Ann Arbor, 1958), first published, 1935, p. 62.

matic limelight. Professor Routh reports that Colet called him,

[16] Routh, *op.cit.,* p. 15.

and 25, More was studying and thinking with scholars ten years
older. If More had been harboring all along a wish for authority, there is little doubt that this wish was encouraged by
such major scholarly recognition of his talent. Talk, words,
language—ancient and modern—the area in which More had
asserted his poetic authority, widened enormously as a genuine
opportunity for leadership and intellectual authority.

What ensured the grip of this opportunity on More's personality were his close friendships in the community of scholars.
Professor Hexter points out that there was a " double bond "
linking the Christian humanists: " a personal bond of comrade-
ship and a spiritual bond of shared sentiment and activity. At
the center, linking both of these bonds together, stood the
single great figure of Desiderius Erasmus." [17] Erasmus, Hexter
explains, believed " above all else " in the " teaching Jesus," [18]
and certainly this is the image which Erasmus' life followed.
More important, this may have been the image More himself
had of Erasmus. The latter was about 30 when he met More,
who was ten years younger. Erasmus was an illegitimate
child,[19] a citizen of no particular country, and a recognized
leader in all countries, wandering, spreading, as it were, the
new gospel of learning and truth. In More's psychology, Erasmus was probably an intermediary figure between More's
wishes for authority and the reality of his capacities. He was a
kind of " big brother " who loved More dearly for a lifetime.
To Erasmus, More wrote, alluding to the former's kind reaction to the *Utopia*, "We two are to my mind a multitude,
as I think I could live happily with you in any solitude. . . .
sweetest Erasmus, dearer to me than my eyes." [20] Subsequently,
More wrote to Erasmus that " Your letter has excited my expectations and I now look every day for our *Utopia,* with the
feelings with which a mother awaits the return of her son from
foreign parts." [21] If More compared himself to a mother, and
Erasmus to the second part of a pair living in solitude, his relationship with Erasmus may be said to have assumed the form of a

---

[17] Surtz and Hexter, *op. cit.*, p. lxiii.
[18] *Ibid.*, p. lxiii.
[19] Chambers, *op. cit.*, p. 69.
[20] Nichols, *op. cit.*, Vol. 2, p. 427.
[21] *Ibid.*, Vol. 2, p. 447.

" Utopian " family, with Erasmus the father-husband-brother. (I will say more about the second quotation in connection with the prefatory poem.) When More died, Erasmus remarked, " In More's death I seem to have died myself; we had but one soul between us." [22]

Erasmus counseled More against political involvements [23] and avoided them scrupulously himself. Although More was sympathetic with this counsel, the deeper wish for power over-rode the sympathy. Perhaps that is why More confided his wish to Erasmus. The fact of his confiding bespeaks their great intimacy, but the content of the vision, in which Erasmus is a mere visitor to the perpetual sovereign, More, underscores the fact that the Erasmian kind of leadership was not altogether satisfactory to More, for whom the philosopher must really be king, and not just a king of words.

We have seen some of the ways in which the wish was frustrated—paternal pressure along with the accident of More's non-royal birth. To cope with these frustrations, More evolved various modes of compromise, in which some of his wishes could be fulfilled part of the time. There were further pressures though from inside him, and these also heavily taxed More's talent—and patience—for compromise.

The main sources of inner frustration were his sexual needs. These exercised an unusual form of pressure in that they contributed to the factors which were already diverting him from study. It is not that his sexual needs were frustrated, but he felt he had to satisfy, rather than renounce them, as he may well have preferred. In the tower, Roper reports that he told his daughter that " if it had not been for my wife and you that be my children . . . I would not have failed long ere this to have closed myself in as straight a room, and straighter too." [24]

---

[22] Quoted in Chambers, *op. cit.,* p. 73. Exact source not given, but 15 August 1535 is the date given. With regard to Erasmus's love for More, Chambers points out the probable pun in the title *Encomium Moriae* (Chambers, p. 101) which, he says, Erasmus thought of on his trip to England in 1509. Certainly, More had the type of personality in which one could simultaneously see the fool and the genius. Chamber's suggestion is consistent with my postulation of More's youthful role as "jester" and poet in his father's house, and with the common connotation of the present-day term "Utopia" as a wise, yet foolish vision.

[23] Nichols, *op. cit.,* Vol. 3, p. 369.

[24] William Roper, *The Life of Sir Thomas More,* ed. E. V. Hitchcock, (London, 1935), p. 76. Quoted by Chambers, p. 307. (In Mildred Campbell, *op. cit.,* 261).

Erasmus characterizes More's choice of sexual fulfillment as
between a "chaste husband" and a "licentious priest," [25] a
choice which suggests More picked the area of repression, rather
than release, chastity over license. Also, in the tower, More
remarked the Carthusian monks " as cheerfully going to their
deaths as bridegrooms to their marriage," [26] thus implicity char-
acterizing marriage as a kind of death. On the one hand,
More's burdens of financial and emotional demands made him
feel that he was missing out on the good life, and on the other,
they fostered guilt that he consumed all his " time in pleasure
and ease licentiously." [27] Perhaps this guilt was motivated by
another of his wishful fantasies: " ' Oh how well could we
three [wives Jane and Alice, and More] have lived together in
matrimony, if fortune and religion would have suffered it. . . .
So death shall give us that thing that life could not.' " [28]
Dame Alice only aggravated More's painful ambivalence, as she
exhorts, " ' What will you doo, that you list not to put foorth
you selfe as other folke doo? . . . By God, goe forwarde with
the first . . . it is ever better to rule then to be ruled.' " [29]
Dame Alice, whom More married some two months after the
death of his first wife in order to provide a mother for his
children, seemed, from this remark, to have been an almost
insidious influence on him, for the remark works to inflame the
impulse in him for power, that he was perpetually struggling
to put down; it exposed his own secret association of the impulse to power with the necessities of being a husband, father,
and provider; that is, Dame Alice probably made him too pain-
fully aware of his own desire to be the best father, the best
provider, the best husband through a more regal, utopian

[25] Nichols, *op. cit.*, Vol. 3, p. 394.
[26] Quoted from Chambers, *op. cit.*, p. 78. Source not given. It is possible to
read this statement as a sarcastic remark, which would have us picture the prospective husbands as grim as doomed monks. This reading is conceivable since More
may easily have shared his father's cynicism about marriage. The trouble comes in
imagining More sarcastic about the monks, though this too, I suppose, is possible.
[27] J. H. Hexter, *More's Utopia: The Biography of an Idea* (New York, 1952), p.
89.
[28] Quoted in Chambers, *op. cit.*, p. 286. These lines are a translation of material in More's Latin Epigrams, for which Chambers gives no specific source. He
does indicate that these lines were intended for More's epitaph.
[29] Nicholas Harpsfield, *The Life and Death of Sir Thomas More* (London, 1932),
p. 95.

path. But this situation obtained only unconsciously. The conscious result of this kind of arousal, however, was that he felt himself becoming involved ever deeper in the " prison " of legal and public life. One of his ways of coping with this irritating, guilt-generating situation was to simulate a monastic life: he secretly wore a hairshirt, sometimes " punished his body with whips," [30] and " led his family in an extensive daily course of pious observances." [31] Monastic austerity was one of his compromises with the multiple pulls of sexuality and family. Thus, the turn of monasticism was the fulfillment of an adolescent wish, an alternate path perhaps to the kind of power he sought. It was the path to intellectual authority and moral-religious superiority. In his conscious life, this functioned as a defense aginst the anxiety engendered by the implications for reality of his even more infantile, probably oral and oedipal wishes for power.

Compromise, defined by these dynamics, apparently characterized his actual choice of wives. Roper tells that in More's prospective wife's family, " his mind served him most to the second daughter, for that he thought her the fairest and best-favored," but he considered it would be " great grief and some shame " [32] to the eldest, so he took pity on her and married her. With regard to his second wife, Erasmus writes, More married her " more for the sake of the management of his household, than to please his own fancy, as she is no great beauty, nor yet young, . . . as he sometimes laughingly says, but a sharp and watchful housewife."[33] Both marriages seem to have been diverted from erotic ends by considerations of duty, first to the Colt family and then to his own. More's mode of compromise was to placate each demand but to remain with a niggling sense of frustration and resented renunciation. It is not psychologically far-fetched to suggest that sexual renunciation of this serious sort is, on the one hand, the symptomatic result of infantile conflict, and on the other hand, a sure sign of painful psychological conflict in other areas of adult life. More was not, perhaps, the compromising sort.

---

[30] Hexter, *op. cit.*, p. 88.
[31] *Ibid.*, p. 88.
[32] Roper, *op. cit.*, p. 6. Quoted in Routh, p. 31. (Mildred Campbell, p. 211.)
[33] Nichols, *op. cit.*, Vol. 3, p. 394.

In his long fight against heresy, and in the circumstances of his death, he was certainly not a compromiser, though with regard to the Act of Supremacy, he tried the compromise of silence. Though he knew it was not true in his case, he argued that silence signified consent in the legal custom.[34] In any case, he did allow his stubbornness free reign at last. He probably suspected the result long before it happened. With regard to Henry, he once remarked that if his (More's) head would get the king another castle in France, it would surely be given. He counseled his successor Thomas Cromwell not to tell the king his own strength, for then " hard were it for any man to rule him." [35] And when he refused to attend the coronation of Anne Boleyn, he predicted that oaths would be required to insure approval of the marriage. All of this apparent foreknowledge of his own fate began to operate in an almost perverse way: By staying in prison, he fulfilled his youthful wish for the cloister. By envying the monks' death row cheer—and by providing some of his own at his execution [36]—More became a cheerful bridegroom instead of a dutiful one. And in going to Heaven, he reached Utopia (where, perhaps, he would also get the forbidden two wives).

In reality, death was no compromise, but the *Utopia* was his best. Here More the poet, the dramatist, the intellectual, the man of State and God, are all given the chance to express their deepest wishes, and to transform the frustrations they engender into a pleasing work of art. Accordingly, the work comprises a multiplicity of generic modes suggesting its " utopian " reach just in its formal range. Furthermore, it seems to make sense that in an individual with so many pulls and genuinely developed aspects of his adult identity, the variety of literary modes must have some correspondence with his many-faceted public personality. While it is difficult to present conclusive proof of this correspondence in a scientific sense, the correlation between the literary modes and the defenses of personality is quite striking and sheds considerable light on the

[34] E. E. Reynolds, *The Trial of St. Thomas More* (New York, 1964), p. 115. Also, Chambers, p. 336.

[35] Roper, *op. cit.*, p. 57. Quoted in Chambers, p. 291.

[36] Roper quotes More on going to the scaffold: "I pray you, I pray you, Mr. Lieutenant, see me safe up, and for my coming down let me shift for myself." In Mildred Campbell, *op. cit.*, p. 279.

psychological ballast of the *Utopia*. From a topical standpoint, the following functions are obviously served: The prefatory poem by the " poet laureate " offers its wish through the adult capacity for puns and verbal byplay. Raphael's Discourse fulfills More's " life-long quest " to " combine the austerity of the cloister with life in the world " [37] through the then-popular format of an exploration journal. The prefatory letters lend the work an air of realism and authority, and the dramatic dialogue surrounding it all justifies the struggle of the self with these wishes and frustrations. The question we are ultimately interested in is: How do these functions tie in with the main psychological motives behind the work?

The following poem is generally cited to enlighten the reader on the pun in the word " utopia."

> The ancients called me Utopia or Nowhere because of my isolation. At present, however, I am a rival of Plato's republic, perhaps even a victor over it. The reason is that what he had delineated in words, I alone have exhibited in men and resources and laws of surpassing excellence. Deservedly ought I to be called by the name of Eutopia or Happy Land.[38]

Although the pun is central, there is much more here. Utopia claims to be a rival and perhaps a victor over Plato himself. There is the further claim that the work goes beyond words, whence the great victory resides in the purported transformation of words into " men, resources, and laws of surpassing excelence." Since the poet laureate is writing in the first person and identifies himself with Utopia, he is also the victor. In his youth, More was a kind of poet laureate who wrote verses of invocation, but in his letter to Erasmus he was also king, stepping beyond Erasmus's acceptance of mere scholarly authority. And, of course, More is the author of this verse. Thinking back to the " foreign parts " quotation given earlier, More, the parent of the Utopia, is also the eagerly awaited son. The creator of the work has fulfilled the wish of the obedient,

[37] Hexter, *op. cit.,* p. 88.
[38] Surtz and Hexter, *op. cit.,* p. 21. Hereafter, pagination from the *Utopia* will be parentheses following the quotations, with indications of page and line.

but inwardly rebellious, son of his father. The reunification of More with his work—which was published abroad—is tantamount intrapsychically to More's being father and son simultaneously. The saving grace of this aggressive wish, however, is the pun Eutopia, a " saving grace " that Hexter actually accepts as a justification for More's wish. That is, the Happy Land is speaking; the Happy Land is the victor; and the Happy Land is real. Who could quarrel with either More or this wish?

In addition to this underlying wish, which I have been tracing throughout More's other activities, there is the *modal* wish, a wish which corresponds to the particular literary mode of its presentation. Because of the word-play and poetic form, we may call the mode of the poem " anal," with the understanding that this rubric will lead us to the *wish* for a *value* of autonomy. In addition to the word-play which marks this developmental style, the infant at this time first conceives of reality as being a combination of himself *plus* a world *outside* himself, a self plus another.[39] Now in More's poem, the margin of victory over Plato is just the increment of reality that More claims for his state. There is an implied critique of Plato's amorphous idealism in More's claim for an extra-verbal reality for his state. More has, in a sense, solidified Plato's fluid idealism—his belief in the primacy of abstract forms. The literary irony that this victory for reality is expressed in a hyper-verbal form is testimony to the anal mode of the victory. The anal-poetic mode and its indisputable felicity thus disguise two wishes, a wish for autonomy and a wish for victory, both stressing the primacy of reality over the ideal. (We will see the anal disguise work more overtly in the Discourse.) The metaphorical and verbal disguises are successful indeed, and have been for four centuries.

But just in case this disguise did not work, we may note that the poem is only part of the preface, and not in the work proper. The poem may not " count " therefore. Yet it might well count since here another disguise or defense takes over. The poem appears in the midst of a group of recommending

---

[39] A change partially brought on by his consciousness of the product that is being separated from him during elimination.

letters by the most important scholars in Europe at the time.[40] Psychologically speaking, however, these letters work to regress further from the anal modality set up by the poem. Along with his inclusion of an alphabet and a map, More's letter to Peter Giles tries to blur the distinction between fact and fiction, and thereby promotes the work's ultimate impulse toward an undifferentiated world. The prefatory material achieves a blending effect, where scholarly authority and felicitous wish form part of the over-arching utopian universe. After reading the prefatory matter, one does not care, in a sense, whether it is all true or false; one is only calmed by the concatenation of goodness, truth, and beauty. The letters work to revoke the distinction between fact and fiction, reality and idealism, by uniting More with his community of scholars and creating the "brotherhood effect" which wants its own utopian world cleansed of the dichotomy between reality and the ideal.[41] The letters and their oral mode function as a disguise as well as a wish. They are a disguise because of their brotherhood and authority value, their appeal to superego forces, and the actual existence of their authors, for the most part, as real people. But they further the by-wish for autonomy and the ultimate oral-incorporative wish for victory by mixing their own reality up with More's poetic fictions and thus asserting the primacy of that one world.

If we accept Professor Hexter's scheme of composition, we should take the Discourse to be the fullest, least qualified expression of More's wishes. It was written outside of England, during leisure periods in his mission to Flanders for Henry. As yet, he was not formally involved with the King; he was Under-Sheriff of London and more or less independent. He was far enough from power to criticize it; and he was close enough to see how much he could do with it. He was thus in an excellent position to speak his mind. Accordingly, the form of the discourse is the least restrictive of all those in the *Utopia.* Peter and More are gathered around Raphael and they are

[40] See Peter R. Allen, "Utopia and European Humanism: the Function of the Prefatory Letters and Verses," *Studies in the Renaissance,* X, (October 1963), 91 107.

[41] Professor Allen (note 40) observes that "the letters, like *Utopia* itself, represent a variety of shades of seriousness," and they pose a "model of the humanistic ideal of combined eloquence and wisdom, delight and instruction."

willing to accept as true almost anything he will say. The ultimate referent for the truth of what Raphael will say, meanwhile, is not anything that exists in reality, but only those motives, dreams, and wishes of the inner Thomas More, now appropriately disguised as a " speaker of nonsense." Raphael's full name itself suggests the dichotomy of the artwork; the surname—that name most important to the real world—denying the authority of all the wishes and dreams—and the given name alluding to the celestial character of the wishes, a naming technique repeating the dichotomy earlier seen in the pun in the name Utopia. In the Discourse, the names' reality recedes from the center of attention and the reality of More's deepest wishes comes to the fore. How do these wishes emerge?

I suggested that one of the basic sources of More's discontent was that he acceded to his father's wishes and became a lawyer. As a result, in Utopia, each youth " is brought up in his father's craft," but if anyone is attracted to another occupation, " he is transferred by adoption to a family pursuing that craft for which he has a liking," and " Care is taken not only by his father but by authorities" that the youth is well placed (127/12 ff.). Although Raphael does not make the connection, he indicates another Utopian principle which, we can see, shows the autobiographical roots of the foregoing principle of adolescent vocational independence. That is, in Utopia, " they absolutely banish from their country all lawyers, who cleverly manipulate cases and cunningly argue legal points" (195/15). Put the two thoughts together, and we have something like, " no one should have to be a lawyer if he does not want to," a principle which would have completely dissolved one of More's greatest misgivings in life.

Significantly, fathers are not banished from Utopia. In the matter of vocation, the custom of paternal leadership is retained. This is understandable, since More had a great stake in his own fatherhood, from the standpoint of both domestic and biological authority. In Utopia, fathers are transformed into benevolent civil authority (or vice versa): " No official is haughty or formidable. They are called fathers and show that character" (195/1). Though the Utopians are not Christians, the ultimate religious force is also a father: they believe in a " certain single being . . . far above the reach of the human mind, diffused throughout the universe . . . in power. Him they call father" (217/15). In his reallocation of paternal authority, More is probably aiming to unite the clerical and intellectual benevolence of Father John Morton and the worldly authority of Father John More, a union that probably occurred to More unconsciously at least from the confluence of the similarity of their names and More's probable wish for such a union.[42]

By and large, fatherhood retains its traditional authority: one may travel " provided he obtain his father's leave " (147/ 15). New buildings are not constantly needed in Utopia because " extravagant heirs " do not let " fall to ruin " " what a father has built " (133/18). And in family religious matters, the father is the confessor for his wife and children (233/25 ff.). The founding of Utopia has a paternalistic or imperialistic cast, but with the familiar justification that it is all for the good. Utopus, " as conquerer . . . brought the rude and rustic people to such a perfection of culture and humanity as makes them now superior to almost all other mortals " (113/7-9). Though More's work as the founding father of Utopia was intellectual, the metaphor of Utopus suggests the violent, power-seeking feelings attached to this work.

In real life, More's authoritarian feelings became visible in his fight against heresy and in his defense of Papal authority. A taste of these feelings can be felt from the discussion of religion in Utopia. While it is true that people who deviate from Utopian religion retain their right to life—though not to public discussion—" if anyone thinks that souls . . . perish with the body or that the world is the mere sport of chance and not governed by divine providence," Utopians " do not regard him even as a member of mankind " (221/32; 233/14). Here are the seeds of More's subsequent religious chauvinism, complete with the now familiar totalitarian habit of reducing deviation to something outside the human species and thereby implicitly expendable.

When Utopia is pitted in any way against the outside world, its authoritarianism is transformed into strict fraternal

---

[42] It is interesting to speculate that in the additional syllable in Morton's name, More may have seen the missing element of fatherhood.

loyalty. This too might be expected from More's biography not only beacuse he almost joined a monastic brotherhood, but also because his involvement with Christian humanism was, as Professor Routh puts it, with a "cosmopolitan brotherhood of learning," [43] a select, elite in-group of scholars having their "own" languages, their own ethics, and even their own New Theology. Certainly More's steadfast affection for Erasmus, Colet, Lilly, and others bepseaks strong fraternal loyalties. In Utopia, enemy generals are fought by "a band of picked youths" who are to "hunt out the opposing general" (211/31) to kill or capture him. War is the opportunity for a fraternal combine to bring down the seat of (opposing) authority. "Huge rewards" are promised to "anyone who will kill the enemy king" (203-5). Whole families come under the ethic of brotherhood: "It is the greatest reproach for a husband to return without his wife or for a son to come back having lost his father" (211/7). That is, if one member of the family is to die, they must all die. Utopians frequently employ mercenaries not simply to save their own lives but because "they would be the greatest benefactor to the human race if they could relieve the world of all the dregs of this abominable and impious people" (209/15). The inner loyalty is almost tribal for "the whole island is like a single family" (149/4). "Wrong done to their friends" (201/34) is severely punished; and if a Utopian citizen "is wrongfully disabled or killed anywhere, . . . if the guilty persons are not surrendered, they cannot be appeased but forthwith declare war. If the guilty persons are surrendered, they are punished either with death or enslavement" (203/10-15). In Utopia, the violence implicit in More's fierce loyalties is exposed in even murderous and vengeful dimensions. His own willingness to die despite the pleas of his family and others who loved him testifies to the reality of these extreme emotions.

Other fulfilled wishes in Utopia elaborate the "father-brother-authority" strain I am tracing. In the idea of communal ownership of food and goods, the (More's?) "single family" is perpetually provided for. But this felicitous situation paves the way for the fulfillment of a more intrapsychi-

[43] Routh, *op. cit.*, p. 17.

cally motivated wish—the abolition of money, More's dependence on which was a constant source of misgiving. Professor Hexter extensively and persuasively documents (from the Discourse section of the *Utopia*) that it was not money *per se* that upset More, but its identification in his mind with pride, pomp, and the sense of personal superiority of the wealthy: [44] " only in man are they [avarice and greed] motivated by pride alone— pride which counts it a personal glory to excel others by super- fluous display of possessions " (139/7) .

But this returns us to psychologically familiar ground. Pride is identified as the ultimate villain in Utopia. Raphael claims that Christ " would long ago have brought the whole world to adopt the laws of the Utopian commonwealth " were it not for the chief progenitor of all plagues . . . Pride " (243-29) . In More's mind, the formula was simple: pride plus money equals power. In Utopia, citizens have neither pride nor money. Their power is communal—or fraternal—and as Professor Rudolph Gottfried points out, there is no king in Utopia.[45] Just as More triumphed over the worldly pride of the " sage father " and over the sergeant whose " harte for pryde/ Lepte in his syde," More triumphs in Utopia over the plague that prevented Christ's rule and becomes the missing savior or king.

If we are to apply the term wish-fulfillment to the content of the Discourse, it would promote my argument to discover an endorsement of the pleasure principle. Raphael does admit that the school of thought that " espouses pleasure as the object by which to define either the whole or the chief part of human happiness " (161/28) seems to be holding sway in Utopia. This endorsement fits interestingly in with the wish-pattern under discussion. Where money disappears from the conventional social and economic areas, it reappears in the pleasure world in two important, related ways: as toys and as toilets. Gold and jewels—adult accoutrements of pride and beauty—are trans- ferred to the world of childhood, where they are common toys; as such they become laughable when visiting ambassadors ap- pear thus adorned. Professor Hexter suggests that this is an

[44] Hexter, *op. cit.,* p. 71ff.
[45] Rudolph B. Gottfried, *A Conscience Undeflowered.* (Lunenberg, Vt.: Stine- hour Press, 1958), p. 7.

autobiographical allusion to More's sense of shame at the role
he just played in Flanders.[46] Yet, the writing of the Discourse
in this period represents More's own indulgence in the childish
game of fantasy-making, playing king and father, particularly.

The shame More felt at the display of ambassadorial gold
is psychologically explained by his association of gold with
eliminative functions—the making of chamber pots out of gold
and silver (153/7). More also classifies sexual pleasure with
the eliminative functions, and we have seen in his biography a
similar shame at the power the sexual function held over him.
The pride associated with gold and sexuality can be equated
with the secret pleasure they must have held for More. In
adulthood, he called this pleasure " pride " and was thereby
able to justify morally his castigation of these pleasures. This
justification takes place in Utopia through the satire involved
in the reduction of gold to toys and toilets. At the same time,
however, the pleasure in sex and money is revealed through
their association with child's play and toilet functions, two
areas which More himself defined as sources of pleasure.

More's repressed and disguised attitudes toward these
pleasures appear in the Utopian scheme for choosing marriage
partners. Viewing one's prospective marriage partner naked
fulfills a kind of oral, voyeuristic character while the metaphor
used to underscore the point suggests a different attitude.
Getting married is compared to purchasing a colt, when one
thoroughly inspects the animal even though the comparative
financial investment is small (189/8). The implication is that
marriage is a much greater financial investment, so one should
certainly inspect the goods first. The commercialization of the
marriage transaction adds an anal trait to the oral, voyeuristic
one. We can document this by referring back to More's choice
of his first wife. Professors Surtz and Hexter, in their notes,[47]
ask if perhaps More had Jane Colt in mind when he used the
metaphor. What More actually had in mind we cannot tell,
and he did write in Latin, where the word " colt " does not
appear. Yet, Roper's story tells us that marriage for More did
indeed involve the choice of a " Colt," a choice in which erotic

46 Hexter, op. cit., p. 38.
47 Surtz and Hexter, op. cit., p. 480.

considerations may have been compromised. The wish expressed in this marriage procedure is that More might have liked to inspect his "goods," and then made his choice, since he is the one making the "financial" outlay. Marriage is really a burden, which brings a host of problems in matters of money, prestige, and sexuality, but which could be solved if marriage were treated as a purchase, where the customer has a free choice. This happens in Utopia; the infantile wishes are fulfilled; that is why it is a "utopian" custom. The complexity of adult life becomes as simple and as pleasurable as child's play, where the child is king.

When More returned from abroad and was offered the position at the Court, speaking his mind brought a new responsibility. His views now "counted" much more than they did before. If Professor Hexter's timetable for the composition of the work is correct, then the need to render the Discourse responsible must have been the motive for writing the Dialogue. The question of advice to a sovereign, which is the main theme of the Dialogue, lends a practical potential to the wish for a Utopian state, while at the same time working out the author's feelings as to exactly how realistic and/or desirable it is.

More explores these feelings through dramatic fragmentation of himself into many figures, a situation quite in keeping with Professor Bevington's hypothesis. From the sheer space devoted to each, it would first seem that the two "polarities" are *persona*, More's and Raphael Hythloday's. The former's position is a moderate one: "What you cannot turn to good you must make as little bad as you can" (101/1). This is a compromise stand which might have been one of More's justifications for his ultimate decision to join the court. Raphael's position is more severe, and from his association with Utopia itself, we are led to believe that it represents a condition of the real world which is corrected by Utopia: "there is no room for philosophers with rulers" (99/10).

Considering Peter Giles in this outer framework of the dialogue suggests that the polarities are not simply between *persona* More and Raphael. Indeed, since More takes a compromise position, we might expect Giles to be at one of the poles. From a topical standpoint, this does not seem to be the case. Giles acts as an intermediary since, as Father Surtz points out, he "introduces Raphael to More." [48] He is described in the *Utopia* in glowing terms as "a young man distinguished equally by learning and character" (49/5). And again as Surtz indicates, he "touches off the whole debate on councilorship." [49] However, part of More's own comments on him, along with the kind of responses Giles offers to Hythloday, indicates that Giles represents a prominent part of More's own mind, a part that perhaps More had some motive to play down.

In introducing Giles, More remarks that Giles is "so polished and so witty" (49/11) that he "made me less conscious than before of the separation from my home, wife, and children to whom I was exceedingly anxious to get back" (49/15). Giles is an audience, but one that acts as a substitute for his family, as a compensation for the domestic security More is now missing in his political enterprises. Although it is possible to construe Giles as a fraternal substitute for the missing dependents, his response to Hythloday suggests that he actually represents More's own reluctant tie to the *status quo*. Giles justifies European civilization on the basis of its only indisputable difference with the New World, its "long experience which has come upon very many advantages for human life" (107/29). Earlier, and in a different context, Hythloday had implicitly answered this objection when he ridiculed royal councilors' sentiments that "it would be a dangerous thing to be found with more wisdom on any point than our forefathers" (59/12). Hythloday's sentiment, in other words, in the earlier as well as the later context is that it is precisely the role of the New Worldians to surpass and make use of the achievements of the earlier, older, more experienced civilization.

The relatively naïve position of Giles then is the set of values that stands opposed to Hythloday, while "More" is an attempt to make his way between the two poles. It is obvious that he values what Giles stands for—his instinctive belief in established civilization, a childlike belief that is perhaps associated with the dependency his own family has on him, and then with his own childlike dependence on his motherly wife,

[48] *Ibid.*, p. cxliv.
[49] *Ibid.*, p. cxliv.

which is in turn associated with his dependence on his father's values. The reason More would perhaps like to suppress this part of himself is that the kind of acceptance of the outer world it engenders is contrary to the rebellious instinct that I think is ultimately governing More's adult behavior. Raphael and the utopian vision represent this instinct—as we have seen in the letter to Erasmus. I would speculate that what Giles represents is indeed the stronger element of More's unconscious life; in the art-work, it is disguised by its scant treatment; in his life, he responded to it with an extremely powerful compensatory rebellion, a rebellion that is in turn disguised by the various puns and jokes and satirical byplay associated with Hythloday.

Ironically, the *persona* More is probably a very close facsimile to what the public knew him as, but one which never really gained a lasting foothold in his personality. This More is capable of considering many viewpoints, such as the belief that " Life cannot be satisfactory where all things are in common " (107/6), which is not the Utopian position. From our psychological perspective, we need not worry whether More " really " believed this, when it makes better sense to say that *a part* of More believed it, and especially when we think we can identify which part.

The third main " part " of More is in Raphael, a kind of Erasmus figure, who would thus represent in the Dialogue More's impulse to scholarship, to the " cosmopolitan brotherhood," to the monastary, and to intellectual detachment, all of whose roots we have already seen in More's youth. Thinking back to the Sergeants' Feast poem, we recall there too a question of " room " for the pedlar, hatter, and sergeant in more learned callings. There was little room for any meddlers in More's poetic activities.[50] We might wonder whether More wanted to be the king or the philosopher, but it is fairly clear that the problem is easily resolved in Utopia, where he would be both.

[50] In Peter K. Marshall's translation, he has "there is no place for philosophy with kings" (New York, 1965), p. 34. Perhaps "utopia" could be substituted for "no place," whence we would have the fulfillment of More's wish: "there is utopia for philosophy with kings." Alas, the Latin uses the word *locus* for "place," and apparently the word *nusquama* would not fit semantically. Yet, the ideas of "no room" and "no where" are not that far apart, regardless of the language.

In order to prove his point about the incompatibility of philosophers and kings, Raphael takes the group back to "his" experience in the home of Cardinal Morton, where he demonstrates that before Morton endorsed his views no one else did, but after the endorsement, they were duly accepted; therefore, what authority says, goes. But the structure of this little scene reveals not the futility of advice, but the ultimate triumph of the rightmindedness of More's boyhood hero, John Morton, to whom Raphael presents his critiques of society. Raphael's antagonist as a "layman, learned in the laws of your country" (67/7) who, after hearing Raphael out, promises to "demolish and destroy all your arguments" (71/28), but is promptly restrained by the Cardinal, put off until "the next meeting" (71/35) which, significantly enough, never comes in the work. A kind of tribunal is set up, where the misery of the public weal, decried by the More-ideal, so to speak, is presented to the opposed emblems of More's searching personality—the Cardinal and his father. The aggressiveness of the latter, framed in the most extreme terms—the threat to destroy *all* of Raphael's views—is duly overcome with equal finality, by the humane Christian hero, the Cardinal. In this "dialogue-within-a-dialogue" Morton's authority is invoked to defeat his father's authority, and thus to justify his (More's) political and social views alongside his humanistic impulses.

In this light, the dramatic situation surrounding *Utopia* can be said to assume a phallic and/or oedipal character. Because, in this phase, the infant first becomes aware that there are more than two people in his society, and that at least one of them is of a different gender, he recognizes that he must cope with the conflicting emotions associated with this particular plurality. In trying to navigate between the conflicting pulls of Giles and Hythloday, More is trying to form an identity by resolving the conflict between a dependency on motherly values—"nostalgia" for his family—and fatherly values—his rebellious desire to be the philosopher king, indeed, to surpass the earlier claimant, Plato, to this throne. Thus, the drama around the *Utopia* is one of self-definition and self-justification. The self that is justified and defined is a variegated one, revealed by the dialogue to be indeed a composite or a compromise construction trying to accommodate opposing impulses.

This is true of the adult identity of any man, but only few men have either the talent or opportunity to express their struggle in so distinct and revealing a form.

To be sure, More's inner struggle is not composed only of two or three identifiable forces. The two figures in the " comic relief " of the Morton dialogue are as much a part of More as are the main figures, and perhaps, like the scantily mentioned Giles, an equally important part. First, it would not be amiss to conclude that any event associated with Morton must have left a lasting impression on More's personality. However, the two figures Hythloday tells about can be intrinsically related to More's youthful experience. Both, in particular, are impecunious parties. The hanger-on in the dialogue is, because of his age, somewhat more parasitical, but he is nevertheless there to offer good wit and interesting opinions, though the opinions are not to be taken seriously. Although the adolescent More's role was justifiable by his youthful seriousness, the analogy is there. The hanger-on arouses the wrath of the friar through the former's impatience with beggars and mendicants, as if the hanger-on were an aristocrat who cannot be bothered with beggars: " ' I am exceedingly anxious to get this person out of my sight' " (83/2). More, we remember, was not disturbed in this way by the poverty of others, but he was precisely so disturbed at his own dependence on money and the need to acquire it. The friar, meanwhile, associates himself with the mendicants in that he too claims state assistance or attention: " ' not even so will you be rid of mendicants unless you make provision for us friars too ' " (83/20). In addition to More's associating himself with the friar's poverty and his tendency to quote scripture, the image of the friar is one of the possibilities of More's future. The sketch of the friar is probably More's own caricature of himself, perhaps as he saw himself in his student days and possibly as his father saw him. Both the hanger-on and the friar are finally laughed out of Morton's household, or at least out of Hythloday's narrative. Finally, the pair might be further analogized to the impotent, sycophantic counsel at court and the noisemaking self-righteousness of the Church—More had more than a finger in both of these institutional pies. This comic pair reveals More's sense of the ludicrousness of his own quandary and demonstrates his ability

to transcend his quandary through such humorous self-awareness. One remembers this habit which he exhibited as he was
going to the executioner.[51] A. R. Heiserman has argued [52]
that a thoroughgoing satiric structure, along with numerous
subtle satirical twists, explain the *Utopia* much more fully than
a frontal ideational analysis of the work. It is clear from More's
unfailing gallows humor (as well as from the comic relief of
the friar and the hanger-on) that his abiding sense of irony
was as deep in his personality as it is in the *Utopia*. Heiserman
suggests that this satirical bent is actually the key to his ultimate
seriousness—his conscious aim " to teach virtue by an attack on
vice." Psychologically, we would say that there is irony in his
attempt to *learn* virture by attacking *his own* vices; it is one of
his key defenses and tools of his impulse to violence; yet, like
his jokes on the threshold of death and his own acceptance of
death, a weapon used perhaps too often against himself.

Rather than any particular dogma—even the Utopian
dogma—a state of profound quandary is justified by the Dialogue. True wishes are sincerely and passionately expressed,
but more than the wishes—the freedom to have them is being
justified, and the right to think them over in public. Only late
in life did More come to any distinct conclusions about where
he stood and abandon the safer habits of compromise, con-
ciliation, and negotiation.

In this context, the last line of the work is a remarkably
accurate confession. The *persona* More observes of Raphael
that

> though in other respects he is a man of the most un-
> doubted learning as well as of the greatest knowledge of
> human affairs, I cannot agree with all that he said. But I
> readily admit that there are very many features in the
> Utopian commonwealth which it is easier for me to wish
> for in our countries than to have any hope of seeing real-
> ized (245-247)

This statement is certainly one of the roots of the work's popularity. Although it contains a hint of double meaning or satire

[51] See note 36.
[52] A. R. Heiserman, "Satire in the *Utopia*," *PMLA*, LXVIII, 163, 174.

in his description and praise of Raphael, it also reveals the wish that all audiences must have in common with the author; the author's feelings are confessed, but the frame of the artwork is retained—the same simultaneity of effect that More achieved in his pageant verses. Father Surtz has observed that the irony of the work " depends not on any express hint but on a secret and shared sympathy of reader and author." [53] There can be little doubt that More achieved a sense of vital fellowship not only with his audience of Latin scholars and intimates, but with enlightened men of subsequent ages as well. This fellowship achieved and achieves for More the cultural prominence and leadership he struggled for in his own age. His work fulfilled the wish that his life could not.

Viewing the *Utopia* as a confessional piece suggests a new perspective on both Christian humanism and the utopian fantasy, as they have remained in our cultural and verbal vocabularies all these years. Christian humanism we can see as an *indignant* demand for ethical and enlightened leadership, a search for authority of informed, learned, and devoted men. As the title of the movement implies, the authority it seeks is a compromise force, one that combines two strains of Western cultural sentiment—one religious and one secular. The correspondence of More's life struggles—from the time he was a teenager writing poetry in his father's household to the moment of self-sacrifice in defiance of his king—with this general predicament of values documents in a new way the fact that at the heart of Christian humanism is the familiar eternal battle of civilization with human emotion. In a sense, the utopian fantasy can be seen as a regressive component of the larger cultural movement. It is a reminder that the wish for power resides in all men, a wish that constitutes the continuous threat of popular rebellion, unless leadership is prepared to distribute equally society's goods and authority. As did More, culture actually confesses the unrealizability of the utopian fantasy. Yet, as seen in so many other areas of civilization—the millenarian movement in the late Middle Ages, in the apocalyptic thrusts of militant Communism and Nazism—many consider it no mere

[53] Surtz and Hexter, p. clii.

fantasy. The wishes that *Utopia* reveals are not very different in sentiment from the barbaric, brutal attempts to take them seriously. Like the apostles of social apocalypse, More was indignant, impatient, angry, and yearning for temporal power to establish his own majority. But More was "civilized" and ultimately "saintly" in that the violence within him was wrought only on himself. Throughout his life, his techniques of concealing his violence—poetry, verbal dexterity, the use and study of classical languages, the dialogic and satiric transcription of his many impulses, and finally his "report" of a non-existent country way off in the inwardly desired "new world"— suggest that art, intellectual refinement, and knowledge offer perhaps the most effective compromise with inner violence and the hope for others to achieve More's majority.

The Personal History of David Copperfield:

A Study In Psychoanalytic Criticism

Leonard F. Manheim

From May 1849 to November 1850, there appeared the monthly installments of the novel by Dickens which has always been accounted the most autobiographical of all his works. It followed closely upon that period of five years during which Dickens had been creating the canon of English Christmas mythology from *A Christmas Carol* through *The Cricket on the Hearth* to the final and little known allegory of memory known as *The Haunted Man.* Its immediate predecessor among the novels—*Dombey and Son*—marked the beginning of a period in Dickens' career as a novelist during which he attempted to make a fierce effort at self-analysis, a determined effort to come to grips with those figures of fact and fantasy which had plagued his conscious and unconscious psyche. In *Dombey* he had tried to exorcise the demon of the primitive father-fear through an attempt to penetrate with sympathy into a three-dimensional "father." Further, he had tried to picture, sympathetically as well, a woman who was no longer virginal but who was neither a freakish maternal image nor a crabbed spinster. He was to try something of the same sort once more when he identified himself with the virgin-image herself in Esther Summerson of the next ensuing novel, *Bleak House.*

In *David Copperfield* the subject for analysis was none other than the author himself—the author, however, in the guise of the mythological hero. Dickens could not and did not succeed in any of these attempted self-analyses, not even in this, one of his most popular works for a full century. That the attempted confession did bring with it a temporary feeling that the load had been lifted through partial catharsis there can be no doubt. There is a certain freeness, an exuberance that runs through *David Copperfield* such as we have not experienced since the days of Mr. Pickwick. And yet it is a queer sort of confession, is it not, in which every element of "truth" is shot through and through with fantasy, dereistic fantasy which is quite as revelatory as is the "confession" itself.

"Whether I shall turn out to be the hero of my own life, or whether that station will be held by anyone else, these pages must show." With these words Charles Dickens opens one of the most famous *Bildungsromanen* in literature. And if David is *not* the hero of his own life, it is not because Charles Dickens did not do his utmost to make him so. There are indeed many points of factual similarity between the two "lives." David must have been born during the early years of the nineteenth century and so must have been about Dickens' own age when he was writing his autobiography. He shares his procreator's initials, in reverse order, a fact which is said to have caused the author some surprise when it was called to his attention. His boyhood reading corresponds closely to that of his progenitor. He attends a bad school with a title not dissimilar to Wellington House; he works as an adolescent under conditions which he considers degrading; he becomes familiar with the law by working in a law office; he learns shorthand and earns his living by reporting parliamentary debates; he uses his newspaper connections to further his ambition to become a writer, and he does become a writer of successful novels and travels on the continent. But there the similarities end. There is not even a hint that the autobiography of the hero is destined to become one of Copperfield's own novels. He insists that "this manuscript is intended for no eyes but mine" and that during his stay in Switzerland (after Dora's death and before he returned to England to marry Agnes) he "wrote a story, with a purpose growing, not remotely, out of his experience, and sent it to Traddles, who arranged for its publication very advantageously." Neither David Copperfield nor Charles Dickens is willing to publish his own life-history without fictional decoration!

At the very opening of the book the pattern is made plain. The hero will follow the pattern of the hero in Rank's analysis of the mythology-pattern.[1] "I was born with a caul," he writes and makes much of the superstitions connected with the relic of such a birth. If the obstetrical connotations of that statement are not plain, let us note that it means that the sac, containing the amni-

[1] Otto Rank, *Der Mythus von der Geburt des Helden* (Leipzig, 1909).

otic fluid in which the foetus lived in its prenatal state, has not burst before delivery, but that it is delivered intact with the infant in it. In the language of the myth, the hero is not "drawn from the waters" one second earlier than is absolutely necessary, that he brings the "waters" into the world with him and is then "born" again by being released from his pre-natal state while he is, paradoxically, already "in the world." (The very superstition connected with the caul indicates its mythological nature; it is supposed to ensure its owner against *drowning*.) His belated exodus from the world of pre-natal omnipotence is followed immediately by other variants on the hero-myth. Once again, the hero is fatherless. In fact, he is fatherless from the moment of his birth, being a posthumous child. In fantasy, he is motherless as well, for Dickens does not miss a single opportunity to point out that Clara Copperfield is a girl-wife, a "mere baby," a virginal figure that at least equals any of the other similar figures with which the earlier works were blighted. If ever there was a virgin birth depicted outside of theological literature, this is it. The pattern is reminiscent of *Oliver Twist*, even though David manages to transcend that former juvenile hero's vapidity. As with Oliver, the father-surrogates and later mother-images crowd in thick and fast. Some have a basis in childhood reminiscence; others in childhood fantasy.

The analytical tendency which arose in *Dombey and Son* makes the father-and-son situation in *David Copperfield* far more explicit. John Dickens, the "villain" who would subject his son to the indignity of factory work, is David's step-father, Mr. Murdstone. Dickens does not wish the reader to miss for one second the implication of the first syllable of his name, for Betsey Trotwood refers to him and his sister as "murdering" villains. "Father" Murdstone, even after the death of David's mother, continues his practice of oppressing and intimidating young and inexperienced wives. Late in the tale, when David renews his old acquaintance with Mr. Chillip, the kindly physician who ushered him into the world, the latter points out "that Mr. Murdstone sets up an image of himself, and calls it the Divine Nature." Thus the omnipotence-fantasy is associated with the ugly father-image.

In David's early youth he is haunted by the double vision of the virginal mother-image in the delicate Clara, existing side by side with the later oppressor-mother in Jane Murdstone. Jane returns to haunt him with a similar vision when she assumes the position of Dora's "confidential friend." The living image of the virgin-mother disappears, however, when David beholds her for the last time on his return to Salem House, but he sees her afterward "in [his] sleep at school—a silent presence near my bed—looking at me with the same intent face—holding up her baby in her arms."

It is not only the nineteenth century but all modern civilization which permits an author to pillory the father-image in the guise of a wicked stepfather. It is but a step further to extend the father-image to other father-surrogates. John Dickens in his guise as improvident father, over-flowery speaker and writer, pretentious pseudo-gentleman, is none other than Wilkins Micawber, Esq., as all the world knows by this time. The picture is no more flattering than is that of Murdstone. I wonder how many readers today are willing to read every word of the flowery utterances, oral and in writing, which flow from Mr. Micawber's lips and pen. Dickens hardly expected them to do so, for in every case in which Mr. Micawber reveals some fact of importance to the course of the plot, that fact is revealed again in simplified form by the author himself. Mr. Micawber is a sweet, lovable old bore of a psychopathic personality. Mrs. Micawber is equally prosy, pretentious, and in addition guilty of the over-protestation that "she will never desert Mr. Micawber," although, as that worthy gentleman points out, no one had ever asked her to do so. The Micawber-Dickens family link, if not sufficiently stressed by the imprisonment for debt (in the King's Bench prison, let it be noted—the Marshalsea will not crop up again until *Little Dorrit*), is riveted more securely by references to David's pawning of the household equipment piece by piece so that the lordly gentleman and his lady may not have to appear in the pawn-shop, by the stress on the pawning of the few pathetic books (not David's books, though), and by Mrs. Micawber's announcement to the world by means of an elegantly-lettered placard (a placard that will appear again in *Our Mutual Friend*) that she is conducting a seminary for young females to which, unfortunately, no young females ever repaired for the improvement of their education.

What is generally overlooked by the Dickens-lovers who revel in the glorious nonsense of the lovable Micawber is the fact that

Micawber is not only a pretentious fool but also, with regard to his own numerous and constantly increasing family, a very bad father. To David he was not so, of course, for David came to him during a period of emancipation from parental restraint and so, in his own new-found self-reliance, could afford to be genially tolerant of Micawber's characteristic imprudence and ambivalence toward Miss Emma, Master Wilkins, the twins, and the new angelic visitor in their midst. Yet even Master Wilkins shares in some of the analytic confession, for does not Mr. Micawber (as John Dickens had done in Charles' youth) comment upon his son's beautiful "headvoice" and extend to him, at a family party which bores the young man to the point of distraction, the option of either going to bed or of favoring the company with a tasteful rendition of "The Woodpecker Tapping"?

But the list of father-surrogates, so far depicted both consciously and unconsciously, does not end with the step-father and the foster-father. Passing over such obvious extensions as the bad schoolmaster, Mr. Creakle, and his "good" prototype, Dr. Strong, as well as the Murdstone and Grinby figures, Mr. Quinion and Mick Walker (Bob Fagin—note the name—of Dickens' blacking-factory days), we find three other characters in this category on whom some comment, more speculative, to be sure, but none the less revealing, should be made.

We know how important is the role of verbal similarities both in psychoanalytic technique and in Dickens' name-giving. Is it not remarkable that Mr. Richard Babley, the harmless old lunatic who is under the protection of that remarkable mother-image, Miss Trotwood, is always referred to as Mr. Dick? Here is the father's whipping-boy, condignly punished by being transformed into an impotent *babbler!*

The clinical picture of Mr. Dick holds together very well. David makes an immediate diagnosis of his condition:

> Mr. Dick . . . was gray-headed and florid: I should have said all about him in saying so, had not his head been curiously bowed—not by age; it reminded me of one of Mr. Creakle's boys' heads after a beating—and his grey eyes, prominent and large, with a strange kind of watery brightness in them that made me, in combination with his vacant manner, his

submission to my aunt, and his childish delight when she
praised him, suspect him of being a little mad; though, if he
were, how he came to be there, puzzled me extremely.
(Chapter XIII)

The symptomatology is revealed little by little. He has marked
distractibility of attention; he has a phobia concerning the use of
his right name; his father and his family consider him a "natural"
(the term is used with just a little of the old superstitious venera-
tion). Then we come to the paranoid delusion concerning King
Charles' head, coupled with the double orientation which causes
him to comment upon the present date and the date of the
martyr-king's execution and to wonder how the King's troubles
could have gotten into *his* head. There is an interesting comment
upon Betsey Trotwood's cooperation with Mr. Dick in his "occu-
pational therapy," for the madman is depicted as being most skillful with his fingers, and Betsey encourages him in his manufac-
ture of toys for the neighboring boys, even to the huge kites
through which he demonstrates the "flight of ideas" by pinning
documents to them as they fly into the air. It is at these times, as
David comments, that he is most relaxed and free from his delusions—as if they were literally carried away from him. The weak
point is, as usual, the nineteenth century etiology, for Mr. Dick is
said to have fallen into his condition as the result of a fever which
followed upon the unhappy experiences of a favorite sister. Miss
Trotwood, who is resolved at all costs to avoid any acknowledg-
ment of Mr. Dick's mental weakness, explains his references to
Kind Charles' head as "his allegorical way of expressing it," saying
that "he connects his illness with great disturbance and agitation,
naturally, and that's the figure, or the simile, or whatever it's
called, which he chooses to use." Miss Betsey seems to understand
the relation between dereistic thinking in the poet and in the
madman! The whole picture taken together would seem to fit a
type of schizophrenia with paranoid trends. The picture is, as
ever, weakened later when Mr. Dick recovers under the strain of
Miss Trotwood's financial decline sufficiently to be able to do
copying work just so long as he keeps his precious memorial close
at hand in which to jot down any references to King Charles' head
which may arise to distract him. He lives in lodgings near those

occupied by David and his aunt, later near the home of David and his wife, and is even enlisted to play an assisting role in the unmasking of Heep. It is a queer sort of recompense, but thoroughly characteristic of the unconscious function of the superego, which permits the writer to satisfy his awakened guilt feelings toward the father-figure by painting another version of this father-image in the role of the "reiner Thor."

Equally rewarding should be our examination of a "good" father-figure, that of Mr. Wickfield, lawyer of Canterbury, father of the "little lamb" Agnes, and employer and dupe of the designing Uriah. Dickens has stressed Wickfield's connection with his own analytical impulse by having Wickfield constantly on the alert for some single guiding motive which he endeavors to detect beneath the actions of each of those with whom he is thrown in contact. Unfortunately, he has no more notion of the true nature of that motive than has Charles Dickens; consequently his analyses always come to grief. Not so Wickfield's self-analysis, however. The Oedipus-situation reproduced in his relations with his daughter seems constantly to plague him. He recollects that his own adored wife died during the girl's infancy because of her inability to withstand the hatred she had had heaped upon her by her own father, or her own sense of guilt at having married one whom her father disliked (for what reason we do not know); and he fixes his love wholly upon that daughter. But that does not bring relief. He finds himself brooding over the effect his daughter's death would have upon him, on the effect his death would have upon his daughter, and this brooding upon death (what we would denominate the incomplete neutralization of the Thanatos-impulse) is so unendurable to him that he seeks refuge in a gentlemanly variety of alcoholism which only adds to his depression, in addition to bringing upon him a sort of alcoholic arthritis, and he falls a victim to the machinations of the villainous Heep. When Heep finally raises his foul eyes toward the lovely Agnes, Wickfield comprehends to a limited degree the meaning of love turned to disease.

'Oh, Trotwood, Trotwood!' exclaimed Mr. Wickfield, wringing his hands. 'What I have come to be, since I first saw you in this house! I was on my downward way then, but the dreary, dreary road I have traversed since! Weak indulgence had ruined me. Indulgence in remembrance, and indulgence in forgetfulness. My natural grief for my child's mother turned to disease; my natural love for my child turned to disease. . . . I thought it possible that I could truly love one creature in the world, and not love the rest; I thought it possible that I could truly mourn for one creature gone out of the world, and not have some part in the grief of all who mourned . . . I have preyed on my own morbid coward heart, and it has preyed on me.' (Chapter XXXIX)

Dickens thinks that he is preaching his usual message of the duty to be "good," to love one's neighbor; in only the tiniest step forward he would have realized the relationship of that sort of universal love to the psychoanalytic revelation of the "economy of love"—"not too little and not too much." Never again was he to come so close to that comprehension. Rarely is he as able to view a father-image with so great a degree of objectivity. Yet we must not fail to note that here again the father who failed to love wisely and truly is subjected to condign punishment, punishment from the hands of one whom he had treated as a son, lifting him up from poverty and lowliness, but only through an unworthy motive, and with inaccurate appraisal of that "son's" motivation.

The freedom which we note in the treatment of the father of one of the virgin-images is lacking in the corresponding figure of one who stands in the position of father to another. Daniel Peggotty loves Emily every bit as much as Wickfield loves Agnes, but his love is not selfish. On the contrary, it is selfless to an almost Christ-like degree. Yet when we come to examine the family circle of the Peggottys, we are impressed by the fact that nobody is related to anyone else more closely than as uncle, niece, or cousin! Yet the set-up is that of father, mother (Mrs. Gummidge), son (Ham), and daughter (Emily). If the Oedipus motive is given free reign, there is no social censor to prevent it, for there is no blood-relationship to cry halt. In Daniel Peggotty we have no attempt at analysis of the father-figure, no attack upon the father as enemy, but the final idealization of what a father ought to be, uncontaminated by social position, unhampered by poverty or indolence, untrammeled by introversion, unhindered by anything which would prevent his being the kind of passionately loving and all-wise father for which the adolescent soul of the author yearned unceasingly.

When the hero, in the words of Menninger's interpretation of the Rank formula[2] proclaims, "I eschew all women except madonnas, for whom I have only reverence, love and devotion," he is casting a large portion of womankind, both married and unwed, into outer darkness. They are for him the pattern of the "common earthly parent" whom he cannot recognize as his own virgin-progenitor. For Dickens they are all queer and odd in sundry ways, either as the faithless servant (Mrs. Crupp), or as the dependent mother who cannot give up the daughter upon whom she relies (Mrs. Crewler, mother of Tommy Traddles' Sophy), or the conniving mother of Uriah Heep, or the vicious mother-in-law of Dr. Strong who has designs upon the virtue of her own daughter, or even unmarried mother-surrogates like the sisters of the late Mr. Spenlow. They are all caricatures of femininity, portrayed vividly enough, to be sure, but never wholly sympathetically. On the other hand, the "humble" mother-substitute who rescues the hero from the bad pseudo-parents (Clara Peggotty) and the regal doting mother who adopts and raises him to a kingly estate (Betsey Trotwood) are the recipients of compensatory traits, super-added to their necessary "queerness" to console the hero for his "terrible wishes" and to make amends and do penance for his sins.

To vary the mythological figure, is not Betsey much like the fairy godmother (divorce the term from its present semantic significance and look at it in its literal meaning) who attends upon the birth of the hero in a fairy-story, then takes offense, disappears, and only returns after a long interval to grant him his "three wishes"? The pattern is even more explicit in the case of the Spenlow aunts, who have what they consider a just cause of complaint for having been slighted at Dora's christening-feast and have remained on cool terms with the family until they take in the orphaned, destitute girl. With respect to Betsey, Dickens goes out of his way time and again to reiterate that her rough and crotch-

[2] Karl Menninger, *The Human Mind* (New York, 1930), p. 315. See also Rank, p. 67.

ety exterior hides a "heart of gold." She imputes all of her affection for David to what the dear child Clara would have felt had
she been alive. In passing, is it not remarkable how Dickens puts
all the blame for their misdeeds upon his "bad" characters? Assuming that which we cannot imagine, that Betsey ever really had
a husband, is it not conceivable that his inability to live on peace-
ful terms with her might have been due in no slight measure to
her peculiarities? Just so David, pictured as an angel-child, might
possibly have appeared otherwise to a stepfather even less cruel
than Mr. Murdstone.

Betsey Trotwood, for all of her denunciation of marriage and
her mortal disappointment with David for not having been born a
girl, is not lacking in affection for some portions of mankind. She
certainly sings the praises of Mr. Dick as a man of unusual sagac-
ity, even over and above the compensatory utterances designed to
distract attention from his obvious mental weakness. She has a
soft spot in her heart for Mr. Wickfield, for she keeps secret the
mode by which she has been deprived of most of her small fortune when she believes that it is Wickfield rather than Heep who
is responsible for its disappearance. Her whole pattern as fairy-
godmother is rounded out when we discover that her later claim
of poverty is exaggerated to "test" David lest his indolence and
pride should ruin him, and that she has secreted a small but still
substantial portion of her fortune throughout the whole time of
David's struggle for financial independence.

David Copperfield, then, is a hero in the mythological sense,
but he is never a hero of a modern novel, never a Raskolnikov,
nor a Hans Castorp, never a Julien Sorel, nor a Daniel Deronda.
And yet there can be no doubt that Dickens in this novel was
trying to penetrate into the mysteries of his leading character.
The trouble was that he could find nothing there because he had
placed nothing there, and he had placed nothing there because he
could not do so without coming directly to grips with those portions of Charles Dickens that he would not and could not bear to
meet. Far easier was it for him to permit the elements in his
hero-figure to be once more spread out among a number of characters, to set off blacks against whites with a few pied colors
thrown in, to create a galaxy of hero-caricatures instead of one
complete hero. This is precisely what he has done. If we examine

Uriah Heep we find that he is everything that David is not, with one single exception—he too reaches adolescence and maturity without the assistance of a father. Uriah has committed the fatal error of rejecting the "good" father-substitute, Mr. Wickfield, modelling himself exactly on his own "bad" father. Dickens pretends to scorn the British tradition of birth and station; yet the greatest element in Uriah's hypocrisy is that he utilizes a pretended humility in his station in order to worm his way out of it and into the "upper classes." Uriah is humble, whereas David is given to pride. But look at the fraud and conniving in Uriah's humility. Uriah is awkward, ungainly, uncouth. Is it to be expected that David should not be proud of his good looks and his gentility when he sees what their opposite has produced in Uriah? David has his period of extravagance and disregard of money. But is not that better than to be so covetous of money that one becomes a usurer and an embezzler like Uriah? Uriah sets David's teeth on edge at first sight. What else could one expect when Dr. Jekyll is confronted with Mr. Hyde? Yet the sum-total is, in David, an unconvincing puppet-like figure of no real vitality; in Uriah, the greatest figure of a hyprocite in all literature since Tartuffe. Note in passing that Dickens, with his craze for "compensatory" character building has given Heep's Christian name to the well-meaning Jewish hypocrite in *Our Mutual Friend.*

David, the mythological hero, makes his series of descents into the pit, only to be resurrected each time into a new and more lovely avatar. He struggles out of the darkness of Creakle's school, the gloom of his mother's death, and the hell of Murdstone and Grinby into the bright sunlight of Betsey Trotwood's affluence. Yet he once more follows the hero-pattern by seeking out the companion of the pit, the hero of his fallen days, his evil genius, James Steerforth. Here again there is a hero-dichotomy. Steerforth has all of the graces of living under his control to a far greater extent than has David. He possesses the savoir faire, the ability to make himself universally loved (by all except the good angel, Agnes, of course), the ability to get on in life with little or no effort. But at heart he is a black villain, for, to him, sex is not the holiest of holies that it is to David. He dallies with it lightly, too lightly, and all is lost. Yet, amazingly enough, David cannot recover from his adolescent infatuation for Steerforth even in the time of his greatest villainy. To

David he is still one to be loved and admired despite his evil ways. Can it, oh, can it be that there is something fascinating about Steerforth's failure to apotheosize the glories of virginity, something that David-Dickens longs for, but can never hope to attain? Or is it conceivable that David sees in Steerforth a means of satisfying the cravings of Eros without the necessity of soiling *any* virgins? The temptation is great to speculate on these possibilities. The literary effect is, once more, to create a great, living character, marred only by the forced and obvious theatricality of his demise with Ham in the great storm at Yarmouth.

And, to balance the picture of David veering toward ruin in his first resurrection, we have the corresponding picture of his neglected and unappreciated schoolfellow, Tommy Traddles, during the period of David's emergence from the double shock of his aunt's financial debacle and his supposedly hopeless love for Dora. It is Tommy upon whom he leans in his need, Tommy who engineers the unmasking of Heep, Tommy who acts as his friend and confidential agent. Yet David does not love Tommy as he loved Steerforth. He finds Tommy's unruly hair trying, Tommy's unfailing good nature something of a bore. He cannot forget that Tommy as a schoolboy received the largest number of beatings from Creakle and took them all cheerfully. Hence he feels that Tommy cannot be the "delicate child of life" that he, David, is; consequently he never identifies himself with him. Thus does David-Dickens excuse his own inability to rise above his oppressing emotions. He envisions Tommy's normal mental and social adjustment as a sort of special gift, rather than something to be attained by his own well-directed efforts. From his schooldays on, Tommy has always "doodled" by drawing skeletons, the reason for which David could not comprehend unless he could be viewed as "a sort of hermit, who reminded himself by these symbols of mortality that caning couldn't last forever."

The last and most shadowy in this galaxy of hero-pictures is Ham Peggotty. He is to heroes what Daniel Peggotty is to fathers, the great Christ-like ideal of humility, forbearance, forgiveness, native nobility, etc., etc., none of which brings him to life for a moment. Could he not see that his patient adoration and abject servitude of little Emily could not have other than a bad end? He had no Marcel Proust to tell him so. Neither did Dickens.

If we have seen in the father-figures, the mother-images, and the hero-portraits the dualism, the dichotomy that arises from an honest attempt at analysis and mental purging of the dregs of the unconscious plus the successful attempts of the psyche to preserve its cherished illusions and to exhibit them in their various fantastic guises, what are we to say of the same double picture which we observe in the author's dealings with the omnipresent virgin-image? The attempt at analysis and catharsis seems to be genuine, but oh, how feeble, for this cherished mirage is most firmly imbedded not only in the mind and "heart" of the author but in the *mores* of his time.

"Why is it," Dickens exclaimed in later life, "that as with poor David, a sense comes always crushing on me now, when I fall into low spirits, as of one happiness that I have missed in life, and one friend and companion I have never made?"[3] If, as seems apparent, something of the same sort of anxiety was plaguing him even when he wrote *David Copperfield,* would it not seem an easy task to find out the source of the lost happiness, the identity of the one companion he has never been united with? Now who could that be in the light of his past history other than the pretty, flirtatious little jilt, Maria Beadnell? No other feminine figure could ever have suggested itself, or have been permitted by the super-ego to suggest itself, to his consciousness. Had he not nursed his romantic, unrequited affection and would he not continue to do so even for the years following *David Copperfield* to such an extent that he would open Maria Beadnell Winter's letter to him years after "with the touch of his young friend David Copperfield when he was in love?" He would even write to Mrs. Winter, five years after he had supposedly routed "Dora's" image from his heart, "Whatever of fancy, romance, energy, passion, aspiration and determination belong to me, I have never separated and never shall separate from the hard-hearted little woman—You."[4] But it would be anticipation to run ahead to the shocking blow Dickens was to receive when his Dora re-appeared in the flesh. We have here to consider the attempt to rid himself of the *succubus* while it is still only a mind-image.

[3] Hugh Kingsmill (Lunn), *The Sentimental Journey: A Life of Charles Dickens* (New York, 1935), p. 170.

[4] Walter Dexter, ed., *Letters to Maria Beadnell* (London, 1936), p. 74.

Good, then! Let the author imagine that his early courtship was a successful one. Let him think that, instead of the mischievous (perhaps jealous) interference of Miss Leigh, he had the kindly, gushing aid of Miss Julia Mills. Let him fancy that his courtship did not have to be placed in the power of the friendly but unimaginative Kolle, but that, when aid was needed, he would have the more intelligent, high-hearted assistance of Tommy Traddles. Then let fiction come to the aid of fact and deprive Maria of her unsympathetic and cruel parents by substituting for them a dead mother and a soon impoverished and deceased father for Dora. What then is to stand in the way of the match? Nothing but a pair of queer maiden aunts, Dora's "Aunt Betseys," and they are soon disposed of.

Good again! David-Dickens is married to Dora-Beadnell. And what occurs at once? He finds that she acts like his image of Catherine Hogarth Dickens at her worst. She is no housekeeper. She cannot manage well. She is silly and romantic, and all this without even Catherine's excuse, a large family of young children. "How silly of me," thinks the author, "to imagine that I would have been happier with Dora. She would probably have turned out just like a real-life wife."

The rest is simple. "Off with her head!" Oh, of course, it is done with great pathos, with something of the genuine tragedy of parting with a cherished illusion, but there is no doubt that Dora, once disposed of as a wife, is better off dead, and that Dickens undoubtedly feels that it is a far, far better thing that he is doing than he has ever done. But when the unconscious aggression has rented itself upon the pathetic ashes of poor Dora, the author cannot face the fact that the image of which she is but a pale replica has not died, and, what is more, will not die. What he yearned for even consciously was the blissful days of the early courtship when he could feel "as to marriage, and fortune, and all that . . . almost as innocently undesigning . . . as when he loved little Em'ly." Dora's great misfortune was that, child-wife though she was, she was wife as well as child and the hideous fate loomed for her, as it had (less consciously) for little Nell, that she might some day become all-wife and no child at all. Just before her final illness, which seems to have followed upon a miscarriage, David has given up his half-hearted attempt to make an adult out of her.

His thoughts mark the high point in the analytical process and require quotation at considerable length.

So ended my last attempt to make any change in Dora. I had been unhappy in trying it; I could not endure my own solitary wisdom; I could not reconcile it with her former appeal to me as my child-wife. I resolved to do what I could, in a quiet way, to improve our proceedings myself; but I foresaw that my utmost would be very little, or I must degenerate into the spider again, and be forever lying in wait.

And the shadow I have mentioned, that was not to be between us any more, but was to rest wholly on my heart. How did that fall?

The old unhappy feeling pervaded my life. It was deepened, if it were changed at all; but it was as undefined as ever, and addressed me like a strain of sorrowful music faintly heard in the night. I loved my wife dearly, and I was happy; but the happiness I had vaguely anticipated, once, was not the happiness I enjoyed, and there was always something wanting.

In fulfillment of the compact I have made with myself, to reflect my mind on this paper, I again examine it, closely, and bring its secrets to the light. What I missed, I still regarded—I always regarded—as something that had been a dream of my youthful fancy; that was incapable of realization; that I was now discovering to be so, with some natural pain, as all men did. But that it would have been better for me if my wife could have helped me more, and shared the many thoughts in which I had no partner; and that this might have been, I knew.

Between these two irreconcilable conclusions; the one, that what I felt was general and unavoidable; the other, that it was particular to me, and might have been different; I balanced curiously, with no distinction of their opposition to each other. . . .

Sometimes, the speculation came into my thoughts, What might have happened, if Dora and I had never known each other? But she was so incorporated with my existence, that it was the idlest of all fancies, and would soon rise out of my reach and sight, like gossamer floating in the air.

I always loved her. What I am describing, slumbered, and half awoke, and slept again, in the innermost recesses of my mind. There was no evidence of it in me; I know of no influence it had in anything I said or did. [sic]

'The first mistaken impulses of an undisciplined heart.' These words of Mrs. Strong's were constantly recurring to me, at this time; were almost always present in my mind. I awoke with them, often, in the night; I remember to have even read them, in dreams, inscribed upon the walls of houses. For I knew, now, that my own heart was undisciplined when it first loved Dora; and that if it had been disciplined, it never could have felt, when we were married, what it had felt in its secret experience.

'There can be no disparity in marriage, like unsuitability of mind and purpose.' These words I remembered too. I had endeavoured to adapt Dora to myself, and found it impracticable. It remained for me to adapt myself to Dora; to share with her what I could, and be happy; to bear on my shoulders what I must, and be still happy. This was the discipline to which I tried to bring my heart, when I began to think. (Chapter XLVIII)

If there is a continuous flow of ambiguity in this analysis; if it represents Dickens in a two-fold attitude toward the lost Dora and the unlosable Catherine, that is exactly what we must expect. Dickens cannot, unaided, penetrate any deeper. He cannot see that what he requires in a wife, she must, paradoxically, lose at the moment she becomes a wife! He sees what he has lost in Dora, but what he cannot see is the inexorable monotonous round in which he re-creates that same fantastic image, loses it in one way or another, and recreates it a moment later. How could we expect in nineteenth century Dickens even so much as an inkling of the suspicion that he must look for the source of his obsession, not to his eighteenth year, not even to his adolescence or childhood, but back to the very inception of the Oedipus-feeling in the various stages of infancy?

For, even apart from Dora, the novel is replete with child-wives. What is worse, they are constantly in the habit of growing up, losing their innocence in one way or another, and joining the

despised class of "the other sort of woman." The fantasy of contamination from this "other sort" is particularly active throughout
the work. Little Em'ly, taking pity on the prime prototype of the
"fallen woman," Martha Endell, must see her and give her aid
secretly, lest even that angelic guardian of her life, Daniel Peggotty,
should learn of the contaminating experience. Ham Peggotty, the
prototype of that Dickens who has found it possible to discuss in
letters with Miss Burdett-Coutts the proper methods for the guidance and reclamation of committed prostitutes,[5] allows the good
deed, while he stands by protectively and offers his purse. Yet
there is a clear hint that the experience has not been a good one for
Little Em'ly, and Martha bitterly reproaches herself with having
been an evil influence in Em'ly's life, and strives to atone for it by
her solicitude for Emily's welfare on her miserable return to London. Little Em'ly, whom David has loved with the only sort of really
"worthwhile" love that Dickens could fully sympathize with, falls a
victim to the secondary hero-prototype, Steerforth, and is lost
forever—or at least until, after her descent into the pit, she is born
again in a new world (Australia) with her beloved "father," Daniel
Peggotty, forswearing love and marriage this time forever.

The fear of contamination is widespread, for kindly Mr.
Wickfield will not extend his indulgence to his beloved Agnes so far
as to permit her to be seen with Annie Strong, when Annie is under
suspicion of harboring extramarital affection for her cousin Jack
Maldon. Good-hearted Minnie Joram cannot bear to see her tiny
daughter even wear a ribbon that once belonged to Little Em'ly.
And so on, and so forth. The only virgin-character who maintains
her childhood charm, with added wisdom and beauty of womanhood, is the shadowy and insubstantial dream-wife Agnes.

The Agnes-Annie connection is tenuous, perhaps, but profoundly illuminating. Before Dickens wrote *David Copperfield*,
eight children had been born to him. Of these, six were boys, two

---

[5] Dickens, in a letter to Miss Burdett-Coutts in 1846, commenting upon cases
of recidivism among the former inmates of the "Home," wrote with some penetration, "This sudden dashing down of all the building up of months upon months,
is, to my thinking, so distinctly a Disease with the persons under consideraton that
I would pay particular attention to it, and treat it with particular gentleness and
anxiety." In the same year he wrote an appeal calling upon these women to enter
the Home voluntarily; he made suggestions for the improvement of its conduct,
even condemning the dullness of the uniforms provided, as late as 1856. (See
Letters to Baroness Burdett-Coutts (London, 1931), *passim.*

girls. Mary Dickens (always called Mamie in later life) had been born in 1838, the year after Mary Hogarth's death. The girl born in 1839 had been named Kate for her mother and Macready for Dickens' actor-friend. No other girl-child was born until the period of *David Copperfield*. A daughter born on August 15, 1850, when *Copperfield* was nearing the close of its serial publication (Dora Copperfield's death is reported in the forty-eighth chapter of a book which ran to sixty-four chapters) was named *Dora Annie*. The resurrection of "Dora" we can well understand; and the reason for some double name is quite apparent, but why Annie? Is it possible that the author saw in Annie Strong the picture of an Oedipus-situation come true, one who gives up the love of one of her own generation in order to remain true to one whom she loves though he is old enough to be her father, whom she loves despite the opposition, trickery, and scheming of her "unnatural" mother? Annie, then, is as far as life can go in producing an Agnes. The Agnes-image, the "little lamb," exists only in the world of dreams and unreality. It was, incidentally, the final cruel trick of fate that it was to be this child, among all Dickens' children, who was to die in infancy!

Nowhere in the novel does scorn and hatred for the fallen woman reach greater heights than in one of Dickens' most violently neurotic women, Rosa Dartle. Not that Dickens endorses Rosa's shrewish denunciations of Little Em'ly for one minute, even though, as we shall see in a moment, he (as author) might have prevented at least one of them. In Rosa, Dickens indicates that he is dealing with the ancient mechanism,

> Heaven has no rage like love to hatred turned,
> Nor hell a fury like a woman scorned.

Rosa is insanely jealous, jealous of Steerforth, toward whom her emotional reaction is markedly ambivalent. She yearns for the days when they were children together, even though it was during those days that Steerforth, in a fit of ungovernable temper, had disfigured her for life. She is bound by ties of mixed love and hatred to her nemesis and benefactor, Steerforth's mother. Steerforth, for whom Rosa herself is a mother-image, an elder-sister prototype, merely endures her existence, showing his unconscious aggression against her only in the inexcusable fact that he

ignores her adoration. Rosa, who seems to have some traces of the
second Mrs. Dombey about her (she, too, can play the harp beautifully when she is in a soft mood), is choked by the spleen of her own
impotence. She finally finds an object to vent it on—Little Em'ly.
She is not content with denouncing the "wayward" girl to David
and even to Daniel Peggotty; she must ascertain when the wretched
creature makes her forlorn return to London, pursue her there,
and then denounce her to her face. But how do we know all this?
David is patiently waiting out in the hall while the cruel tongue spits
venom at Steerforth's misguided little would-be lady. And he does
not interrupt Rosa, for he fears to let Em'ly see anyone of her
former acquaintances until Daniel Peggotty arrives, so that she may
throw herself into his protecting arms. So David stands by, in
ridiculous impotence, and Dickens has the satisfaction of a certain
sort of secondary sadism at the expense of one who would trade
her virginity for gold and position, even though she be one whom
he had once loved! Nothing is left for Rosa but to return to the
woman who stands for everything that is James Steerforth and who
has yet seen fit to set herself up in opposition to the son who
resembles her so closely, to denounce the mother of her beloved
James in equally biting terms when the erring young man's death is
reported; yet to remain with the older woman in her final drifting
into senility and weakness. Rosa occupies a queer position within
the Dickens categories of women. He should sympathize with her,
but he doesn't; she should be admirable, but she isn't. The result is
a most felicitous character-portrayal.

   David Copperfield is Dickens' greatest *Bildungsroman,* his most
titanic effort at self-revelation and self-analysis, balked and frustrated at every turn; yet emerging at times with a violent grasping
at literary and artistic realism which is unequalled in his own
works, unequalled in nineteenth century British fiction, and
hardly bettered anywhere in the field of the novel. If the analytic
impulse which created it was practically spent when it was being
written, we cannot be too critical. How could we expect even so
much from Dickens in the light of his own neurotic drives, in the
light of the times in which he lived, and especially in the light of a
deliberate, conscious attitude which could allow him to write that
he could never dream of his characters, since "it would be like a
man dreaming of himself, which is clearly an impossibility. Things

exterior to one's self must always be the basis of dreams"?[6] If he had known that it is impossible for one to dream of anything *but* one's self, then perhaps he would not have been Dickens. To a greater extent than others knew, perhaps to a greater extent than he knew himself, he was dreaming of himself when he wrote *David Copperfield,* although it cannot be said in all honesty that he was *writing* about himself. There was no book which he wrote with which he was more loth to part. In the original preface to the book he protested that he could not "get sufficiently far away from it . . . to refer to it with composure which this formal heading of Preface would seem to require." In the preface to a later edition he continues in the same vein.

> My interest in it was so . . . strong, and my mind was so divided between pleasure and regret—pleasure in the achievement of a long design, regret in the separation from many companions—that I was in danger of wearying the reader with personal confidences and private emotions.
>
> Besides which, all that I could have said of the Story to any purpose, I had endeavoured to say in it.
>
> It would concern the reader little, perhaps, to know how sorrowfully the pen is laid down at the close of a two-years imaginative task; or how an Author feels as if he were dismissing some portion of himself into the shadowy world, when a crowd of the creatures of his brain are going from him for ever. Yet, I had nothing else to tell; unless, indeed, I were to confess (which might be of less moment still), that no one can ever believe this Narrative in the reading more than I believed it in the writing.
>
> So true are these avowals at the present day, that I can now only take the reader into one confidence more. Of all my books, I like this the best. It will be easily believed that I am a fond parent to every child of my fancy, and that no one can love that family as dearly as I love them. But, like many fond parents, I have in my heart of hearts a favourite child. And his name is *David Copperfield.*

Many a favorite child has been far less worthy of the love lavished upon him by a fond parent.

[6] *Beadnell Letters,* p. 14.

Kafka and Dickens:
The Country Sweetheart

Mark Spilka

At one point in his diaries, Franz Kafka noted an enormous debt to the English novelist, Charles Dickens. In technique and detail, his first novel, *Amerika,* was "a sheer imitation" of Dickens' *Copperfield*: "The story of the trunk, the boy who delights and charms everyone, the menial labor, his sweetheart in the country house, the dirty houses, *et al.,* but above all the method. It was my intention, as I now see, to write a Dickens novel, but enhanced by the sharper lights I should have taken from the times and the duller ones I should have got from myself . . . "[1] This passage was first explicated by E.W. Tedlock, Jr., in a splendid article called "Kafka's Imitation of *David Copperfield*."[2] Tedlock concentrated here on the five specific parallels, and explained four of them as follows: "The story of the trunk" referred to David's loss of his trunk, by theft, on the way to Dover, and to Karl Rossmann's loss of his box, again by theft, on the road to Rameses; the "delightful boy" was Steerforth, for Dickens, and Mr. Mack for Kafka—two sophisticated, patronizing figures who attract and baffle their naive admirers; "menial labor" referred to the warehouse chapters in *Copperfield,* and to the lift-boy chapters in *Amerika;* while "the dirty houses, *et al.,*" included the tenement where David finds the abandoned Emily and the apartment house where Karl is imprisoned by two vagabonds. As for "method," Tedlock rightly pointed to the "moral and emotional ambiguity" in each author's work, and to their common use of "the technique of the grotesque." His one difficulty was with the "country sweetheart" item, for which he attempted three different explanations, none of them quite ade-

[1] *The Diaries of Franz Kafka, 1914–1923,* ed. Max Brod, trans. Martin Greenberg and Hannah Arendt (New York: Schocken, 1949), p. 188.
[2] *Comparative Literature,* VII (Winter 1955), 52–62. Other comparisons of these novels include Rudolf Vasata's "*Amerika* and Charles Dickens," *The Kafka Problem,* ed. Angel Flores (New York: New Directions, 1946), pp. 134–139; Roy Pascal's "Dickens and Kafka," *The Listener,* 26 April 1956, pp. 504–506; and my own "*Amerika:* Its Genesis," *Franz Kafka Today,* ed. Angel Flores and Homer Swander (Madison: University of Wisconsin Press, 1958), pp. 95–116.

quate. My aim in the present paper, then, is to account more fully
and accurately for the troublesome parallel, and to demonstrate
its relation to each writer's method.

Kafka's interest in this theme begins with an early fragment,
"Wedding Preparations in the Country." As that story opens, young
Eduard Raban is plainly reluctant about visiting his fiancée. He is
expected that evening at her country home, but as he stands in an
open doorway, waiting for the rain to stop, he dreams of various
ways to avoid the journey:

> "And besides, can't I do it the way I always used to as a child
> in matters that were dangerous? I don't even need to go to
> the country myself, it isn't necessary. I'll send my clothed
> body. If it staggers out of the door of my room, the stagger-
> ing will indicate not fear but its nothingness. Nor is it a sign
> of excitement if it stumbles on the stairs, if it travels into the
> country, sobbing as it goes, and there eats its supper in tears.
> For I myself am meanwhile lying in my bed, smoothly
> covered over with the yellow-brown blanket, exposed to the
> breeze that is wafted through that seldom aired room. The
> carriages and people in the street move and walk hesitantly
> on shining ground, for I am still dreaming. . . .
>
> "As I lie in bed I assume the shape of a big beetle, a stag
> beetle or a cockchafer, I think. . . . The form of a large
> beetle, yes. Then I would pretend it was a matter of hiber-
> nating, and I would press my little legs to my bulging belly.
> And I would whisper a few words, instructions to my sad
> body, which stands close beside me, bent. Soon I shall have
> done—it bows, it goes swiftly, and it will manage everything
> efficiently while I rest."[3]

Eduard's macabre scheme suggests the regression image from a
later story, *The Metamorphosis,* and stamps his reluctance as a form
of arrested adolescence. Like the giant vermin in that novella, he
wants to avoid adult responsibilities by forcing others to assume
them. There is a curious precedent for this in *David Copperfield,*
where the carrier Barkis is unable to propose directly to Nurse

[3]*Dearest Father*, ed. Max Brod, trans. Ernst Kaiser and Eithne Wilkins (New York: Schocken, 1954), pp. 6–7.

Peggotty, whose cakes and pastries have aroused his marital appetite. Instead, he asks young David to send her the cryptic message that "Barkis is willin' " and later "that Barkis was a-waitin' for a answer." Barkis lives close to the nurse himself, but like Eduard Raban, he sends a child's "body" on his marital errands. There is something childish, as well, about his preference for "apple parsties" and his fear of direct speech with maiden ladies. There is even something dreamlike and vague in his actions, as if he somehow expressed a part of David's inmost self. And from the evidence in the novel, it seems he does. When David's mother is about to marry Murdstone, for instance, it is Barkis who takes the boy away from home, and waits silently in his cart while the mother kisses him goodbye; and later, when the boy goes to school, he waits in silence as the motherly Peggotty embraces David: "After another and a final squeeze with both arms, she got down from the cart and ran away . . . without a solitary button on her gown. I picked up one of several that were rolling about [relates David], and treasured it as a keepsake for a long time."[4] It is then that Barkis makes his famous proposal, through David, to the woman who already substitutes for the boy's mother. It seems almost superfluous to add that David, too, waits silently outside, while Barkis and Peggotty get married, that he dreams that night about dragons, and awakens next morning with Peggotty calling to him, as usual, from beneath his window at Yarmouth, "as if Mr. Barkis the carrier had been from first to last a dream too."[5]

As this development shows, it is hard to tell whether Barkis sends David to do his courting, or whether David sends Barkis to marry his nurse, as a proxy for his own desires. In either case, the split in the sender's mind would have appealed to Kafka, whose hero suffers from a similar disturbance. Of course, there is no question of direct influence here; the point is, simply, that Kafka first connects the sweetheart theme with reluctant courtship and sexual arrest, and that Dickens provides examples of a similar complex.

In both *Copperfield* and *Amerika,* however, the sweetheart theme is fused with economic concerns. In Kafka's novel, Karl

[4] *David Copperfield* (New York: Modern Library, 1950), p. 66.
[5] *Ibid.,* p. 157.

Rossmann travels to the country with the businessman, Mr. Pollunder, to meet his daughter Clara. As they drive through New York City, the main roads are blocked by a demonstration of metal-workers on strike, and their car is diverted by mounted police into side-alleys. But Karl ignores the evidence of economic strife, and leans back happily on Mr. Pollunder's arm: "the knowledge that he would soon be a welcome guest in a well-lighted country-house surrounded by high walls and guarded by watch-dogs filled him with extravagant well-being."[6] Karl's trip is based on Chapter XXVI of *Copperfield*, in which David goes to the country with his employer, Mr. Spenlow, to meet his daughter Dora. David too enjoys his journey, as his employer defines their profession as "a privileged class," and explains legal folderol as a quiet family game, with expenses falling on the clients, and with the price of wheat highest when lawyers are busiest. David is baffled by the connection between law and wheat, but he defers to his employer and makes no objection. "I was not the man to . . . bring down the country," he declares, for like Rossman he sides for the moment with a privileged class. In Kafka's novel, however, the economic conflict seems more visual and dramatic, thanks to the "sharper lights" derived from modern times.

As I have already hinted, the lights applied are Freudian as well as Marxist. When Pollunder drives off with Karl, they sit close together in the car, and Pollunder holds the boy's hand while they talk, or puts his arm around him. At the house itself he again encircles Karl and draws him between his knees; and at one point he leads him away from an apparent rival and blows his nose for him. Karl himself compares Pollunder's lips with his daughter's, and seems anxious to lure him away, in turn, from his massive colleague, Mr. Greene. These two lecherous elders are further abetted by the aggressive daughter, Clara, who wants Karl to come to her bedroom, with her elders' approval. Thus Karl resembles an innocent victim of a sexual free-for-all, or better still, a sexual charade, though he also contributes to this charade without his conscious knowledge.

With the same perfect innocence, David enacts a comparable charade in *Copperfield*. In the early chapters, he has been cut off

---

[6] *Amerika*, trans. Edwin Muir (New York: New Directions, 1946), p. 49.

from his mother by his wicked stepfather, Mr. Murdstone, and by the latter's prim, self-righteous sister. As David himself explains, this conflict turns on his spelling lessons:

> Shall I ever forget those lessons? They were presided over nominally by my mother, but really by Mr. Murdstone and his sister, who were always present, and found them a favourable occasion for giving my mother lessons in that miscalled firmness which was the bane of both our lives. . . . I had been apt enough to learn, and willing enough, when my mother and I had lived alone together. I can faintly remember learning the alphabet at her knee. To this day, when I look upon the fat black letters in the primer, the puzzling novelty of their shapes, and the easy good-nature of O and Q and S, seem to present themselves again before me as they used to do. But they recall no feeling of disgust or reluctance. On the contrary, I seem to have walked along a path of flowers as far as the crocodile book, and to have been cheered by the gentleness of my mother's voice and manner all the way. But these solemn lessons which succeeded those, I remember as the deathblow at my peace, and a grievous daily drudgery and misery. They were very long, very numerous, very hard . . . and I was generally as much bewildered by them as I believe my poor mother was herself.[7]

Under this new external pressure, the boy flunks his lessons and is beaten for his failure. David bites his oppressor's hand, however, and for this he is locked in his room five days and cut off from his mother in the most literal sense. His confinement resembles that of Gregor Samsa, in Kafka's story, *The Metamorphosis,* and suggests once more the close affinity of these authors.[8] But more pertinently, it directly parallels David's later predicament, when his relations with Dora Spenlow are abruptly severed. For the agent of that severance is none other than Miss

---

[7] *David Copperfield,* p. 55. As this paragraph suggests, Dickens recounts here his own early memories of a childhood Eden with his mother, which was interrupted when his father sent him to work at a blacking warehouse, and all his "early hopes of growing up to be a learned and distinguished man" were crushed. Now Murdstone suppresses David's drive for learning, as Dickens projects resentment of his father's action into fictional form.

[8] See my article "Kafka's Sources for *The Metamorphosis,*" *Comparative Literature* (Fall 1959).

Murdstone, who suddenly reappears in the novel as Dora's paid companion and protector. Dora herself is a frail, charming, helpless girl, who resembles David's childish mother,[9] while her father is a businessman like Murdstone, who at one point had employed David in his wine warehouse. In this sense, the entire cast from the early chapters has reassembled, in symbolic guise, to reenact the early crime. Thus, when Miss Murdstone discovers David's letters to Dora, she exposes him before the employer-father, the engagement is broken off, and David is deprived once more of an oedipal attachment:

> I submitted, and, with a countenance as expressive as I was able to make it of dejected and despairing constancy, came out of the room. Miss Murdstone's heavy eyebrows followed me to the door—I say her eyebrows rather than her eyes, because they were much more important in her face—and she looked so exactly as she used to look, at about that hour of the morning, in our parlour at Blunderstone, that I could have fancied I had been breaking down in my lessons again, and that the dead weight on my mind was that horrible old spelling-book with oval woodcuts, shaped, to my youthful fancy, like the glasses out of spectacles.[10]

This connection with his spelling lessons is revealing, for Miss Murdstone's disapproval of them has just been matched by her disapproval of the love letters. As I have already shown, David had been beaten by his stepfather for that early lapse, and then kept in isolation from his mother. Now another father defeats him, and stands between him and the girl he loves. The sexual charade is complete, and along with it, the thematic parallel with Kafka's novel. In both stories, a young man journeys to the country with a commercial father and becomes entangled there in a bizarre charade, expressive of his arrested development. In both stories, that is, the theme of economic subservience is expressed through sexual immaturity: for the moment, the fathers triumph in both realms,

[9] This view of Dora and David's mother as childish counterparts is now fairly common. Cf. Jack Lindsay, *Charles Dickens: A Biographical and Critical Study* (London: Andrew Dakers, 1950), pp. 289–290; and Gwendolyn B. Needham, "The Undisciplined Heart of David Copperfield," *Nineteenth Century Fiction*, IX (September 1954), 89.

[10] *David Copperfield*, p. 583.

and the sons are kept in economic and sexual servitude. Karl is shoved out of the country house to join two vagabonds, while David continues his legal work with no hope of marriage.

If the sexual parallel seems more thematic than circumstantial, this is only because Karl stands at an earlier stage of development than David; his troubles are bisexual rather than oedipal, and they derive from an earlier portion of Dickens' novel and involve a different sweetheart. Because Tedlock thinks here in terms of character alone, he fails to catch this clever synthesis. In Clara Pollunder he sees first "a comically modern reversal" of Dora Spenlow—an aggressive, knowing, and violently athletic girl, and her delicate, foolish opposite. His third solution, that Little Em'ly is the country sweetheart, seems even less convincing; but it is only tentatively held and can be thrown out here as peripheral and irrelevant. His second brief suggestion seems quite valid, however, since the scornful and capricious Estella, in *Great Expectations,* more directly resembles the perplexing Clara. Even her mysterious country home, with its grotesque banquet chamber, dark, winding corridors, and wanderings by candlelight, strongly suggests the country house in *Amerika.* Then too, young Pip is commanded to play with her by the strange Miss Havisham, while Karl is virtually ordered to "have a pleasant time" with Clara. In the course of such play, both boys disguise their mortification before taunting sweethearts, and both engage in violent struggles. But Pip's restraint with Estella is not self-imposed, like Karl's with Clara, and he does prove more handy with his fists, in defeating another boy, than the absurdly ineffectual Karl, who is quickly thrashed by Clara.

What seems interesting here is the recurrence of the same set of elements in both novels—the mysterious house, the taunting girl, the mortified boy, and the violent struggle. Yet a similar set occurs in *Copperfield* itself, when David visits the home of Steerforth and meets his would-be sweetheart, Rosa Dartle. Rosa loves to confound her listeners with sharp-edged questions and insinuations: "Is it really so?" she always asks. "I want to know so much." She also plays the harp reluctantly before Steerforth and David, and, when Steerforth pretends to be touched by her playing ("Come, Rosa, for the future we will love each other very much!"), she strikes him and throws him off "with the fury of a wildcat," and then bursts from the room.[11] Towards the end of the novel, she breaks into another violent rage, this time against Little Em'ly, her rival for Steerforth's love.

Rosa's violence is the result of sexual and emotional frustration. She is about thirty years old, and as even David guesses, she wants to be married. On her lip there is a scar, however, the "gift" of Steerforth, who threw a hammer at her when a boy, out of mere exasperation. For David, this scar becomes the sign of mysteries beyond his grasp. When he settles down in his room at night, for instance, he suddenly finds "a likeness of Miss Dartle looking eagerly at [him] from above the chimney-piece":

> It was a startling likeness, and necessarily had a startling look. The painter hadn't made the scar, but *I* made it; and there it was, coming and going—now confined to the upper lip, as I had seen it at dinner, and now showing the whole extent of the wound inflicted by the hammer, as I had seen it when she was passionate.
>
> I wondered peevishly why they couldn't put her anywhere else instead of quartering her on me. To get rid of her, I undressed quickly, extinguished my light, and went to bed. But, as I fell asleep, I could not forget that she was still there looking. "Is it really, though? I want to know;" and when I awoke in the night, I found that I was uneasily asking all sorts of people in my dreams whether it really was or not—without knowing what I meant.[12]

In *Amerika* Kafka seems to solve the puzzle of what David meant. For David's sexual innocence is clearly mixed with fear and revulsion—and with repellent fascination. Karl Rossmann shows a similar mixture when he resists the frankly sexual invitation of Clara Pollunder and attempts to escape from her into the darkness of his bedroom. But Clara pursues him there (even as Rosa's likeness pursues David) and then shoves him about in her fury, throwing him down violently onto a sofa, threatening to box his ears, and nearly choking him: " 'Cat, wild cat!' was all that Karl could shout in the confusion of rage and shame which he felt within him. 'You must be crazy, you wild cat!' "[13]

[11] *Ibid.*, p. 457.
[12] *Ibid.*, p. 313.
[13] *Amerika*, p. 61.

Later Karl plays the piano, very reluctantly, before Clara, when suddenly Mr. Mack calls to him from a nearby room, where he sits in his nightshirt in the middle of a huge double bed. Mack falsely compliments him on his playing, just as Steerforth fakes the effect of Rosa's music; but Karl is more disturbed by the revelation of illicit love between Mack and Clara—even as David is disturbed by the implications of Rosa's violence. All of which makes Rosa the most likely source for Kafka's sweetheart. It seems relevant, at the least, that she treats David like an innocent child, in conjunction with Steerforth and the mysterious servant Littimer, while Karl is treated like a child by Clara, Mack, and the old servant with the lantern. It was David's sexual innocence, and not his later affair with Dora, which seems to have attracted Kafka. At Steerforth's home he is immersed in sexual violence, and like Karl he is repelled and fascinated by what he sees. Indeed, the whole nexus of adolescent feeling seems to inform these chapters, since David's great affection for Steerforth, and the effeminate nickname, "Daisy," which Steerforth gives him, only add to the pattern of sexual ambiguity and set a precedent for Rossmann's adolescent fondness for Mack, Pollunder, and his Uncle Jacob.

It seems plausible, then, that Kafka's note about "die Geliebte auf dem Landgut" includes various portions of Dickens' novel: the first trip to Dora Spenlow's, the charade device which follows, and the scenes at Steerforth's home which are interspersed with all these chapters. This mixture of material is typical of Dickens, who had little control of the movement of his early novels; but in *Copperfield* there does exist a kind of psychological order, imposed from within by Dickens' unsuspected urgings. With the help of Freudian lights, Kafka was able to improve considerably upon this order: in successive stages, his hero moves through bisexual and oedipal love to sexual maturity. Yet to cite his advantage is not to disparage Dickens so much as to place him historically, and to give him full credit for psychological depths which are generally denied him. There is no need to agree fully, for example, with Roy Pascal's judgment that "[Dickens'] books are full of things and persons, surging up and sinking from sight, helping and hindering the hero, yet constituting a world essentially separate from his inward self, only temporarily and accidentally related to it . . .

[while] in Kafka ... each incident is symbolic of the total situation. The outer world is a projection of the inner, and Karl's
inner world determines the character of his experiences. Hence
the formal unity of Kafka's works, as contrasted with Dickens'
'barbaric senselessness,' as Kafka calls it."[14] In the first place,
David's inner world very often determines the character of his
experience, in a naïve but powerful way: in his early exclusion
from his mother, in his proxy courtship of Nurse Peggotty, in
his repellent fascination with Rosa Dartle, and in the later charade with the Spenlows, we have excellent examples of a controlling inward force which Pascal ignores—examples, moreover,
which Kafka himself chose to imitate, and which figure forth the
very "method" he admired. In the second place, there is some
doubt as to whether Kafka could have written *Amerika* without
these examples. If he speaks of Dickens' formlessness, he adds at
once that he has been able to avoid this fault, thanks to his
weakness as an artist, and, *wiser* for his epigonism.[15] And before
this, he cites a pattern of incidents which is strongly marked in
Copperfield, and which gave him a readymade order to work with.
After all, if Kafka enjoys an aesthetic advantage, he does so only
because Dickens has broken the formal ground before him; and
if his psychological perceptions are keener and surer, still, it was
Dickens' naïve vision which enabled him to see with greater clarity. Consider simply all the "country sweetheart" parallels: the
common approach to reluctant courtship, the fusion of sexual
and economic themes into a single psychic experience, the gro-
tesquely comic quality of the sexual charades, the awareness of
adolescent fears and ambiguities, the progression of both heroes
toward emotional maturity, and most inclusive of all, the childlike view of a world controlled by harsh parental figures. As
Eduard Raban remarks, in "Wedding Preparations in the Country": "a book that I was ... reading recently taught me more
about my little journey than you could imagine."[16] Though the
reference is obscure, it seems to apply, with compelling force, to
Kafka's reading of *David Copperfield.*

[14] Roy Pascal, p. 504. For further discussion of these issues, see my essay
"*David Copperfield* as Psychological Fiction," *The Critical Quarterly* (Winter 1959).
[15] *Diaries, 1914–1923, p. 189.*
[16] *Dearest Father, p. 30.*

David Copperfield Dreams of Drowning

E. Pearlman

When Betsey Trotwood comes to London to tell her nephew that she is financially ruined, and that he must henceforth shift for himself, David Copperfield is not unnaturally shocked and distraught. His sleep is nightmarish, as it often is (more than twenty of his dreams are recounted in the novel). He imagines himself

> hopelessly endeavouring to get a license to marry Dora, having nothing but one of Uriah Heep's gloves to offer in exchange, which the whole Commons rejected; and still more or less conscious of my room, I was always tossing about like a distressed ship in a sea of bedclothes.[1]

The rejection by the Commons is a form of public humiliation, not infrequent in dreams; it is also a close echo of a preceding incident. Just prior to Aunt Betsey's arrival, David had encountered Edward Murdstone at the offices of Spenlow and Jorkins. Murdstone had at that moment procured a license to marry a beautiful girl " just of age "—a girl, we are to understand, very like David's mother. The fantasy of seeking and failing to get a marriage license is clearly a re-enactment of this event. Again David competes with Murdstone, and again he fails, just as he had failed in competing with him for the attention of Clara Copperfield. Equally revealing is the object which David offers to the Commons—" one of Uriah Heep's gloves." The implication is that David, now deprived of the status that accompanies financial well-being, unconsciouly acknowledges his new kinship with the unpropertied social climber Heep. But is there any significance to the glove itself? Dickens, most economical of novelists, frequently defines characters in terms of objects, as for instance Jane Murdstone is denoted a sadist by her iron beads (" fetters " to David). Heep's hand, and by association his gloves, are a metonym for his character, for his body, for his sexuality. The gloves figure prominently in the scene in which

[1] XXXV, 566. Page references are to the convenient Penguin edition of Trevor Blount (1966).

Heep reveals his desire to marry Agnes (an action with a number of ironic parallels to David's wooing of Dora). " He was close beside me, slowly fitting his long skeleton fingers into the still longer fingers of a great Guy Fawkes pair of gloves " (XXV, 436). He was " so humble in respect of those scarecrow gloves, that he was still putting them on, and seemed to have made no advance in that labour, when we got to my place." Heep's incomplete penetration of the glove is a marvellous image of sexual aggression, none the less nauseous for its futility. But the key terms in the passage are " scarecrow " and " Guy Fawkes," which categorize Heep as repulsive and sub-human and also suggest that he is a scapegoat slated for ritual expulsion. The dream hints at the depth of the relationship between David and Heep, one aspect of which is that Heep is freighted with the baser elements of human nature which are apparently missing from David's character. David and Uriah are, in psychological terms, " splits." But a close reading of the novel, with special attention to the unravelling of fantasies, shows that David Copperfield is split not twofold but triply, and that James Steerforth is as important in David's psychological life as is Heep.

On the night of David's first meeting with Uriah Heep, his sleep is also troubled by dreams. In his odd circular office at Canterbury, the villainous clerk has fearfully suggested that David is ambitious to usurp his place in Wickfield's firm. David denies such an intention. Heep leaves the office by an outside door, and extinguishes the light. As he is about to return to Wickfield's home by a connecting passage, David falls over Heep's stool.

> This was the proximate cause, I suppose, of my dreaming about him, for what appeared to me to be half the night; and dreaming, among other things, that he [Heep] had launched Mr. Peggotty's house on a piratical expedition, with a black flag at the masthead, bearing the inscription ' Tidd's Practice,' under which diabolical ensign he was carrying me and little Em'ly to the Spanish Main, to be drowned. (XVI, 293)

The controlling form of this dream of drowning is flashback, or regression, to childish fantasies based on the semi-surreptitious reading of picaresque adventure. For an imaginary moment, David is once again one of Smollett's seagoing heroes, or " Captain Somebody of the Royal British Navy " (IV, 106). Sometime in daylight and sometime in dreams, David longs to be a great heroic figure (" Whether I shall turn out to be the hero of my own life . . ."), and the Spanish Main is one of the demesnes of great men. It is, in fact, the part of the world Dickens had sent Walter Gay, the hero of *Dombey and Son* (1848) to seek his fortune. But David's odyssey is landlocked, and he comes no closer to the sea than to study nautical law at Doctors' Commons. Even in the dream, he does not command the ship. David is a passenger; Heep is the captain.

But a closer look at the dream reveals that a third person, shadowy but nevertheless real, is also present. For it is Steerforth, not David, who carries off little Em'ly and drowns. David fantasizes for himself the role that Steerforth enacts or, stated another way, Steerforth represents that part of David which desires to philander and seduce. As a child, David had wished to marry Em'ly; now older and wiser, he recognizes that a gentleman does not marry a fisherman's niece. The fantasy reveals what society and civilization make David deny, even to himself. The dream of drowning, then, contains David and the two men who stand for alternative moral paths, and at least in the world of dreams, symbolize parts of the self. Uriah Heep represents what David fears he is or might become; Steerforth, briefly, stands for what David wishes to be, but can neither achieve nor reject.

In terms of the dream, all three men " drown," and this too has an obvious significance. The traditional association between water and sexuality is not unknown to Dickens, as is clear from the splendid comic excess of the account of David's infatuation with Dora.

> If I may so express it, I was steeped in Dora. I was not merely over head and ears in love with her, but was saturated through and through. Enough love might have been wrung out of me, metaphorically speaking, to drown

anybody in; and yet there would have remained enough within me, and all over me, to pervade my entire existence.[2] (XXXIII, 535)

Drowning is not only a way of dying—it is the plunge into the sea of passion; its ineluctable corollary is that sex and sexual passion are dangerous and destructive. Therefore Dora dies of the consequences of miscarriage—she dies of the love that is " wrung out of " David. The association between water and passion permeates the novel. Little Em'ly, for instance, is first seen running " along a jagged timber " which protrudes over the water, as if " springing forward to her destruction." David tells us that he is " afraid of her falling over " (III, 86), but in the dream, exercising the prerogative of the unconscious, he falls with her. She elopes across the water, and Steerforth even christens his clipper (" clip her ") the *Little Em'ly*. The rechristening of the *Stormy Petrel* is transparently an emblem of her fall. In fact, a number of the highly sexed, and therefore potentially or actually immoral figures in the novel are drawn to the water. Martha Endell, a prostitute, tries to commit suicide in the river. Jack Maldon, the principal threat to the marriage of impotent Dr. Strong and his child-bride Annie, says that " when a plunge is to be made into the water, it's no use lingering on the bank " (XVI, 287), and he plows the sea as far as to India and back. Maldon is a swashbuckler, a parody of Steerforth, and a ne'er-do-well even at seduction. He attempts to violate Annie's virginity, but only succeeds in taking her cherry-colored ribbon.[3] A more effective plunger is Steerforth himself—a great lover of the sea, naturally adept at sailing, a " nautical phenomenon " (XXII, 383). Mr. Peggotty remembers his name as Rudderford, and the confusion is a Dickensian manner of definition. David, who magically cannot drown,

---

[2] The extension of this metaphor leads to delectable but submerged puns, as when David says of his love that its "profundity was quite unfathomable" (XXXIV, 551). Or note Julia Mills's use of the term "the Desert of Sahara" to indicate trouble between the lovers.

[3] Dolly Varden is also decked in cherry when she is molested by "Hugh of the Maypole" in *Barnaby Rudge*.

and Agnes are specifically identified as land—chaste—characters by the second components of their surnames.[4]

The medium of the dream is water; the primary subject is Uriah Heep, who is a sexual, an economic, and a moral threat to David. In terms of simple male rivalry, Heep opposes David for the hand of Agnes, just as another Uriah was once a rival of David for possession of Bathsheba. Repulsive in himself, Heep is more loathsome when considered as a partner for Agnes. It has been suggested that Heep's physique bears the iconology of the habitual masturbator; [5] whether or not this is true, there is certainly something indecent about him. In this novel, a male character's genital is occasionally represented by his hand. Old Dr. Strong's, for instance, " did nothing for itself " (XVI, 282); nor is it accidental that when the oedipal struggle between David and Murdstone comes to a crisis, Murdstone is bitten on the hand. Heep's hands are long, dangly, and wet, and he manipulates them constantly.

> It was not fancy of mine about his hands, I observed; for he frequently ground the palms against each other as if to squeeze them dry and warm, besides often wiping them, in a stealthy way, on his pocket-handkerchief. (XVI, 291)

Heep's writhing, rufous, snaky appearance suggests flaccidity rather than self-abuse. His Christian name, no less than his appearance, associates him with micturition. " Heep " might refer to a heap of money, but again the excremental reading is the more likely.[6] Indeed, tradition tells us that the two are the same (cf. Mr. Merdle and the dust-heaps in *Our Mutual Friend*). Heep, though, is not an anal character in Freud's sense,

---

[4] The meaning of David's name is unclear. I would derive it from Edward Moor, *Suffolk Words and Phrases* (London, 1827), which Dickens used as a source for Yarmouth dialect. Moor defines "COPPEROZE. The common red field poppy" (86). The conjunction of "copper" and "field" is persuasive, especially since Dickens rejected such names as "Topflower" and "Flowerbury" for his hero. Cf. also Steerforth's "Daisy." Flowers seem to have been on Dickens' mind.

[5] Steven Marcus, *The Other Victorians* (New York, 1966), p. 19.

[6] Cf. also Traddles. Moor defines "Trattles—or trottles. The globular excrementitious droppings of sheep. The following are the similar words I have met with. *Tirdles* or *treadles*, or *treddles*, the dung of a sheep. *Trettles*, the dung of a rabbit or coney." Perhaps Durdles in *Edwin Drood* should be mentioned here.

although he does participate to some extent in the type. Taken as a whole he is, to put it as simply as possible, repulsively cloacal. He therefore represents a kind of immature or diseased or perverted sexuality which David finds sometimes attractive—"[he] had a sort of fascination for me " (XVI, 290) ; " I was attracted to him in very repulsion" (XXV, 443–4)—but more often despicable. When David dreams that Heep launches him, the latent meaning is that he is initiated into a new world of dangerous and potentially degenerate sexuality. It is also clear that David would be willing to launch himself, but can only deal with his desires when he scapegoats them onto Heep (it is, after all, David's dream). Heep is not scapegoat only, but the Yahoo within David, projected outward.

Heep also causes David distress of a social order, for in essence Uriah is Mealy Potatoes with social pretensions. David lives in fear that he might lose gentlemanly status and fall again into the proletariat. The special nightmare of Murdstone and Grinby is not the loss of education—it is the horror of manual labor and low associations. Had David not run away to Dover, and succeeded in becoming a gentleman through the transforming magic of his Aunt, his path through life would have been the same as Heep's. The dream is very clear on the subject, for in it David is an unwilling participant in Heep's enterprise. David dreams that Heep " had launched Mr. Peggotty's house on a piratical expedition, with a black flag at the masthead, bearing the inscription, ' Tidd's Practice.' " The " piratical expedition " is the means by which Heep attempts to clamber upward—the foray into Wickfield's accounts. " Tidd's Practice " is the law book that Heep pores over, and therefore an appropriate symbol for his ambition.[7] The ship itself is

---

[7] Heep's intercourse with "Tidd's Practice" is just a bit disgusting.

I found Uriah reading a great fat book, with such demonstrative attention, that his lank forefinger followed up every line as he read, and made clammy tracks along the page (or so I fully believed) like a snail. (XVI, 290)

But a "tid" in Victorian slang is a woman, and Heep's molesting of Tidd suggests an unpleasant sexual practice.

"Have you been studying much law lately?" I asked, to change the subject.

"Oh, Master Copperfield," he said, with an air of self-denial, "my reading is hardly to be called study. I have passed an hour or two in the evening, sometimes, with Mr. Tidd." (XVII, 311)

The "air of self-denial" is deliberately unpersuasive, and the idea of passing "an hour or two" with Tidd is curiously suggestive.

a telescoping of the Wickfield and Peggotty residences. They are comparable: in the Peggotty home (a boat), a complete family appears to be in residence, yet there is no relationship of real intimacy until the doomed engagement of Ham to Em'ly. At Wickfield's, Agnes is surrogate wife to her father—a chaste and slightly insane relationship later duplicated by that of Mr. Peggotty and Em'ly in Australia. Each family is initially free of sexual passion, but in the course of the novel each is invaded, the one by Steerforth, at David's invitation; the other by Heep, who exclaims to David: " To think that you should be the first to kindle the sparks of ambition in my umble breast! " (XXV, 438). Both invasions are disastrous in their consequences; both lead to " shipwrecks "; both are alluded to in the dream.

Heep is also, as the dream reveals, " diabolical "—an Iago-like figure who enjoys villainy for its own sake, and whose hatred for David is as intense as its motivation is obscure. His devilishness is part of a religious content of the novel that has never been fully explored.[8] Steerforth, for instance, is the " bad angel "—the misleader of youth in attractive shape. Heep is Vice in form as well as fact. Agnes, the good angel (Dickens is consistent in his use of morality nomenclature) is also, as her name suggests, *agnus*. Clearly David does not want Heep to creep and climb and intrude into her fold. But Heep is also parody Christ. He preaches " umbleness," but his humility is false and hypocritical. The great scene in which David slaps Heep and dislodges a tooth is a burlesque of true Christianity. Heep literally turns the other cheek.

> " Copperfield," he said, " there must be two parties to a quarrel. I won't be one. . . . I forgive you. . . . I'm determined to forgive you. But I do wonder that you should lift your hand against a person that you knew to be so umble." (XLII, 686-7)

His humility and fraudulent forgiveness are designed to arrogate power to himself. Heep is also " subtle," a " devil," and generally snaky. In addition, he is designed to be a Jew in

---

[8] The theme is touched on by J. Hillis Miller in *Charles Dickens: The World of his Novels* (Cambridge, 1958), p. 157.

everything but fact. His red hair, as Dickens well knew, is a
theatrical badge with antecedents in Judas, Shylock, and Fagin.
In *Our Mutual Friend,* Dickens conveniently splits Heep into
Fledgeby and Mr. Riah. Fledgeby works on much the same principle as Heep—exercise of power over the " better " people by
exploiting weakness and acquiring privileged information,
while Mr. Riah preserves Heep's " Christian " name. Another
of the complex reverberations that make Heep terrifying is his
connection with death. He is " cadaverous " and has long " skeleton " hands. He generally wears " decent black," and his
mother continues to wear weeds throughout the novel, although
even at the time of David's dream, her husband had been dead
four years. Heep's father, incidentally, was a sexton and like
Gabriel Grub in *Pickwick Papers,* probably also a gravedigger.
The association explains why Heep appears in the dream as
an angel of death.

Another property of Heep's that is connected with the
dream is his stool. The clerk, it will be remembered, lives in
a " little round tower that formed one side of the [Wickfield]
house " [9] (XV, 275). His room is circular, and he sits, with
Tidd, on a high stool. The stool is associated with his ambitions
and David, characteristically, trips on it. In fact, the stool is
the catalyst that precipitates the dream.

> Being, at last, ready to leave the office for the night, he
> asked me if it would suit my convenience to have the light
> put out; and on my answering, ' Yes,' instantly extin-
> guished it. After shaking hands with me—his hand felt like

---

[9] The "image cluster" involving towers (Dickens calls Heep's stool a tower), the
sea, and dreams is recapitulated when the subject again turns to drowning (Steerforth's).

> I now approach an eventide in my life, so indelible, so awful, so bound by an
> infinite variety of ties to all that has preceded it, in these pages, that, from the
> beginning of my narrative, I have seen it growing larger and larger as I
> advanced, *like a great tower in a plain,* and throwing its fore-cast shadow even
> on the incidents of my childish days.
>
> For years after it occurred, I *dreamed* of it often. I have started up so
> vividly impressed by it, that its fury has yet seemed raging in my quiet room,
> in the still night. I *dream* of it sometimes, though at lengthened and uncertain
> intervals, to this hour. *I have an association between it and a stormy wind, or the
> lightest mention of a seashore, as strong as any of which my mind is conscious.* (LV,
> 854, my italics)

a fish, in the dark—he opened the door into the street a very little, and crept out, and shut it, leaving me to grope my way back into the house: which cost me some trouble and a fall over his stool. This was the proximate cause, I suppose, of my dreaming about him, for what appeared half the night, and dreaming. . . . (XV, 293)

This is Dickens at his best. Every element in the description combines primary meaning with deeper reference. Here is Heep, under the guise of serving David's convenience, inconveniencing him severely. Here is Heep, cribb'd confined, cabin'd, opening doors " a very little." His personality is as locked up as that of Shylock, or Barkis, or Tulkinghorn. Or Heep as snake, creeping about; as an odious sexual creature, waiting until the light is extinguished to shake hands. And there is the symbolic fall over the stool which represents Heep's economic power, and which also seems to carry a sexual reference. It is like the stool in Dr. Strong's school on which Mr. Dick sits. " He always sat in a particular corner, on a particular stool, which was called 'Dick' after him" (XVII, 310). Mr. Dick parodies Heep's pretensions, as his *Memorial* is a parody of David's autobiography and Dickens' *roman à clef*.[10] And though it is Sterne and not Dickens who is generally thought to be novelist of stools and corners, the import of a stool named Dick is clear.

Uriah is for David a nightmare of a special kind. He is ostentatiously immoral, sexually diseased, and socially unacceptable. Steerforth is the opposite. Aristocratic in manner if not in fact, he is unconcerned with what preoccupies David: respectability, love, duty, work. He is clearly modeled on Shelley (a try at Oxford, curls, physical beauty, elopement with a member of the underclass, heroic drowning).[11] David, hyp-

---

[10] Dr. Strong's *Dictionary* and its search for "Greek roots" is another example of parodic authorship. It is linked to Mr. Dick's *Memorial* by the simpleton's delight in it, and by a curious detail. "Adams, our head-boy, who had a turn for mathematics, had made a calculation, I was informed, of the time this Dictionary would take in completing, on the Doctor's plan, and at the Doctor's rate of going. He considered that it might be done in one thousand six hundred and forty-nine years, counting from the Doctor's last, or sixty-second, birthday" (XXXIV, 293). The *Memorial* is obsessed with the execution of Charles I, A. D. 1649.

[11] And the first boat that appears in *David Copperfield* is called the *Skylark*.

notized, fails to notice his abundantly obvious faults. He does
not see that Steerforth's exploitation of him is as offensive as the
viciousness of employers, waiters, coachmen, and schoolteachers.
" I feel as if you were my property " (XX, 348) , says Steerforth,
who is nothing if not frank. David becomes his " plaything "
(358) and finds the unequal relationship satisfactory. The
colonial-colonizer relationship never changes. And, as is characteristic of members of an exploited class, David identifies with
his idolized victimizer, especially when Steerforth acts out the
wish that is revealed in the dream. " I had never loved Steerforth better than when the ties that bound me to him were
broken " (XXXII, 516) .

David and Steerforth share adolescent crushes on each
other. Later the two share love objects. Dickens flirts with this
classic homosexual theme, but does not take it very far. Little
Em'ly is loved by both, and so, in a less obvious way, is Rosa
Dartle. Steerforth seduces them both; David loves them both,
but loves them passively, unsuccessfully, and therefore morally.
Miss Dartle is one of Dickens' angry women, not so magnificent
as Edith Dombey, not so perverse as Miss Wade. She is fero-
ciously jealous of the women in Steerforth's life, and she is
also jealous of David. When David first comes to the Steerforth home, he learns the story of Miss Dartle's remarkable
scar—the mark that cuts through her lips.

> ' Why, the fact is,' he returned, ' *I* did that.'
> ' By an unfortunate accident! '
> ' No. I was a young boy, and she exasperated me, and
> I threw a hammer at her. A promising young angel I must
> have been! '
> I was deeply sorry to have touched on such a painful
> theme, but that was useless now.
> ' She has borne the mark ever since, as you see,' said
> Steerforth, ' and she'll bear it to her grave, if she ever rests
> in one—though I can hardly believe she will ever rest
> anywhere. She was the motherless child of a sort of cousin
> of my father's. He died one day. My mother, who was
> then a widow, brought her here to be company to her.
> She has a couple of thousand pounds of her own, and saves

the interest of it every year, to add to the principal. There's the history of Miss Rosa Dartle for you.'

'And I have no doubt she loves you like a brother?' said I.

'Humph!' retorted Steerforth, looking at the fire. 'Some brothers are not loved overmuch; and some love—but help yourself, Copperfield.' (XX, 352)

The passage is brimming with suggestions.[12] Miss Dartle's scar is an emblem of the sexual violation which was produced by Steerforth's hammer and which passed through her lips (i. e., *labiae*). Her restlessness allies her to Steerforth and Maldon and suggests that she is among those fated to "drown." The sudden death of Rosa's father, so casual in report, is reminiscent of the death of Mr. Spenlow. David, of course, is attracted to women with weak or absent fathers. In the closing exchange, David, fishing for information, intimates that the relation between Steerforth and Rosa ought to be that of brother and sister. This is rejected, and the implication of the aposiopesis is what we later learn directly from Miss Dartle: that Steerforth has "used" her, and continues to use her at his whim. The parting expression—"Help yourself, Copperfield" is entirely apt. Steerforth is willing and anxious to share.

Miss Dartle is about thirty years old, which is the same age as the elder Miss Larkins, after whom David's heart launches still another of its undisciplined impulses. The first stirrings of lust for Rosa come when he spends the night at Steerforth's home. He is surprised to discover his room dominated by a portrait of his new love, and again he is transfixed by the scar.

It was a startling likeness, and necessarily had a startling look. The painter hadn't made the scar, but *I* made it; and there it was, coming and going; now confined to the upper lip as I had seen it at dinner, and now showing the whole extent of the wound inflicted by the hammer, as I had seen it when she was passionate. (XX, 356)

---

[12] Some of which have been elucidated by Mark Spilka, *Dickens and Kafka, a Mutual Interpretation* (Bloomington, Indiana, 1963), to which this passage is indebted.

The wound which grows larger with passion is a cliché of
Victorian pornography, and the italicized " *I* made it " enforces
the identity with Steerforth, as David, in fantasy, duplicates the
act of violation. The sexual import of the passage is implicit
not only in metaphor, but in the very rhythm of the sentence,
especially in the phrase, " coming and going." David's repressed and stylized imaginings are parallel to the content of the
dream of drowning—David would do what Steerforth can do.

But Steerforth is more than the conventional gentleman-
seducer. How frequently does David refer to his wasted powers,
to his easy learning and bored novelty seeking. He is rather
a precursor of Des Esseintes than a successor to Lovelace. And
there is a hint of perversity here too—the same that is implicit
in the notion of drowning together.

> ' You haven't got a sister, have you? ' said Steerforth,
> yawning.
> ' No,' I answered.
> ' That's a pity,' said Steerforth. ' If you had had one, I
> should think that she would have been a pretty, timid,
> little bright-eyed sort of a girl. I should have like to have
> known her.' (VI, 140)

The implication of Steerforth's remarks are as clear as is the
effeminate nickname which he gives to David—" Daisy." And
perhaps this is the solution to what has been considered a puzzle—what exactly does Steerforth find attractive about Em'ly?
Steerforth is more interested in David than he admits, and of
all the daisies in the field he chooses a girl most like David—
his " sister."

David Copperfield's dream of drowning is then a path into
the central structural pattern of the novel, which is the rich
and complex relationship between David and two complemen-
tary figures. Dickens is an extraordinarily subtle novelist,
though the depth of his psychological vision is not as apparent
as that of the novelist of manners whose fiction is dense with
the involuted analysis of personality and motive. Here, Dickens
has created a brilliant tripartite relationship; perhaps its im-
mediacy is accounted for by the same reasons that made this

novel a " favorite child." And if an understanding of his method can only be effected by dwelling on details and trifles, then we must fall back on David's own observation, that " trifles make the sum of life " (LIII, 838).

Raskolnikov's Motives: Love and Murder

Edward Wasiolek

W. D. Snodgrass' reading of *Crime and Punishment*[1] brought into the center of attention a whole part of the novel that had largely been ignored by the " classic " explanations of Raskolnikov's motives. He was the first to perceive the tangled and bruising relations between Raskolnikov and his mother, and the first to perceive that the landlady and the pawnbroker are displaced representations of Raskolnikov's mother, so that in striking at the pawnbroker Raskolnikov was striking symbolically at the mother. Before Snodgrass' article was published, very little had been said about the relations between mother and son, and almost nothing about the part these relations play in the murder of the pawnbroker, even though one-fourth of the novel concerns Raskolnikov's relations with his mother.

The sections dealing with Raskolnikov and his mother show hidden aggression towards each other. The mother is intent on reminding Raskolnikov how much she and Dunia have sacrificed for him and how much they are willing to sacrifice for him. Although the mother dwells on her love and affection, she reminds him subtly of his subjecting them to misery and hardship through his refusal to continue his studies and to support himself at the university. Raskolnikov in turn has passively and intentionally revolted against the burden of his mother's love and sacrifice by defeating her expectations of success. He gives up his studies, refuses to find work, and permits himself to fall into dependence and degradation.

The punishing relations between mother and son may not be immediately perceptible, but the powerful emotional ties between them and between brother and sister are clearly visible in a number of scenes. When Raskolnikov receives the letter from his mother in part I, chapter 3, his hands tremble; he is

[1] W. D. Snodgrass, "Crime for Punishment: The Tenor of Part One," *Hudson Review*, XIII (Summer 1960), 202–253.

visibly perturbed during the reading and then rushes out of his room in a half-demented state. When he first sees his mother and sister in the narrative time of the story, he faints, a psychic defense against the painful reality of their presence.

Snodgrass' analogy between the mother and the pawn-broker implies that Raskolnikov has a murderous hostility toward his mother. Raskolnikov himself tells us that he hates his mother and sister: Near the end of part III, he says to himself: " Mother, sister—how I loved them! Why do I hate them now? Yes, I hate them, I feel physical hatred for them. I can't bear them near me." [2] Snodgrass supports the tie between mother, landlady, and pawnbroker by pointing out that each is a widow, each is accompanied by a younger woman (Dunia, Natalya, and Lizaveta), that Raskolnikov places himself in a position of indebtedness to each of the women, and that Raskolnikov has fantasies of violence against each. Snodgrass summarizes the resemblance between the three women: " For if Raskolnikov has intentionally picked Alyona Ivanovna to stand in the image of Pashenka, he has picked both to stand in the image of his mother. They form a triumvirate of older women, each accompanied by a younger woman, each a widow. From each, Raskolnikov has asked and received something; to each he is indebted. They hold his spirit as a pledge. They seem to him tormentors, since it is on their account that he torments himself. When Raskolnikov strikes down the pawn-broker with an axe, he will strike at Pashenka, but he will also strike behind her at the image of his greatest creditor, his mother." [3] Snodgrass might also have pointed out what may be the most telling evidence of all in connecting the pawn-broker and the mother. Near the end of part III and following the passage in which Raskolnikov expresses his hate for his mother and sister, he slips imperceptibly in his reflections from talking about hating his mother to talking about hating the " old woman." He says, " Ah, how I hate the old woman now! I feel I should kill her again if she came to life!" The shift from mother to pawnbroker is evidence of how they are asso-

[2] All quotations from *Crime and Punishment* are from the Garnett translation, Modern Library edition.
[3] Snodgrass, p. 219.

ciated in his mind; even more significant: it is not possible to establish from the word " old woman " which woman he is referring to. It is in all probability an intentional ambiguity.

Snodgrass' brilliant perception of the similarities between the three women is, I believe, established convincingly. There are a number of other points of similarity which Snodgrass does not mention and to which I will come later on. The more pressing question, however, is why Raskolnikov felt such murderous rage against his mother and why he had to expend such hate in a displaced and disguised way. The answer lies partly in the social, religious, and ethical prohibitions of a society that inhibits one's expression of hostility toward a loved one, especially against a parent. But, it is not merely a matter of external checks. The child finds it painful to permit himself the conscious thought, let alone an action of violence against a parent. Since the hate, by the law of psychic economy, has to go somewhere, it will tend to be displaced on someone else, chosen as a surrogate for the loved one, or, as is also quite frequent, it will be expended against oneself. The more violent the hate and the closer the loved one, the more hidden and more remote will be the object against which the hate will be expended. Such remote expressions are necessary to protect Raskolnikov against the pain of directly expressed hostility.

The same kind of veiling can be observed in regard to his sister and his relationship to the landlady's daughter and to Lizaveta. Such concealment can be explained by the need to protect himself against a conscious admission of erotic affection for his sister. Dunia, like her mother, is a strikingly handsome girl, robust in body, intelligence, and temperament. The landlady's daughter is sickly, passive, and mentally somewhat undeveloped. The pawnbroker's sister is even less attractive physically and less developed mentally: she is ungainly, a halfwit, and she passively endures the outrages of the older sister and the sexual aggressions of various men. It is significant that the disguises progress toward overtness of sexuality, since Raskolnikov " loves " the landlady's daughter in a compassionate and spiritual sense, but the pawnbroker's sister is repeatedly and coarsely seduced by other men.

By and large, the displacement both of mother and sister

is constructed to move toward an overt expression of what is hidden. Such progression can be discerned to control a number of traits. Raskolnikov is indebted, for example, to each of the women, and there is a progression toward active manipulation by him of that indebtedness, that is, toward a revelation of his part in " choosing " the indebtedness and consequently of progression toward the consciousness of what he is doing. His indebtedness to his mother seems at first to be the result of untoward circumstances; but on closer examination, it is possible to see Raskolnikov's passive part in contracting the indebtedness. His role in arranging his indebtedness to the landlady, and then blaming her for punishing him, comes out quite clearly when, later in the novel, we hear Razumikhin's version of the facts. As for his indebtedness to the pawnbroker, he actively and openly arranges to make himself the indebtor and her the debtor. The same progression from the hidden to something open can be seen in the physical traits of the three women. The mother is a strikingly beautiful woman (her name Pulkheriya means beautiful), the landlady is in Raskolnikov's eyes unattractive (although we learn later from Razumikhin that she is quite attractive), and the pawnbroker is ugly and hateful. He feels oppressed and tormented by his mother, but carefully refrains from expressing to himself what he feels; he feels tormented by his landlady and says so; and he goes out of his way to dwell on the hateful and tormenting qualities of the pawnbroker. We go from hidden hate to overt hate, as we go from mother, to landlady, to pawnbroker. The point of such a progression is an indication of the disguises that Raskolnikov must go through before he will permit the hate and hostility to rise in his consciousness. Snodgrass failed to point out the progressions, but they support his basic identifications.

It is clear that Snodgrass is acquainted with psychoanalytic concepts, even though he never mentions Freud or psychoanalysis or uses any technical terms. Such basic concepts as displacement, defenses, reaction formation, projection, introjection, and internalized aggression lie just below the surface of his argument and his conclusions. There is the possibility that he did not choose to name them or use them more explicitly to avoid the automatic and uncritical negative reactions that such terms

and methods often arouse in literary audiences. More probably, his psychoanalytic knowledge came not so much from
explicit acquaintance as from the general diffusion of Freudian
concepts in our culture. The latter surmise is supported by the
fact that he never mentions Freud in the long article, but does
mention Edmund Bergler and Simone Weil. Bergler would have
taken him to Freud, and Weil away from Freud and to the generalized philosophical and religious conclusions which finally
neutralize, and in my opinion, distort, his psychoanalytic perceptions.

It is not Snodgrass' reluctance to use psychoanalytic terms
that I have reservations about, but his failure to make the most
of his excellent analogy by the use of systematic psychoanalytic
thinking. This failure led him to miss that opposites like beauty
and ugliness (mother and pawnbroker) and moral robustness and
frailty (sister and pawnbroker's sister) can also be similarities.
It also led him to miss the supporting progressions, which the
psychoanalytic process of displacement of painful experiences
projects on to increasingly remote surrogates. In the article,
Snodgrass veers from the psychoanalytic implications of his
analogy to vaguely social-moralistic conclusions. This shift is
particularly perceptible in Snodgrass' explanation of Raskolnikov's motives, toward which the entire article moves. The
groundwork is laid for a new and different explanation of
Raskolnikov's motives; yet the conclusions that are drawn from
psychoanalytic perceptions bring his argument back to familiar
and inadequate social-moralistic explanations.

Snodgrass himself summarizes his four-part explanation of
Raskolnikov's motives at the beginning of the article as " the
desire to achieve punishment which will reinstate him as a
worthy member of a moral universe." Such an explanation may
be true on a moral and philosophical level, but Raskolnikov's
drama is not only a philosophical treatise but also a painful,
torturing personal drama. Snodgrass' conclusions do not explain adequately what the experience means to Raskolnikov,
and don't do justice to his own perceptive analogy between
mother and pawnbroker. Raskolnikov's personal drama has to
do with the hostility he suffers and provokes in regard to his
mother, and the symbolic attempt to resolve the hostility by

striking out against the mother. There is a hiatus between Snodgrass' perceptions and his conclusions. Much of the article has to do with Raskolnikov's relations with his mother, but the conclusions are restricted to a social and religious context.

It is true that Raskolnikov attempts to do with society what he has done with his mother, to implicate it in his suffering, to raise in his consciousness a conception of society which aggresses against him, so that he may be justified in striking out against it. He tells Sonia more than once, as he tells Dunia near the end of the novel, that he has done nothing more in murdering the pawnbroker than society does as a matter of course. He pursues the punishment of society so that he can feel victimized, and thus justified; and on a deeper level, so that by the punishment he may be, as Snodgrass suggests, forced back into the fold of humanity. The same drama can be seen as pursuit of punishment for religious ends, or at least Sonia raises it to this level. He aggresses against God, so that God will show the limits of freedom and moral law. Without raising the question of relative importance, I would maintain that the personal drama comes before the social and religious dramas. The grudge that is elevated into aggression against society and God is first a grudge and aggression against his loved ones, and it is Snodgrass' reading that has permitted us to glimpse what the sources of that grudge may be. His feelings run high against the society that has " degraded " him, but his feelings run deeper against the family he feels has degraded him.

Snodgrass' translations of the personal drama into social and religious terms can be seen in his reading of the mare-beating dream. His conclusion about the dream is the following:

> The dream shows Raskolnikov to himself as a man too feeble in drawing his burdens, yet entirely too strong in punishing himself for that failure. Thus he is stuck on a treadmill of guilt and rage where he is beating himself to death for being stuck. At the same time, the dream shows him a world which has the same characteristics: all good characters are weak or victimized. (The dream contains but disguises the fact that these characters have chosen to be either weak or victimized). Meantime, " the worst are

full of passionate intensity." The only active role in the
dream belongs to such destroyers as Mikolka. Raskolnikov's
drama tells him that he must choose either murder or
suicide, either kill or be killed.

The interpretation assumes that we can make a neat distinction
in the dream between the victimized and the victimizers. Yet
this is not so, even by the identifications that Snodgrass himself
gives us. He perceives correctly that the mare (the victimized
creature in the dream) stands not only for the teen-age girl on
the boulevard, (Dunia, Sonia, Marmeladov), and the mother,
but also for Raskolnikov and the pawnbroker. He sees also that
the pawnbroker is to be identified with Mikolka (the victimizers
and the destroyers), but he does not see, or at least does not
mention, that the mother, the landlady, Dunia, and Marmeladov can also be identified with the destroyers and the victimizers. Much of Snodgrass' article, after all, shows us how art-
fully his mother, and to a lesser extent his sister, have victimized
Raskolnikov, and how by analogy Marmeladov has, through
his passive actions, victimized his daughter Sonia and his wife
Katerina. If Raskolnikov, the pawnbroker, the mother, the
sister, and Marmeladov are both Mikolka and the mare, both
victimizers and victimized, how can we come to the conclusion
that the dream shows Raskolnikov that he " must choose either
murder or suicide; either killed or be killed? " Who are the
murderers and who are the victims? Snodgrass sees also that
Raskolnikov comprises all the actors in the dream, but he fails
to see that this is evidence against his conclusions that the drama
shows us a Raskolnikov who must choose between a world in
which one is victimized or one in which one is the victimizer.
In order for Raskolnikov to have a choice between victim and
victimizer, between suicide and murder, Raskolnikov must be
able to separate himself from what is being represented. The
dream does not show us, as Snodgrass suggests, Raskolnikov
and a state of things outside of Raskolnikov. The choices have
already been made and the dream shows us what they are. The
pawnbroker, landlady, Sonia, Dunia, Lizaveta, Marmeladov,
Katerina have the meaning Raskolnikov assigns to them.

What Snodgrass has done is " rationalize " the dream, giving it a general character of an intellectualist sort. What the dream actually shows us—and we must always remember that it is Raskolnikov's dream—is Raskolnikov killing his mother, the pawnbroker, and the landlady, and in turn being tormented and killed by them. Most of all, it shows us a Raskolnikov who is killing himself, who is tormentor and tormented, victimizer and victimized, killer and being killed. Since it is he who assigns the roles to the mother, landlady, pawnbroker, they exist as meanings within him; they are what he has decided them to be. In killing them, he attempts to kill what they mean in him, and what they mean to him is that they are his tormentors and victimizers. But in striking at them, he strikes at himself. If they are his tormentors, he does not silence the tormenting by tormenting, but only increases it because he is both tormentor and tormented. The dream shows us that the ferocity of hostility against his real or imagined tormentors is also directed against himself. We are shown no contemplative Raskolnikov in the dream observing a state of things that asks him to choose between murder and suicide. The dream gives him no choices at all, but it does dramatize the futility of doing both; the blow against others is struck against himself. Raskolnikov will tell us later the same thing: that in killing the old hag, he had killed himself, and the symbolic reenactment of the killing of the pawnbroker, at the end of part III, tells us again that he had not been able to kill the pawnbroker within himself, even though she has " actually " been killed. What he had not been able to kill is the pawnbroker within him.

Still, if I am correct in stating that the dream shows us that Raskolnikov, in striking at others, is striking at himself and that the punishment of the tormentors is a punishment of himself, I will have corrected Snodgrass' interpretation of the dream, but I will not have met the objections I brought forth to his social-religious conclusions. Snodgrass tells us that Raskolnikov desires punishment for the deep sense of shame and wrong he feels within himself, but he does not tell us what that shame and wrong are. I have indicated that Raskolnikov has attempted to punish his tormentors, and has succeeded only in punishing himself, but I have not explained why he feels he must punish his tormentors with such ferocity and why Dostoevsky felt it necessary to translate the punishment into self-punishment. Why does Raskolnikov feel that he must kill the pawnbroker and through her symbolically the mother? What moves him to pursue punishment and self-punishment with such relentless and undeviating ferocity? What is it that has persuaded him that the experiment will be a failure before it has begun, so that it is not really an experiment but only a confirmation. And a confirmation of what?

II

Near the end of the novel Raskolnikov says to Dunia: " Oh, if only I were alone and no one loved me and I too had never loved anyone! Nothing of all this would have happened." This is a tantalizing and mysterious statement, made after the crime and the agony and somewhat in the cold reflection of everything that had happened. If we take this statement literally, Raskolnikov is saying that " love " caused everything: the guilt, the search for punishment and the attempt to alleviate the guilt by murdering the pawnbroker and symbolically the murder of the mother. If we turn to his relationship to his loved ones,— his mother and sister—we find ample evidence that his love for them and theirs for him are entwined with a great deal of hostility and aggression. It is their sacrificial love that drives him to the half-demented fury with which he leaves his little room and rushes out into the street muttering to himself; it is this same sacrificial love that causes him to throw Luzhin out of his room without a provocation that is commensurate with the ferocity of Raskolnikov's reactions. It is their presence that causes him to faint, that provokes him to express hatred for them, and that leads him to flaunt his relationship with Sonia before his mother. We can explain his reactions by saying that he feels victimized by the sacrificial love of mother and sister, for such love predetermines what he will be and what he must be, just as Marmeladov is victimized by Katerina by her insistence that he be like her imagined first husband. Marmeladov is permitted only the identity that Katerina Ivanovna will give him: the dutiful, sober husband who resembles her first husband, or at least as she imagines him to have been. Raskolnikov is permitted only the identity that mother and sister give him: the dutiful son, hard-working, morally undeviating, and destined to bring security and honor to them. Marmeladov tells Katerina by his destructive actions that she must accept him as he is and not as she thinks he ought to be. Since she refuses to relinquish the Marmeladov she has formed in her mind, he destroys the image by acting out another Marmeladov. His destructive acts are both aggression and appeal. The aggression is against the Marmeladov she insists he must be, and his appeal is to be accepted for what he really is. Something of the same aggression and appeal can be seen in Raskolnikov's relations with his mother. It is as if Raskolnikov were saying to his mother: I am not what you think I am, I am even the very opposite. I am not the ideal son, I am secretly the hateful son. You have the ideal image, but I am the vicious reality. Indeed, he says this in almost the same words in the notebooks.[4]

Raskolnikov's revolt against the burden of his sister's and mother's love and against the constraint of his freedom, implied by their expectations, gives us what would seem to be an adequate explanation of his furious actions. Such an explanation would justify the subplot of the Marmeladovs and even more important would explain why it is necessary to strike out symbolically against the mother in killing the pawnbroker. But the explanation is wrong, or at least inadequate, because it assumes that the sacrificial love is a cause, when it is really an effect. The burdensome sacrificial love is something that Raskolnikov has chosen, not something that has driven him to other choices. He *chooses* to drop out of school, to be poor, to lie for days with an empty stomach in his coffin-like room; in short, he chooses the very conditions that provoke his mother to sacrifice and Dunia to become a governess at the Svidrigaylovs, to suffer near rape and disgrace, and then to choose legal prostitution with Luzhin. And if he chooses the sacrificial love, the love cannot be the cause of his agony and his guilt.

---

[4] *The Notebooks for "Crime and Punishment,"* ed. and trans. Edward Wasiolek (Chicago: The University of Chicago Press, 1967), p. 48. "N. B. *About the mother.* She loves me because she sees in me everything beautiful, an unattainable ideal, but if she were to find out, then she would come perhaps to hate me very much. (Lack of faith, doubt, estrangement from his Mother. From his Mother. From his sister, all the more.)"

The situation is complicated, of course, and not as schematic as I have put it, for both theory and the actual narrative line of the novel show that there is an interaction between Raskolnikov's provoking his family to sacrifice and his suffering from such sacrifice; but, whatever the part that the choice plays—and it plays some part—it is clear that something other than the burdensome sacrificial love moves him to the murder.

In attempting to get at this something other, we cannot overlook the dense web of erotic relations that exist in the novel. Psychoanalysis will lead us, of course, to some erotic relationship against which the individual will protect himself in various ways. One such way is to intellectualize and consequently impersonalize the painful content. It cannot escape our attention that Raskolnikov's overt motivations, to be a benefactor of family and humanity or to be a superman exempt from the normal constraints of law, are such intellectualizings and impersonalizations. Raskolnikov seems to be saying: I did the murder because I am a special and heroic personality. Such a possibility is substantiated by the frequent outbursts of abuse against himself.

In attempting to get at the explanation of why Raskolnikov should feel himself to be hateful, I have no intention of reducing the complexities and refinements of Raskolnikov's drama to an oedipal complex. I have too much respect for literature to make it—and especially this novel—an example of static and abstract psychoanalytic generalizations. Nor do I think that psychoanalysis—when applied to life or to literature—leads one to such crude oversimplifications. If I can add to Belinsky's dictum " Life is higher than art," I would say that literature is " higher " than psychoanalysis or indeed any set of propositions that we frame to explain life or literature. Freud and psychoanalysis, however, have added immensely to our store of hypothetical generalizations about psychology; and since psychology is inevitably part of literature, it would seem both rational and academic to take such propositions into consideration.

Dostoyevsky lived in a society which repressed direct sexual expression, and his difficulties with editors in using even the mildest of sexual terms are evidence that the taboos were strictly enforced. Yet, it is remarkable how much of a sexual nature he expressed in the novel, although necessarily in disguised and oblique form. Snodgrass touches on sexual implications of the murder in a few casual remarks, such as the spasm that Raskolnikov experiences as he fumbles with the keys and attempts to open the old hag's trunk. But he quickly translates the sexual content into metaphors for Raskolnikov's self-abuse: " Yet, because of Raskolnikov's deep identification with Alyona Ivanovna, the murder must finally be seen not as an act of sexual violence directed against another; but rather as an act of self-destruction and 'self-abuse.' " But the image of Raskolnikov rummaging under the old women's bed, and below the clothes in the trunk to get at her " treasure," (a word that is used in colloquial Russian for a woman's sexual favors) should not be ignored. Less obvious but perhaps more significant, the aggression of mother against son and son against mother is played out not only on economic and career levels, but also on a sexual level. Raskolnikov's choice of women he falls in love with is calculated to give hurt to his mother and to provoke her aggression against them. We are told that Madame Raskolnikov so disapproved of his choice of the landlady's daughter that she was happy when the girl died. Similarly, she disapproves of Sonia and is convinced that Sonia is at the bottom of all their misfortunes. In a scene, reminiscent of Hamlet's behavior at the dumb show when Hamlet aggresses against his mother by choosing to lay his head on Ophelia's lap and to talk to her in coarse sexual terms (instead of responding to his mother's invitation to sit next to her), Raskolnikov insists on inviting Sonia, when she comes to invite him to the funeral dinner, to enter his room and sit in the presence of his mother, to the mother's obvious discomfort and disapproval.

There is evidence, also, of an erotic relationship with his sister. Raskolnikov has chosen women to fall in love with who would least remind him of his sister. Dunia is robust in body and mind, and the landlady's daughter is weak in both. Dunia is firm and willful, Sonia is timid and self-effacing. There is no expressed antagonism on the part of Dunia toward Sonia in the novel, but such antagonism is expressed in the Notebooks: " The sister becomes Sonia's worst enemy; she sets

Razumikhin against her; gets him to insult her; and afterward when Razumikhin goes over to Sonia's side, she quarrels with him." [5] There are too, on several occasions, signs of embarrassed and ambiguous affection between brother and sister. But perhaps the most telling evidence for such a suppressed erotic relationship is to be seen in Raskolnikov's behavior toward Dunia's two suitors. The gratuitous rage Raskolnikov feels against Luzhin bespeaks of feelings that are pent up, barely restrained, and powerful enough to break through the politeness and courtesy of social intercourse. Raskolnikov's feelings against the actual attempted seducer of Dunia, Svidrigaylov, are less intense. To be sure, he warns Svidrigaylov to stay away from his sister, but he does this in a relatively calm and rational way. There are no unreasoned and uncontained outbursts against Svidrigaylov, even when the latter describes in detail how he attempted to seduce Raskolnikov's sister. Indeed, when Svidrigaylov tells how he attempted to seduce Dunia, and how there was a point in which she seemed to be giving in, Raskolnikov listens to the long narrative without interrupting Svidrigaylov. We can only conclude—given his propensity to break out emotionally on many other scores—that he listens with rapt attention and enjoys the narrative vicariously. How does one explain the viciousness of his response to Dunia's legal fiancé and the mildness of his response to Svidrigaylov's dishonorable advances? One explanation would be that Svidrigaylov had been repulsed by Dunia and is therefore not an imminent threat to whatever erotic feelings he has for his sister, whereas at the time of his violent outburst against Luzhin, Luzhin was the legal fiancé and seemed to be on his way to obtain legally what Svidrigaylov had failed to do directly. But there is another explanation. If we are to take Dostoevsky's words in the Notebooks literally that Svidrigaylov is supposed to represent one side of Raskolnikov and that Svidrigaylov is an overt expression of what is unexpressed in Raskolnikov, then it would seem that we would have to look at Svidrigaylov's sexual aggressiveness as in some way an externalization of what is hidden in Raskolnikov's unconscious.

[5] *The Notebooks for " Crime and Punishment,"* p. 46.

Critics (myself included) have taken Dostoevsky's words as justification for seeing Svidrigaylov as a philosophic embodiment of Raskolnikov's desire to be above morality. Svidrigaylov is the bronze man Raskolnikov had hoped to become by the murder. If we can use Svidrigaylov as a symbolic equivalent for hidden philosophical and moral motives in Raskolnikov, then we cannot deny them as symbolic equivalents for other motives, among which the erotic motives loom large. Svidrigaylov has murdered, as Raskolnikov has murdered; he whips his servant and his wife, as Raskolnikov symbolically whips the landlady, and as he beats his mother and sister in the Notebooks. Svidrigaylov is indebted to his wife, as Raskolnikov contrives to indebt himself to the landlady, pawnbroker, and mother. Svidrigaylov has violated and apparently caused the death of a young girl, and has on at least two occasions attempted to violate Raskolnikov's sister. Raskolnikov may be repelled by the dirt Svidrigaylov has surrounded himself with, but he is also attracted to it, as the meeting between them in the tavern makes abundantly clear. Svidrigaylov understands this and regales Raskolnikov with stories of his sexual exploits in a manner of complicity.

But it is not only Svidrigaylov who represents the hidden impulses of Raskolnikov, but also Sonia. Again both the Notebooks and the structure of the novel are explicit on this point. If we can use Svidrigaylov as a dramatic externalization of hidden sexual motives in Raskolnikov, it would seem that Sonia cannot by any stretch of the critical imagination find a place in such an explanation. Dostoevsky himself in the Notebooks indicated that they should be taken as opposite externalizations of Raskolnikov,[6] and the dominant critical tradition has seen Raskolnikov as torn between his " Sonia principle " and his " Svidrigaylov principle." I believe this interpretation to be correct, but again they are opposites on more than philosophical and moral grounds. We must remind ourselves that Sonia is a prostitute, and it is only to her, a prostitute, that he is ineluctably drawn. What Raskolnikov cannot get over is that Sonia

[6] Svidrigaylov is despair, the most cynical. Sonia is hope, the most unrealizable. (Raskolnikov himself should express this.) He became passionately attached to both. *The Notebooks for " Crime and Punishment,"* p. 244.

is a prostitute but is unsullied and remains pure. What fascinates him is her "clean-dirtiness." She represents for him a resolution of what is clean and what is dirty; she redeems in his eyes the dirty life she has been forced to lead, and it is this redemptive quality that attracts him to her.

I am aware that it may go against our aesthetic sense to think of Sonia in sexual terms, especially in view of the fact that she has been discussed almost exclusively in spiritual terms. But she is a prostitute and is looked upon by Lebeziatnikov and the Marmeladovs' landlady as morally unfit to live in the apartment house. Since Raskolnikov's erotic feelings for his mother are deeply repressed and highly displaced, one would expect that they would be permitted expression only under the most exceptional circumstances and would be projected on someone who would not arouse erotic feelings. Sonia is such a person; her sexuality is barely perceptible and disguised by the unquestioned spirituality of her nature. In addition, Dostoevsky dramatizes the confession scene so that the reader may understand it both in spiritual and sexual terms. As Raskolnikov prepares to confess to Sonia, he turns pale, sits down on Sonia's bed, and his whole body shivers; at the same time, Sonia begins to pant and her face becomes paler and paler. When Sonia understands that Raskolnikov is the murderer, she shudders convulsively and sinks " helplessly on the bed."

The deep grudge that Raskolnikov feels against his mother and in a less intense way against his sister is a grudge against their "love for him and his for them." But the love is not just the sacrificial love of his adult years. Below the sacrificial love, there is the original love, which he had to bear and struggle against without the aid of the interdicting father. The deep grudge would be then against the repugnant and hateful thing that he had fantasized, and which he had to suffer alone. It is this love which he must punish and for which he must punish himself. It is the hateful mother within him that he attempts to destroy, but which he cannot destroy without destroying himself.

The imagery of the novel and especially of the mare-beating dream suggests a Raskolnikov who attempts frantically and futiley to cut out something repugnant within himself. It is not the pawnbroker or the mother he attempts to kill but the meaning of the hateful mother within him. If he can kill part of himself, he will become whole again; if the hateful and repugnant Raskolnikov can be cut out, the beautiful Raskolnikov will remain. But the hateful thing will not be cut out. The dream of the mare-beating shows us that the punishment creates only more punishment. The dream is not only a symbolic matrix of the contradictory relationships which love occupies in Raskolnikov's conception of himself and his loved ones, but it is also a suggestion of " the cure." It tells us not only what is wrong, but also what will make it right. Raskolnikov not only kills the mare (himself, the pawnbroker, the mother, the landlady), but he also weeps for it and then caresses it and them. The little boy in the dream still exists in the mature Raskolnikov, and it is the little boy that could provide the redemptive strength. What the dream shows symbolically is Raskolnikov—the little boy—kissing (forgiving) the hurt that he is inflicting on the mother-pawnbroker-landlady-sister, and the hurt that Raskolnikov, the adult, inflicts on himself. And this is what the novel shows us, by way of Sonia's intercession: that it will not be by rejection and force that he will be made whole again, but by acceptance-forgiveness: the forgiveness of his mother and of himself, the first step of which is the confession to Sonia. He must come to love and forgive the hateful and repugnant mother within him, and consequently that part of himself; and he does this by way of Sonia, who is not only the religious redemptrice, but also the psychological redemptrice. The hateful mother within him is not only the mother of sacrificial love, but also the mother of sensual love. By loving Sonia, the prostitute, he accepts the dirtiness of love, because it is not actually dirt, no more than it was with his mother, though the fantasies of childhood made it so. Sonia is the living embodiment of " clean " dirtiness, of corruption that is redemptive. She takes him back to his real self and his whole self, not the beautiful and abstract self he had imagined and which he had elevated into grounds for striking out against others and against himself. In order for the mind-soul-psyche to become whole again, the good mother and the hateful mother have to become one, and the good Raskolnikov and the evil Raskolnikov have to become one. What is half-confessed in his dream is wholly confessed to Sonia, and Sonia asks him to do the final thing: to confess it to everyone. What is hidden must become open, because it is by becoming open that the self reclaims itself.

The overt motives Raskolnikov gives to explain the murder of the pawnbroker are rationalizations and, in psychoanalytic terminology, defenses against what he fears is ugly and hateful in himself. Raskolnikov sees himself and wants to be someone free of the old Raskolnikov. The motivations are aspirations, in fantasy, yet real as aspiration, to a total freedom. The explanation of the old Raskolnikov, the hateful and repugnant Raskolnikov that I have given in erotic and sexual terms, can be reconverted, if one wishes, into ethical terminology. What he discovers is that he cannot deny the old Raskolnikov, and that the freedom he aspires to is bought at the price of self-destruction, and that "true" freedom is bought at the price of acceptance of the old slavery. Beauty and ugliness, freedom and responsibility, become one in the acceptance of oneself. Perhaps this is what Dostoevsky meant by forgiveness and suffering. Such a conversion into ethical terminology—though correct—empties the drama of some of its specific content, for one must still ask: freedom from what and the acceptance of what slavery? There is enough in the novel to suggest that the specific content, in some part, is erotic and sexual and that the consequent translations of such impulses into guilt and shame come to color the conscious and conventional love of son and mother, brother and sister. The fantasies and experiences of childhood leave deep and ineradicable channels in us, through which flow the experiences we later characterize as religious, social, economic, and practical. It is astonishing that Dostoyevsky was able to perceive this dramatically, but it was not astonishing to Freud, who on the occasion of his seventieth birthday paid the extraordinary tribute to Dostoyevsky acknowledging, with generosity characteristic of him, that everything he had discovered was already to be found in Dostoyevsky's works.

Summary

W. D. Snodgrass in " Crime for Punishment: The Tenor of Part One " made an important contribution to the understanding of Raskolnikov's motives by suggesting that the pawnbroker was a displaced representative of the mother and that Raskolnikov, in killing the pawnbroker, was striking symbolically against the mother. Snodgrass failed to pursue the psychoanalytic implications of this perception and brought back his interpretation of Raskolnikov's motives to familiar moral and psychological conclusions.

The repressed eroticism and hostility that Raskolnikov feels for his mother is expressed more fully and in finer structural detail than Snodgrass suspected: the situations, imagery, and character traits are constructed to move from concealment to overtness as one proceeds from mother to landlady and pawnbroker. Sonia may be considered to be a sexual as well as a religious redemptrice, since she embodies, in Raskolnikov's eyes, "clean-dirtiness." She permits him to come to terms with the hateful and repugnant mother he had fantasized within himself and had attempted unsuccessfully to cut out of himself.

The Creative Surrender:

A Comment on "Joanna Field's"* book *An Experiment in Leisure*

Anton Ehrenzweig

In my experience as an art teacher I found that creative sterility may be the result of ego rigidity impeding the free flow of mental imagery. The student cannot relax his all too deliberate control of the medium, nor can he tolerate any failure in realizing preconceived ideas; he is thus unable to absorb new stimuli arising from his work in progress. It follows that the art teacher's task is to make the student's personality more flexible and so to develop his latent creativity. What precisely these creative ego changes are is difficult to say. The analyst is more concerned with resolving the id conflicts which stand in the foreground and call for all his skill; he will be inclined to let the sublimations that follow on the resolution of id conflict look after themselves; he may consider creative development an educational rather than an analytical task. The art teacher, who is in better position to observe creative ego changes, lacks the conceptual tools to describe them for us. Yet the artist's never ceasing search for creative stimulation reveals itself as every bit as dramatic and painful as is the psychoanalytical exploration of id conflict and ego defenses.

It is our good fortune that Marion Milner, who finally became a psychoanalyst herself, continued her life-long search for creativeness without interruption by her psychoanalytical training. She felt that her creative search as an artist was something apart from her growing understanding of her id fantasies. For this reason, perhaps, she never bothered to reformulate more technically her creative experiences, which she had gathered in her first two "Joanna Field" books, written before her psychoanalytical training. Her first book *A Life of One's Own*[1] mainly dealt with the shedding of conventional clichés that had cluttered up her life;

*Pseudonym for Marion Milner.

[1] Joanna Field [Marion Milner], *A Life of One's Own* (London: Penguin Books, 1956. Published originally in 1934.)

her second book *An Experiment in Leisure*[2]—as she called her creative search—dealt with finding truly potent imagery to replace the abandoned clichés. In my view this change in the character and function of mental imagery represents the crucial creative change in the ego. It needs only to be put into more technical language to make clear that Marian Milner has described a new approach to an ego psychology of creativeness.

We know how artists are apt to scan the world for potent images to give a new impetus to the flow of their imagination. These images do not serve them so much as "picturesque motifs,' i.e., as substitutes for free invention, but rather as a means for keeping their eyes fresh and their sensibility sharpened; unlike motifs, creative images need not become part of the actual composition. They merely act as catalysts for setting the creative process going and ultimately may lead to the invention of quite different ideas and shapes.

Marion Milner, too, soon gave up her search for motifs and instead scanned the world, her memory, and her imagination for more significant imagery, in a sustained effort to enhance her general sense of reality and beauty. As she was already to some extent familiar with psychoanalysis, she was aware that the strength of such images did not derive from their conscious meanings, but from their ramifications in the unconscious. But even their unconscious symbolic meanings did not fully explain their creative potency. They are mainly images of suffering and death deeply embedded in sado-masochistic fantasy and centered round Frazer's theme of the 'Dying God.'[3] For their role as creative catalysts their infantile symbolism mattered but little; as they entered the creative process they even lost their burden of anxiety and guilt. Marion Milner says, "the still glow that surrounded some of these images in my mind, images of the burning god, of Adonis and Osiris, did it come because they satisfied surreptitiously some crude infantile desire that I ought to have left behind long ago? I could not believe that it was so, for I had enough psycho-analytical experience to recognize the feeling of disreputable desires. ... But the kind of thinking that brought these

---

[2] Joanna Field [Marion Milner], *An Experiment in Leisure* (London: Chatto & Windus, 1937).

[3] James Frazer, *The Golden Bough*, abr. ed. (London: Macmillan, 1947).

other images was of a quite different quality, it had the feeling of greatest stillness and austerity." Of course, the guilty satisfaction of the id may coincide with the creative changes within the ego. In Marion Milner's words, it is "quite possible that the image of killing the human representative of a god could directly satisfy primitive desires to inflict pain, or to destroy authority that thwarted one's desires; but at the same time it could simply fore-shadow the truth of a purely psychic process for which no more direct language was available," that is to say, the process of creative change within the ego, or more specifically the participation of self-destructive (ego) instincts in that process.

It is strange that so many creative minds today should still derive so much inspiration from Frazer's anthropological speculations. When he first put forward the archetype of the Dying God —Osiris, Adonis, Attis, and all the others—he hoped that he had found the primitive content of religion from which all later more complex religious beliefs would have evolved. When he wrote, half a century ago, cultural anthropology was still dominated by Darwin's discovery of evolution; cultural anthropologists tried to do for the prehistoric evolution of the human spirit what physical anthropologists had done for the evolution of the human body; they tried to reconstruct the primitive origins of the various branches of culture. Today the search for cultural 'origins' is dis-credited and Frazer's work stands neglected by his fellow anthro-pologists; not so, however, by poets, artists, and other creative minds for whom Frazer's imagery has lost none of its appeal.

I feel that the wheel of scientific fashion may turn once again. It may be true that Frazer's attempt at reconstructing the origin of religion has failed, but his real discovery goes beyond his con-scious project; it shows that the theme of the Dying God is suf-fused into an unlimited number of cultural institutions. His dis-covery of unity behind superficial diversity does not so much point to a common origin in prehistory as to a common root in the unconscious. It appears that any creative stimulus, whether underlying religion, or social growth, or the development of art and even science, has this common unconscious denominator.

Freud knew and admired Frazer's work; but apart from occa-sional reference (e.g., in "The Theme of the Three Caskets"[4]), he

[4] Sigmund Freud, "The Theme of the Three Caskets," *Standard Edition*, XII.

did not try to evaluate the universality of the Dying-God theme, perhaps because he himself had independently found the universal theme of Western religion and social institutions in the Oedipus Complex. Freud also proffered a specific 'oceanic' ego condition as the root of all religious experience. We now know that an oceanic condition is found in any creative activity. As Marion Milner pointed out in a recent paper[5] the oceanic fusion between inner and outer world is needed for successful symbol formation; the lack of differentiation in the oceanic state leads to new symbolic equations, and to new creativeness. Freud would have thus described both the source of creativeness in the id—the Oedipus Complex—and the ego condition specific for creativity—the oceanic state. These two aspects of creativeness do not correspond genetically. The imagery of the Oedipus situation presupposes clear differentiation between the roles of father, mother, and child and is far removed from the lack of differentiation in the oceanic fusion.

The imagery centered round the Dying-God theme comes far nearer to this undifferentiated state. Not only does the mother imago—Isis, Kybele, Astarte—stand alone opposite her dead son lover, but their images are interchangeable, indicating a lack of sharp differentiation between them. Freud's highly significant contribution to the Dying-God theme was to extend it to fully inverted situations: the image of Lear, carrying his dead daughter Cordelia, stands for the Mother Goddess carrying her dead son, the Walkyrie carrying the dead warrior. In my view, Orpheus conducting Eurydice from death also inverts the situation of the Death Goddess conducting her son to death. (Unless one takes account of the increasing lack of differentiation in near-oceanic imagery, interpretation is bound to go astray; I hope to give a fuller description of structural levels in imagery in a forthcoming book.)

The sado-masochistic content of the Dying-God theme, its voluntary acceptance of self-destruction, appears directly related to the structural disintegration of imagery on the oceanic level. We now understand Marion Milner when she said that the Dying-God theme did not so much represent id fantasy as certain ineffable changes in the ego during the onset of creativeness which

[5] Marion Milner, "The Role of Illusion in Symbol Formation," in *New Directions in Psycho-analysis*, ed. Melanie Klein (London: Tavistock, 1955).

she aptly calls creative 'surrender.' What is felt emotionally as a surrender to self-destruction in the image of the Dying God is really a surrender to the disintegrating action of low-level imagery, which dissolves the hardened surface clichés while consciousness sinks towards an oceanic level.

Long ago, Silberer described this double aspect of imagery as related both to the id and the ego. The reveries during falling asleep may symbolize id fantasy, but at the same time they may reflect the changes of the ego in transition to the sleeping state. I myself found that, whenever I resisted falling asleep, images tended to become turbulent and unstable, sometimes catastrophic in content, in contrast to the calm imagery of a gradually sinking consciousness. Similarly, the creative state if unresisted (in a mental gesture of 'surrender'), may come smoothly and at once acquire the austere stillness of which Marion Milner speaks; it will then lack the chaotic savagery which occurs whenever creative 'fury' has to overwhelm the ordinary state of consciousness.

The double aspect of low-level imagery has been implicitly appreciated by other writers. Bertram Lewin, in his exposition of the 'dream screen,' referred to the lack of definite content as well as of structure in certain dream images; these at first sight appear merely an empty billowing screen waiting to be filled with more definite structure and content.[6] Lewin ingeniously suggested that this screen has to be related to a very primitive state of ego functioning during the oral stage when the child perceived the mother's breast not as part of a solid body, but as a disembodied film billowing in empty space. The failure to see the mother as a solid object points to a near-oceanic state of perception. (See my theory of plastic perception later on.)

It is difficult, if not impossible, to visualize such undifferentiated imagery in the normal state of consciousness; hence the impression of emptiness. Primitive imagery of low differentiation will act very disruptively on ego functioning, particularly if the disintegration of surface functions is resisted. The emotional experience of self-destruction then corresponds to genuine psychic reality. I am inclined to attribute great significance to Ida Macalpine's and R.A. Hunter's views on the disruptive effect of

[6] Bertram Lewin, "Sleep, the Mouth, and the Dream Screen," *Psychoanalytic Quarterly*, 15, (1946).

bisexual fantasies of procreation where sex differentiation becomes suspended and the roles of id and external world become reversed.[7] (The husbandless mother of the Dying God is, of course, related to a primeval bisexual creator.) The writers argue—in my view convincingly—that the famous schizophrenic Schreber defended himself not so much against an unconscious homosexuality, as Freud thought, as against the ego-disruptive effect of a fantasy where he was neither man nor woman, but some sort of primeval hermaphrodite being destined to give birth to a new mankind. This fantasy, apart from its relation to the Dying-God theme, approaches the lack of differentiation in the oceanic state where a single ego literally contains, or creates, the entire universe.

Normal surface consciousness, with its precise, narrow focus, cannot surrender to such undifferentiated fantasy, and the fear of self-destruction adhering to the fantasy is partly explained by its threat to the surface functions. Hence the vision also resists verbalization. It proves Schreber's genius that he was in fact able to verbalize his fantasies during his recovery. No doubt, he had to subject them to some kind of secondary elaboration which he himself called only "approximately" correct, in order to make them comprehensible to the surface mind, as we have to do with all low-level memories, dreams, daydreams, and creative visions. (I will later argue that the main function of secondary elaboration is to remove the ego-disruptive effect of low-level imagery.) But even so, Schreber would have first to surrender his healing surface mind to the threat of renewed disruption. This surrender is not altogether dissimilar to the "creative surrender," particularly as we must accept Schreber's autobiography as creative work of a high order. His achievement is not diminished by the fact that his continuing illness forced him to accept the fate of the Dying God, that is to say, the id-aspect of his fantasy, when he connived in being emasculated in order to recreate mankind in his role of a bisexual being. What mattered for his creativeness was his facing of the ego-disruptive effect of his fantasy.

Eric Simenauer tells us that Rainer Maria Rilke also suffered from bisexual fantasies of procreation which he at first resisted.[8]

---

[7] Ida Macalpine and R.A. Hunter, "Observations on the Psychoanalytic Theory of Psychosis," *British Journal of Medical Psychiatry,* 27 (1954).

[8] Eric Simenauer, " 'Pregnancy Envy' in Rainer Maria Rilke," *American Imago,* 11, no. 3 (1954).

He met Lou Andreas-Salomé, the friend of Nietzsche and Freud; she encouraged him to surrender to his fantasies. Simenauer claims that only after this surrender did Rilke become a true poet; he was able to verbalize unspeakable fantasies without disguise. His *Book of Hours* contains the prayer for the appearance of the true hermaphrodite to give birth to the God of Death. Rilke exclaims fervently, "Give the last proof to us, make the crown of your strength appear and give us man's real motherhood." Anatomical details of this strange mother are not omitted. The point, as in the case of Schreber, is that the creative effect of Rilke's surrender does not lie in an acceptance of homosexuality, but in the submission to the ego-disruptive effect of the fantasy involving great amounts of anxiety. Unlike Schreber, Rilke does not articulate his fantasy into precise, obscene imagery, but succeeds in keeping its undifferentiated ambiguity; he is so able to express at the same time also the poet's longing for true creativeness which is felt as motherhood. (See later the dangers of a secondary elaboration into unambiguous precise surface imagery.)

Robert Graves gives us what almost amounts to a recipe for poetic creativeness on very similar lines. He paraphrases the Dying-God theme in the image of the White Goddess who kills her son-lover.[9] The poet has to submit to this death in love whereupon the cruel Goddess will turn into the Muse and give him creativeness. If Graves proclaims all true poetry to be love songs to the killing Goddess, he does not—and this is the often repeated point—elevate sado-masochistic fantasy to the sole theme of poetry, but proclaims the creative value of an undifferentiated imagery where love, birth, and death becomes a single theme.

Freud studied the structural difference between different levels of ego functioning in his investigation of the secondary dream elaboration. While in the creative surrender the undifferentiated low-level imagery overwhelms the articulate surface imagery, the opposite holds good for the secondary dream elaboration. There the conflict between divergent structural principles ends in the victory of the articulate surface functions. When, after waking, we try to remember a dream, the surface mind will automatically cast the fluid and indefinite dream images into a more precise mold;

---

[9] Robert Graves, *The White Goddess* (London: Faber & Faber, 1948).

gaps are filled and incoherent details eliminated. Admittedly, the censorship of the superego will guide this articulation process so as to repress the traces of unconscious dream fantasy; but this interference of the id-superego conflict does not alter the fact that the transformation of the dream imagery is inevitable, owing to the conflict between two structural principles inherent in ego functioning. This is a conflict within the ego which could well be called "autonomous" (by analogy with Hartmann's concept of autonomous ego functions) in the sense that this dynamic ego tension or conflict can be usefully studied and described without reference to id-superego conflict.

The "resistance" against the disruptive effect of low-level imagery is equally autonomous from id-superego conflict, and the deep anxiety—often masked by ego rigidity—which may be aroused by the threatening break-through of low-level imagery, may arise independently of any resistance or anxiety which the sado-masochistic id fantasy attaching to this imagery may call up. As we have seen, the resistance and anxiety are directed against a catastrophic shift of consciousness to an undifferentiated, near-oceanic level. This shift exaggerates a basic rhythm inherent in ego functioning; shallower and quicker shifts between different structural levels constantly occur in normal ego activity, but go unnoticed. No spectacular disruption and anxiety arise from the continuous oscillations. I have followed Varendonck, Schilder, and recent writing on Gestalt psychology in assuming a split-second oscillation of perception.[10] Varendonck, without the help of laboratory tests, concluded that every single perception is preceded by a forgotten moment of dream-like hallucination which is repressed as soon as the articulate rational image emerges into consciousness.[11] Later laboratory experiments confirmed this view; the exposure of images is reduced to split-seconds when no articulate image can be formed. Schilder interpreted the dream-like distortion and ambiguity of these tachistoscopic glimpses as primitive, undifferentiated types of perception similar in structure to infantile vision.[12] If the split-

[10] Anton Ehrenzweig, *The Psychoanalysis of Artistic Vision and Hearing: An Introduction to a Theory of Unconscious Perception* (London: Routledge, 1953).

[11] J. Varendonck, *The Evolution of the Conscious Faculties* (London: George Allen & Unwin, 1923).

[12] Paul Schilder, *Mind: Perception and Thought in Their Constructive Aspects* (New York: Columbia University Press, 1942).

second exposure is cut down still more below a certain threshold, conscious perception fails altogether and the projection screen remains empty, for the surface mind, that is. It was found that observers still reacted to them as though they had unconsciously (subliminally) perceived them. Guesses as to the possible content of the unseen exposures produced a significant number of correct or unconsciously related solutions. Though the superego may well influence the symbolic distortion of these guesses, it cannot explain the repression of low-level perception as such. It appears that the consciously perceived distortion and diffusion of split-second exposures increases near the threshold to such an extent that conscious articulation fails altogether. We have to describe this as a 'structural repression' inherent in the stratification of ego functioning, which is autonomous from the superego's repression, just as we had described the anxiety and resistance against low-level imagery purely in terms of structural ego conflict without reference to id and superego. The existence of a structural repression explains why we know so little about low-level perceptions, whatever their content; if they are allowed to penetrate into consciousness at all they may appear empty, as does the dream screen to the average dreamer.

Varendonck already recognized the structural similarity of tachistoscopic glimpses and the more profound oceanic vision of the creative state. There the normal ego oscillation is enlarged into a catastrophic breaking up of the surface clichés during the creative surrender, and the slower rhythm swings down to the oceanic level where all differentiation ceases. Hence flexibility of ego functioning is the essence of creativeness; the artist is at home on many levels of the mind and can make his consciousness regress at will. I have described in a recent paper[13] how the painter periodically diffuses his narrow focus into a broader, apparently empty stare through which he is able to comprehend the entire structure of his work down to the smallest detail within a single glance, an impossible feat for surface vision. What on the surface seems an empty stare, really, on an unconscious level, teems with undifferentiated imagery which will give birth to a new flow of invention.

[13] Anton Ehrenzweig, "The Mastering of Creative Anxiety," in *Art and Artist* (Berkeley and Los Angeles: California University Press, 1956).

The creative use of imagery, then, depends on the free flexible ego rhythm swinging out between widely distant levels. Images will be constantly immersed into oceanic undifferentiation and brought up again to the surface in a newly articulated shape, a new symbol for a cluster of unconscious images with which it was brought into contact. It is in this manner that I understand Marion Milner's assertion that the first stage in the creative use of symbols must be a temporary giving up of the discriminating (differentiating) ego, which stands apart and tries to see things objectively and rationally and without emotional coloring.[14] When this surface ego is abandoned, the way to oceanic undifferentiation is open. The imagery sinks to a lower structural level, where it loses its precise definition and sharp boundaries and merges with other images into new symbolic equations; then as the ego rhythm rebounds, the melted image recrystallizes and reassumes an independent existence, while, on the lower level, it still remains equated with, or diffused into, the other images which it now merely 'symbolizes.' A symbol will remain usable and creative only by being constantly remolded in the interaction between different levels of ego functioning.

We understand now why ego rigidity, which interferes with the free swinging out of the ego rhythm, will also interfere with the successful use of symbols and with creativity in general. As mentioned in the beginning, art teaching can break this deadlock by resolving ego rigidity and the unconscious anxiety masked behind it. That educational methods should succeed in this is perhaps explained by our assumption that the ego conflict underlying the rigidity can arise independently of id conflict and can therefore also be resolved without touching the id conflict. Marion Milner showed how a gesture of surrender may overcome the rigidity of surface functions by exposing them to the disruption by low-level imagery. Of course, a pathogenic id conflict may reinforce the dissociation of low-level imagery; if the imagery serves to symbolize pathogenic id drives, the ego's rigidity and resistance against low-level imagery will also serve as a defence against the id. This need not make the art teacher's task hopeless. If an ill artist is able to tolerate great amounts of anxiety and face his id

---

[14] Milner, "Role of Illusion in Symbol Formation."

conflict, he still may be capable of performing the creative surrender, integrate his low-level imagery with his surface functions
and thereby resolve a creative sterility based on the dissociation of
his ego functions. Then the pathological id conflict will noisily
dominate his consciousness, and the misleading impression is
aroused that an artist's creativeness comes from id conflict and
neurotic illness; this impression makes artists fear undergoing
psychoanalytical treatment and cherish their neuroses. But their
fear is only justified inasmuch as the psychoanalytical resolution
of id conflict may well leave behind an autonomous ego conflict
with its sterilizing effect on creativeness. The art teacher, on the
other hand, must tread warily in softening the student's rigidity,
expressed in his all too careful, all too deliberate use of his medium; in the beginning a less controlled, more spontaneous han-
dling of the medium may bring on overwhelming anxieties which
were hidden behind the ego rigidity. Marion Milner in her artistic
beginnings did not have the aid of an understanding teacher; in
her second and third "Joanna Field" books she reports the severe
anxieties which she had to face after she had abandoned clichéd
imagery in a catastrophic reversal of ego functioning.[15] The creative surrender is not always so dramatic a gesture. The art
teacher will gradually lead his student towards freedom, trying all
the way to gauge intuitively the amount of anxiety the pupil can
bear and the integration of ego functioning already achieved.[16]

I have said that the sado-masochistic imagery accompanying
the creative surrender conforms with psychic reality. If the surface functions are too rigid their collapse may indeed lead to total
ego disintegration. This often happens with schizophrenic imagery, which is over-concrete, over-precise, over-rigid. It would be
wrong to consider the precise concreteness of schizophrenic imagery as primitive in the sense that it corresponds to an infantile,
normally unconscious mode of ego functioning; the opposite is
nearer the truth. The schizophrenic cannot tolerate the undifferentiation of primitive low-level imagery because to him the normal periodic disintegration of surface imagery means total ego
destruction; indeed when a schizophrenic artist's creative spell

---

[15] Field [Milner], *Experiment in Leisure:* and Joanna Field [Marion Milner], *On
Not Being Able to Paint* (London: Heinemann, 1950).
[16] Ehrenzweig, "Mastering Creative Anxiety."

ends, due to a worsening of his illness, his rigid precise imagery crumbles away without transition into complete structureless chaos. Marion Milner, in her paper given to the nineteenth International Psychoanalytical Congress 1955,[17] showed that excessive fear of undifferentiation, particularly of a confusion between the body openings, can prevent the ego's regression to an oceanic state and so preclude a creative use of symbols. A vicious circle can be set up; the ego rigidity prevents the oscillation of ego functions between different structural levels and so leads to a progressing dissociation between surface and depth functions, and to an increasing anxiety lest the surface ego be overwhelmed whenever low-level functions are stirring. A similar anxiety besets certain patients suffering from insomnia; they cannot relax conscious ego control because, unconsciously, they equate the temporary lapse of surface functions with death itself. A certain modicum of dissociation between surface and depth functions is inevitable as a result of the secondary elaboration processes transforming symbols into cliché which will become independent from unconscious fantasy. My point is that creativity is improved to the extent to which the dissociation can be overcome. We could speak of a "horizontal split" in the rigid ego structure which is remedied by setting free the oscillation between the dissociated levels of ego functioning, thereby leading to a new "vertical integration" of the ego.

It is the undifferentiated structure of low-level imagery and not its sado-masochistic content which brings creativeness. If through secondary elaboration such images are cast into concrete and precise Gestalt, they may turn into perverted or criminal fantasy and bring moral degradation instead of inspiration. Schreber's fantasies verged on a concrete wish for castration, while Rilke preserved some of the ambiguity inherent in undifferentiated imagery which prevented it from becoming a motif for purposeful behavior. Marion Milner comments on the perennial abuse of creative imagery in organized popular religions and in the self-consciously archaistic cults of National-Socialism, "the whole history of popular religions could . . . be looked upon as a

[17] Marion Milner, "The Communication of Primary Sensual Experience (The Yell of Joy)," *International Journal of Psychoanalysis,* 37 (1956).

materialization of the image; and once it was no longer looked upon as a truth of spirit, but instead a truth of external fact, then it became the instrument of all kinds of exploitation, lustful, political, social, the instrument of crudest infantile desire. . . . "

The creative mind will unceasingly discard the secondary elaborations of his creative imagination, but he cannot prevent the secondary elaboration from taking place; it is inevitable owing to the constant rhythmical interaction between different levels of ego functioning. As in the secondary dream elaboration, the surface mind will automatically focus on the undifferentiated images emerging into consciousness and recast them in its own precise mold. It will thereby deprive them of their original disruptive effect, but at the same time also of their creative power. No creative image can possibly retain its catalyst function for any length of time so that the creative mind will remain for ever on the look-out for new potent imagery. Marion Milner, in her book, takes us right inside this eternal search; image after image is brought up from a rich storehouse of dreams, myths, and childhood memories, each with a new promise of final revelation; but in the end we are told that the quest was all and the answer nothing. We are left with a final sense of despair which, however, is a good beginning for the attitude of surrender, a letting go of all purpose and planning and a growing trust in the guidance of the unconscious ego.

The creative surrender has two features which are of theoretical interest. At first sight they seem to contradict each other; the surrender brings a deepening of the reality sense, but at the same time it possesses a manic quality, a feeling of oceanic, cosmic bliss which strangely contrasts with the imagery of suffering and death. Uncreative, rigid personalities often suffer from a flatness of the reality experience which, in my view, is due to the horizontal ego split. In my analysis of artistic perception[18] I expanded Freud's explanation of the vividness attaching to certain dream images so as to cover any kind of perception; the plastic vividness of perception in general would depend on its extension into the depth of the unconscious ego. The more unconscious material goes into a perception the more vivid it will appear consciously. Now, a horizontal dissociation of ego functioning will isolate sur-

---

[18] Ehrenzweig, *Psychoanalysis of Artistic Vision and Hearing.*

face perception from its unconscious matrix; imagery will be pressed into existing cliché unnourished by unconscious fantasy. The result is that perception becomes flat and unreal. This is well brought out by the facts of depersonalized vision. Depersonalization splits off and ejects the unconscious substructure of our imagery, hence the wonderful all-over clarity of depersonalized vision: no dark corners and nooks are left in the peripheral field of vision where unconscious fantasy normally seeps through unobserved. (Devereux has first drawn attention to the relation of peripheral vision to unconscious fantasy.)[19] But at the same time, depersonalized vision is flat and unreal. We understand now why the creative surrender—where the unconscious substructure erupts and ejects the surface clichés—will give us a deepened sense of external reality.

The creative surrender will also advance our understanding of psychic reality through the emotional experience of self-destruction. We have seen that the periodic disintegration of surface functions in the creative state involves a genuine act of psychic self-destruction from which the uncreative somehow shirks away. This self-destruction remains emotionally unnoticed as long as the self-destructive phase of ego functioning is smoothly absorbed into the ego oscillation between different levels; then the death instinct working within the ego remains mute as Freud described it. But if ego rigidity has to be resolved by a catastrophic reversal of ego functioning, the radical ejection of the surface ego is emotionally felt as death itself. Marion Milner maintains that the facing of this experience is a test for a full acceptance of death as part of reality. She recalls that in Spanish bullfights the killing of the bull is called 'the moment of truth.' Hanna Segal told me that she considered the emotional acceptance of death as a fact to be a condition of creativeness. In her paper "A Psychoanalytical Approach to Aesthetics,"[20] she tells of patients who were impeded in their creative ability for this reason; one patient felt an overwhelming need for preserving her body, which she experienced as being half-dead already. In a way, all uncreative persons do this

---

[19] George Devereux, "A Note on Xyctophobia and Peripheral Vision," *Bulletin Menninger Clinic,* 13, no. 3 (1949).

[20] Hanna Segal, "A Psycho-analytical Approach to Aesthetics," in *New Directions in Psycho-analysis,* ed. Melanie Klein (London: Tavistock, 1955).

quite literally by clinging to their rigid, half-dead clichés at the
expense of low-level fantasy, which alone could infuse life and
richness into their reality experience. It would appear that the
emotional realization of death as a fact is not so much a condition
of creativeness as the result of the creative surrender to partial
ego-destruction, which the uncreative cannot tolerate.

It may seem strange that we should have to surrender our
rational surface functions to the irrational depth mind in order to
advance our understanding of death and of reality in general. Is it
not generally held that only our rational conscious mind, but not
the unconscious, knows of death? But it is only the unconscious id
which ignores time and death; we have seen how the unconscious
ego constantly experiences disintegration and death in its rhythm
of waking and sleeping, and, more important, in the rhythm of
creativeness. Very likely the unconscious ego rhythm gives us also
our sense of time, and we can thus enlarge Freud's saying that
time might be the mode in which the ego works. The uncreative
who resists, or flattens, the ego rhythm, owing to his deep fear of
both the unconscious ego and of death, also denies the flow of
time and fails in his emotional acceptance of dying as a fact.

The second already mentioned feature of the creative surrender seems to contradict its value as reality experience; it is its
distinct manic quality. The killing of the bull, the sacrifice of the
Dying God, have no depressive feeling about them; death, once
accepted, becomes a feast of cosmic bliss, of liberation from bond-
age. This manic experience is connected with the ego fusion
achieved in creative surrender which heals the ego split—not by
ejecting the superego as happens in pathogenic mania—but by
ejecting the dissociated surface crust. Adrian Stokes has rightly
drawn attention to the constructive role which a manic experience
plays in creativity, a role which equals that played by the Depressive Position as described by Melanie Klein.[21] The feeling of
'otherness,' of precise differentiation, experienced in the Depressive Position, has to be balanced by the manic feeling of 'same-
ness,' of undifferentiation, where the boundaries between outer
and inner world melt away. Marion Milner, as already mentioned,
maintains that the oceanic fusion is a prerequisite for the fusion

[21] Adrian Stokes, "Form in Art," in *New Directions in Psycho-analysis,* ed.
Melanie Klein (London: Tavistock, 1955).

of images into symbolic equations and for successful symbol formation in general.[22] A child patient re-enacted in his play the archetypal ritual of the Dying God when he solemnly burned a toy soldier with a deep sense of mystery; this sacrifice meant the creative surrender of the common-sense ego that watches over the boundaries between things and between outer and inner world. Here is the very opposite of a manic denial; here is a scene of communion between consciousness and the undifferentiated matrix of all creative imagery through a bacchantic ritual of sacrifice and death.

I have always felt that an exclusive stress on the Depressive Position as the source of creative activity did not take account of the almost biological rhythm between mania and depression, where mania appears on the same level as depression, as a fundamental human attitude. Once we accept this equal status of mania, we are able to discern cooperation rather than antagonism between the polar attitudes; creative depression would lead to an horizontal integration between ego nuclei split vertically on the same structural level. Creative mania supplements this healing process by the vertical integration between different ego levels, through overcoming the horizontal split and restoring the free rhythm of ego functioning on which creativity depends.

[22] Milner, "Role of Illusion in Symbol Formation."

Yeats's "Second Coming": What Rough Beast?

Richard P. Wheeler

"The Second Coming" is often regarded as a powerful poem, having special force even in the work of a man acknowledged to be a writer of much powerful verse. Denis Donoghue, speaking broadly of Yeats's poetry, argues that "the sense of power is the most pervasive sense at work in the poems," a power before which the reader must "bend the knee." [1] Harold Bloom, in a discussion of "The Second Coming," concerns himself primarily with "the nature of its power" (p. 317).[2] Bloom points to serious confusions in the poem; its peculiar twistings of Christian myth make the poem "a masquerade of Yeats's Gnosticism in Christian terms" (p. 342). He concludes that "the power of *The Second Coming* is not called in question by these smaller questions, but perhaps its artistry is" (p. 323). This paper investigates the power of "The Second Coming" in terms of the role played by the experience of power as a necessary dimension of human relationships, particularly in the conditions of infancy and childhood.

Bloom writes: "There is something in the power of *The Second Coming* that persuades us of our powerlessness" (p. 324). This reading assumes a radical split between the imagination that created the poem and those that are stirred by readings of it. The poem presents an image of destructive, historical force before which we, as readers, are helpless, but with which Yeats, as creator, is identified. Yeats participates in a sense of power that his readers experience as hostile and alien. As Yvor Winters has it: "Yeats approves of this kind of brutality."[3]

Certainly "The Second Coming" presents an ominous image of historical process. I find the poem distressing, often,

[1] *William Butler Yeats* (New York: The Viking Press, 1971), p. 5.
[2] *Yeats* (New York: Oxford University Press, 1970).
[3] *The Poetry of W. B. Yeats* (Denver: The Swallow Press, 1960), p. 10. Quoted in Bloom, *Yeats*, p. 323.

particularly as I move away from the experience of reading it, or saying it over to myself, and move toward a consideration of what it tells me about the direction of history. In so far as "The Second Coming" presents a poet/prophet's privileged insight into historical possibility, in Bloom's phrase, it "persuades us of our powerlessness."

But I repeatedly find that reading "The Second Coming" offers an experience very different from the sobering prospect of the poem's prophetic claim. Its power is not a power over me, nor a power held up portentously before me, but a feeling of power which in some way I share. Furthermore, I think that this response—my participation in a sense of power generated by the poem—is typical for many readers, and is an important factor in this poem's enormous impact on readers of the last five decades. "The Second Coming," I will argue, is a powerful poem because it imparts a sense of power. Why this should be so is not immediately clear.

"The Second Coming" presents a vision of cultural destruction, or disintegration, that has made a nearly authoritative claim on the imagination of twentieth century readers shaken again and again by a history of anxiety and violence. Countless readers have experienced as authentic the prophetic image of historical reality the poem conveys. I will be less concerned, however, with the poem's presentation of historical crisis as objective possibility than with the ego-states through which that crisis is registered, the subjective postures through which the poem confronts the reality it imagines. The vision of history that the poem articulates is shaped significantly by unconscious factors that were deeply rooted in the poet's mind long before the poem was written, and which are intimately implicated in our response, as readers, to it.

I will attempt to show that "The Second Coming" builds upon a deeply repressed fantasy of omnipotent, destructive rage, called into service to master an experience of intolerable, infantile helplessness. This fantasy underlies and enforces the poem's meaning as historical myth. Our collaboration in this fantasy, as readers, enables the poem to impart a sense of power. That "The Second Coming" can also enforce our sense of "powerlessness" is an apparent paradox that may be better

understood once the place of the poem's unconscious significance within its total meaning has been further explored.

The opening section of "The Second Coming" presents
an external world which is chaotic, frustrating, and dangerous:

> Turning and turning in the widening gyre
> The falcon cannot hear the falconer;
> Things fall apart; the centre cannot hold;
> Mere anarchy is loosed upon the world,
> The blood-dimmed tide is loosed, and everywhere
> The ceremony of innocence is drowned;
> The best lack all conviction, while the worst
> Are full of passionate intensity.[4]

This vision of cultural destruction mirrors an inner experience
of impending psychic catastrophe. "Fear for oneself," writes
Weston La Barre, provides "the pattern of fears for the
world."[5] The inner anxiety conveyed in these lines was shaped
by situations independent of the social, historical conditions
that bring it to expression in the mode of poetic prophecy, however appropriate that anxiety may be in conveying the quality
of experience in catastrophic historical conditions.

The crisis of self presented in the first section of the poem
has its roots in crises of early infancy, when the psychological
range of the experience of power swings from omnipotence to
utter helplessness. The strong emphasis on imagery of disintegration, the totalistic sweep of the historical metaphor, and the
either/or thinking of "best" and "worst" suggest an unconscious situation that originates in the oral stage. D. W. Winnicott summarizes some components of the distress an infant
undergoes in the oral stage of development when the maternal
presence is experienced as hostile and rejecting rather than
fulfilling:

> the sense of going to pieces,
> the sense of falling forever,

---

[4] Quotations from Yeats's poetry are taken from *The Collected Poems of W. B.
Yeats*, rev. ed. (New York: The Macmillan Co., 1956).
[5] *The Ghost Dance* (New York: Doubleday and Co., 1970), p. 313.

the feeling that external reality cannot be used for
  reassurance,
and other anxieties that are usually described as
  'psychotic.'[6]

This list indicates feeling states that are central to the poem's
first section. Those lines depicting external chaos convey the
fragmentation of symbiotic unity into a perceived reality of
terror both imminent and immanent. The " sense of going to
pieces," of things falling apart, is conveyed in the image of the
falcon spiralling out of control, and generalized in the expression " the centre cannot hold." Impulses arise independently
of inner control, and will not respond to it (" The falcon cannot
hear the falconer "). The " sense of falling " appears with great
force (in an inverted form characteristic of the tendency of
dreams to represent by opposites) through the vertiginous sense
of vast height conveyed by the same image, the falcon reeling
beyond the reach of the falconer's command. Perhaps it need
hardly be added that the external reality of " anarchy " and
" the blood-dimmed tide " has been stripped of its capacity to
offer reassurance, though the importance of that transformation
of benign reality in an infant and in that part in all of us that
remains infantile can scarcely be overestimated.

The crumbling historical world of " The Second Coming "
builds on this infantile situation of utter helplessness experienced as fear of annihilation. The roots of this fear in infantile
frustration help shape the key destructive image of the poem's
first section: " Mere anarchy is loosed upon the world,/The
blood-dimmed tide is loosed, and everywhere/The ceremony
of innocence is drowned; . . ."

This image of anarchy and terror is grounded psychologically in the oral-sadistic, or second oral, stage of infantile
development, when good and bad potentialities both for the
self and for the vaguely differentiated external world are created
out of the dissolving symbiosis of infant and mother. Sadistic
fantasies of this stage are generated by frustration and newly
perceived separation, and mobilize powerful aggressive protests.

[6] "The Relationship of a Mother to Her Baby," *The Family and Individual
Development* (New York: Basic Books, 1965), p. 18.

This aggression is directed against the offending object, the mother, or mother's breast or mother as feeder, since the mother as a separate, whole person does not yet exist in the infant's awareness. But the fantasy content of this attack begets its retaliatory counterpart in its object, as the infant projects his hostility onto the only world he knows. The mother's breast, mutilated in the child's aggressive fantasy, responds in this fantasy not with the desired love and milk but with a " blood-dimmed tide " which threatens to overwhelm or swallow up the aggressor. "The ceremony of innocence," the benign situation of fulfillment and fusion at the breast, is lost, and the life-sustaining succor becomes a means of overpowering the infant. The "drowning" of "the ceremony of innocence" is a malevolent transformation which parodies the "oceanic feeling" that Freud traced to the experience of oneness in which self and mother (world) are as yet undifferentiated. The longing for this " fusion of self and object, . . . mouth and breast felt as fused into one,"[7] is the deepest need expressed in the poem, although it is only expressed through images which convey its failure. That fusion is the center which " cannot hold," which fragments into the anarchy of uncontrolled aggressive drives turned against the vulnerable infant self.

There are two controlling images in the first section of " The Second Coming," the image of the falcon reeling out of control and the image of the " blood-dimmed tide " which drowns " the ceremony of innocence." The nature of the anxiety elaborated in each of these images is significantly different. Each registers a separate response to the failure of maternal symbiosis. As the first of these controlling images, that of the falcon " turning and turning in the widening gyre," gives way to the second, the image of the " blood-dimmed tide," the centrifugal gestures of spiralling flight and things falling apart

[7] Marion Milner, "Aspects of Symbolism in the Comprehension of the Not-self," *International Journal of Psychoanalysis*, 33 (1952), 184. Brenda Webster finds an image in which "blood becomes a substitute for the desired milk" in an early draft of Yeats's play "The Shadowy Waters," "Yeats's 'The Shadowy Waters': Oral Motifs and Identity in the Drafts," *American Imago*, 28 (Spring 1971), 5. This useful paper also finds in early drafts of the play another psychological motif that figures prominently in "The Second Coming." The character Forgael, invested with deeply frustrated oral drives, "wishes to destroy the world itself and replace it with fantasy: 'Oh eagle-headed race . . . quench the world'" (p. 6).

give way to a concentration of malevolent forces which converge on the "ceremony of innocence." In lines one through three, falcon and falconer alike dissolve into the process of disintegration. The line "Things fall apart; the centre cannot hold" crystallizes that process and impersonally conveys the action of fragmentation. There is very little violence expressed in these lines, and little that is specifically touched by a sense of human suffering. The hardly emphasized humanity of the falconer, even, gives way to the more abstract imagery of "things" falling apart. The prospect of massive violence, however, is "loosed" in the next line: "Mere anarchy is loosed upon the world." The orientation within the realm of things is also drastically altered in lines five through eight. In these lines, key words and phrases (particularly "blood-dimmed," "ceremony of innocence," "best," "conviction," "worst," and "passionate intensity") carry the poem clearly into a human, if catastrophic, realm.

The image of the spiralling falcon suggests what Harry Guntripp sees as "the basis of all schizoid characteristics, the deep secret flight from life, . . . "[8] The violence of "the blood-dimmed tide," however, implies an embattled engagement with life, in which the self is powerless. The image of flight defends against this situation of powerlessness within a hostile world. But in the order of the poem, flight precedes violence, the defense precedes the situation that calls it into being. A further purpose is served by this ordering, which is in itself defensive. Schizoid flight, although undertaken as a defense, ultimately poses a danger of total disengagement from life that may be more threatening than the violence of a world to which the self may remain in personal contact. As the metaphor shifts, the direction of regression is turned around; the ego-state abandoned for schizoid flight is retrieved. This ordering moves the poem from a fantasy of the self lost in fragmenting things to a fantasy of the self at the center of a human, if malevolent, world. In the schizoid state, all sense of coherent, human self is forfeited. In the malevolent state, the self exists and is confirmed by a hostile reality that encloses it, but which threatens to overwhelm it. It is through this world of dangerous, overwhelming, "passionate intensity" that the poem moves into its second section, seeking an alternative to the hazardous defense of schizoid withdrawal.

The opening lines of the second section declare the intolerability of the condition expressed in the first section and the need for some form of release from it:

> Surely some revelation is at hand;
> Surely the Second Coming is at hand.
> The Second Coming!

The incantatory force of these lines imposes ritualistic stasis on the frenzied energies of the first section and evokes the image about to make its appearance. Like a magical conjuration, these lines serve to create and concentrate the visionary power capable of apprehending the mysterious intruder from another order of reality:

> Hardly are those words out
> When a vast image out of *Spiritus Mundi*
> Troubles my sight: . . .

The "vast image" itself is presented with forceful Yeatsian economy:

> somewhere in sands of the desert
> A shape with lion body and the head of a man,
> A gaze blank and pitiless as the sun,
> Is moving its slow thighs, while all about it
> Reel shadows of the indignant desert birds.

These lines freeze in their solemnly measured rhythms the swift perceptual rhythm of astonished visual discovery. The poem's gaze first takes in the vague and barren spatial orientation "somewhere in sands of the desert," then perceives the bestial and masculine features that give the image shape. Moving yet closer, the poem's vision is startled by the beast's gaze, "blank and pitiless as the sun," and withdraws just enough to remark the shape's slow movement. Finally circling shadows of desert birds enter the retreating perspective.

As this vision unfolds, Yeats develops images that bind intimately the sight being presented with the subjective states demanded of the viewer. As the beast stares out with blank and pitiless gaze, we are invited to look intensely, as if fascinated, at this terrible gaze. The shadows of desert birds which circle about the shape are made to convey—particularly through the force of " reel "—the sense of recoil into uncontrolled dizziness or giddiness imparted by the vision. This reeling effect is intensified by the jarring convergence of different kinds of movements that shape our experience of these lines. The lines which present the vision unfold slowly and portentously, and create, particularly at first, a sense of awesome stillness:

> somewhere in sands of the desert
> A shape with lion body and the head of a man,
> A gaze blank and pitiless as the sun, . . .

But this stasis is broken by the slow, massive movement of the beast's thighs, almost as if an image with photographic stillness is suddenly perceived to move. This ponderous slowness, the slowness of the centuries, then gives way to the whirling protests reflected in the shadows of the desert birds. All this is taken in by the perceptual movement which first focuses vaguely on the desert, then moves in to view the beast itself, and its gaze, and finally recoils from this view, to end abruptly when " the darkness drops again."

The image of the staring, slowly moving beast and the image of the circling shadows suggest the two movements that characterize the first section of the poem. The concrete image of the terrible beast " moving its slow thighs " recalls the more abstract " mere anarchy is loosed upon the world." The reeling shadows of desert birds recall " turning and turning in the widening gyre," an abstract image made concrete in the image of the falcon reeling out of control. These echoes of key images orient the vision of the beast in terms of the defenses of the poem's first section. Significantly these defenses are restored to the order demanded by the logic of regression, the paranoid situation (rough beast) giving way to the deeper schizoid defense (reeling shadows). The poem here presents in small a regressive maneuver that the larger movement of the poem defensively reverses.

Further consideration of the complexly determined beast image provides insight into the infantile roots of the poem's anxiety content and into the defensive strategies through which that anxiety is mastered. The following properties of the image are particularly important: the beast emerges out of the darkness, as an intruder, bringing into the night the terrible desert sun; only its visual properties are presented—shape, gaze, and movement—and these convey its power; the power conferred on the beast is intensified by its " blank and pitiless " gaze; the entire movement of the beast is represented by the movement of its thighs; it is surrounded by shadows of reeling desert birds, smaller creatures that look on in helpless, indignant protest; the beast has the shape of a sphinx. A heavy emphasis on acts of looking connects many of these elements. The poet looks on and is troubled by what he sees; the birds look on also, with indignation; the beast itself looks out with " gaze blank and pitiless as the sun." Indeed, the lines that precede the appearance of the image serve to " stage it;" they direct us to look intensely at what is about to be presented. The line that ends the vision suggests a curtain falling between spectators and a stage: " The darkness drops again."

These strongly emphasized acts of looking—the visionary looking of the poet, the fierce gaze of the beast, the indignant, onlooking birds, the stage-like setting of the vision—together with the sphinx-like shape of the beast, tend to confirm a meaning in this creature that Géza Roheim discovered in the sphinx figure of mythology. " The Sphinx," Roheim observes in a study of the Oedipus myth, ". . . is the father and mother in one person, and a representation of the two fundamental tendencies of the Oedipus situation which are awakened in the child when he observes the primal scene."[9] The sphinx-like beast is a composite image which builds unconsciously on the fascination and the threatening power of parental sexuality for the child's ego.

[9] *The Riddle of the Sphinx* (London: The Hogarth Press, 1934), p. 22. Although the Theban sphinx has female breasts and the Egyptian sphinx that Yeats evokes has the head of a man, this difference does not affect the significance of the beast image as a representation of a primal scene fantasy; either sex may provide the manifest form without altering the unconscious content. I suggest a reason for the male features of this sphinx-image later in this paper.

A primal scene experience " is likely to connect the ideas of sexual excitations and danger." A frequent misinterpretation of the primal scene on the part of the child is to view "sexual intercourse as a cruel, destructive act."[10] The dangerous, destructive associations of sexuality are stressed in the beast image of the poem, but sexuality does not appear directly at all—although it informs the image of the crouching beast " moving its slow thighs." The very slowness of the beast tends to remove the image from the violence of the primal scene fantasy out of which it grows. This slowness serves a purpose similar to that of complete stillness in the wolf dream of Freud's famous " wolf man " patient, which also disguised a primal scene fantasy.[11] The wolf dream, however, conveyed a terror for Freud's patient that was not reflected in its manifest form, which represented an attempt to hide the violence of the latent content. The poem, while disguising latent content, carefully intensifies the power of the image to convey terrible force.

The beast image as a whole concentrates and conveys the threatening power which the child associates with parental sexuality, and reserves its defenses for disguising the unconscious sources of the anxiety. The location of the activity " somewhere in sands of the desert " spatially distances it from the intolerable proximity of family associations, while keeping it within reach of the prophetic eye. Temporally, too, the image is removed from its roots in the continual present of the unconscious and becomes an omen of future calamity, of something that has not already happened, or is happening, and which may, therefore, be anticipated. A child's animism, which Fenichel cites as one source of confusion in primal scene fantasies, appears in the creature's lion body. The " shadows of the indignant desert birds " register the child's protest, and his helplessness.

One unconscious meaning behind the image of the rough beast, then, is that of a primal scene fantasy, a repressed infan-

[10] Otto Fenichel, *The Psychoanalytic Theory of Neurosis* (New York: W. W. Norton, 1945), p. 214.

[11] "From the History of an Infantile Neurosis," *Standard Edition*, XVIII. Freud traced this dream to an actual experience of observing parental intercourse, although it is not necessary to assume such an experience behind a primal scene fantasy.

tile association of destructive power with the real or imagined
spectacle of parental sexuality. Such fantasy material may present, according to Fenichel, a threat " beyond the capacity for
mastery as yet developed"[12] in the child's adaptive ego, and
thus may force a regression to more primitive psychological
stages. One such regressive experience has already been offered
in the poem's first section. The malevolent reality presented
there registers in a primarily oral context the threatening
power of the primal scene fantasy. The image of " the blood-
dimmed tide " condenses the primal scene threat with the
threat of oral annihilation. One possibility for eluding the
force of this threat is the schizoid flight that informs the image
of the spiralling falcon, an image echoed in the circling desert
birds. But this defense, I have argued, is rejected by the total
movement of the poem.

In order to discover how this threat is managed it is necessary to assume, as Freud demonstrated of dreams, that a single
image can carry unconscious meanings that are totally different,
even contradictory. In this case, the image of the rough beast
presents not only the ego-shattering force of a primal scene
fantasy, but also the means of coping with that threat. In this
second context, the ego is identified with the rough beast as
destroyer of a world which has become intolerable. This second
meaning belongs primarily to the deeply regressed oral stage,
and represents an alternative defense against the failure of
symbiosis which is so important in the first section of the poem.
Instead of passive helplessness before a separate, hostile reality,
or schizoid flight from that reality, the beast image in this context represents the total rage of the child forced to perceive
separateness through frustration. The destructive force invested
in the image of the beast expresses what Marion Milner calls
the " hate that is inherent in the fact that we do have to make
the distinction between subject and object."[13] Its psychotic
analogue is the " repressed hatred," subjectively felt to have
the force of " omnipotent malevolence " or " all-powerful de-

[12] Fenichel, *Neurosis*, p. 214.
[13] *On Not Being Able to Paint*, 2nd ed. (New York: International Universities
Press, 1957), p. 68. Quoted in Norman N. Holland, *The Dynamics of Literary Response* (New York: Oxford University Press, 1968), p. 338.

structiveness " that Harold Searles has found in his work with schizophrenic patients.[14] The crisis of losing "a subjectively omnipotent oneness"[15] with the mother generates a rage that itself possesses the subjective quality of omnipotence. Denied " omnipotent oneness " with a benevolent world, rage becomes the vehicle for a re-birth, a second coming, of that omnipotence in malevolent form.

In the context of this unconscious meaning—that of a total, destructive attack on a frustrating world, the world perceived as hostile other—it is important that Yeats invests the sphinx-like beast with male features, since the image expresses an aggressive wish elaborated through the development of infant into boy into man. The " gaze blank and pitiless as the sun " not only suggests unconscious word play (sun/son), but reflects the vital role played by the eyes and looking in the oral stage of development. Moreover, the agent of destruction crawls on all fours, and thus conveys the body image of a young infant invested with fantasied omnipotence. In this context, the reeling shadows of desert birds dramatize the world's helpessness before the omnipotent attack of the outraged infantile ego.

An unconscious identification with the beast image, felt as an expression of deeply repressed rage or hatred, enables the poem to impart a sense of power to its readers, the sense of power this paper set out to trace. Into this unconscious identification with the destructive power of the beast flows another source of gratification. The primal scene fantasy is threatening in large part because of its projective content; it expresses Oedipal wishes which have in themselves become sources of anxiety. The release of the aggressive wish against the frustrating mother carries with it also the force of the sexual wish for the Oedipal mother and gives the beast (as son) the envied power of the Oedipal father. With this convergence of Oedipal and oral contexts, the conquered world represents both the bad mother created out of the experience of oral frustration and desired mother of the Oedipus stage.

---

[14] "Schizophrenia and the Enevitability of Death" (1961), *Collected Papers on Schizophrenia and Related Subjects* (London: The Hogarth Press, 1965), p. 500.
[15] "Scorn, Disillusionment and Adoration in the Psychotherapy of Schizophrenia" (1962), *ibid.*, p. 612.

The ending of the poem places the vision of the beast in broad historical context. Twenty centuries since the birth of Christ have been troubled from the first by something in the very nature of their beginning. But the hour draws near for a new epoch to supersede the Christian era.

> The darkness drops again; but now I know
> That twenty centuries of stony sleep
> Were vexed to nightmare by a rocking cradle,
> And what rough beast, its hour come round at last,
> Slouches towards Bethlehem to be born?

The emphasis on "rocking cradle" and birth brings the conditions of infancy particularly close to the poem's conscious concern with cultural catastrophe.

Richard Ellman has observed of these lines:

> The final intimation that the new god will be born in Bethlehem, which Christianity associates with passive infancy and the tenderness of maternal love, makes the brutishness particularly frightful.[16]

The conflict of tenderness and brutality, of Christianity and the terrible new age, concentrates in the impending clash of vast cultural forces the key elements of the poem's unconscious dynamics. It is particularly important that the poem relates "nightmare" and "rocking cradle" causally, insists that the source of terror was bred in the apparent peace of the culturally hypostatized infancy of Christ, for this connection of infancy and terror reflects precisely the unconscious link that this paper has sought to establish. Suggestive also is Roheim's association of the mythical figure of the Night-mare with the sphinx-figure as a representation of those desires mobilized by a primal scene fantasy (*Riddle*, pp. 55-56). This connection suggests that the poem's vexing "nightmare" which disturbs sleep echoes the primal scene context that informed the image of the beast. The anxiety state conveyed in "stony sleep" thus extends, in the form of dread, both unconscious contexts inferred above

---

[16] *The Identity of Yeats*, 2nd ed. (New York: Oxford University Press, 1964), p. 260.

with regard to the sphinx-image, the Oedipal anxiety of the primal scene fantasy, and the oral anxiety of separation. But the era of stony sleep will be displaced by the era of the rough beast, born in the same city of maternal love.

What rough beast? The rough beast here carries the transforming power of infantile rage and Oedipal triumph discussed above. What the beast will bring, besides omnipotence, is not stressed in the poem, and is not important to the fantasy. Its function—in the arena of history and in the arena of inner conflict—is to supersede the vexing nightmare brought on by the "rocking cradle." If the beast is, in Ellman's words, "particularly frightful" because it promises to destroy the world of "passive infancy and maternal love," it is especially gratifying because it releases an aggressive wish to destroy the inner torment created in response to the failure of maternal love. The aggressive beast as projected, destructive ego supplants passive infancy when passivity comes to mean helplessness and intolerable separateness rather than the fulfillment of omnipotent oneness.

In exploring the imagery of historical catastrophe presented in "The Second Coming" for fantasies that are linked to childhood situations of traumatic magnitude, my aim has been to understand the unconscious roots of the sense of power that the poem imparts to its readers. Stated very briefly, I have tried to show that the poem utilizes a fantasy of omnipotent rage to master a situation of intolerable helplessness. The reader's unconscious participation in this destructive fantasy is at the core of that sense of power. But the poem does not let its readers off quite so easily as this analysis suggests.

The total rage or hatred that is expressed unconsciously is common, potentially, to all people. But such massive aggressive longings necessarily jeopardize one's very place in even the most primitive social contexts. In the earliest social relationship, they rouse "the fear that one's hate will destroy the very person one needs and loves, a fear that grows into guilt" (*Schizoid Phenomena*, p. 25). Guilt, in this sense, results from the necessary turning back of that hatred against the self in which it originates. "The Second Coming" evades this guilt, momentarily, by dividing the self into discrete parts. In the reading I have offered, the most important parts are the projective fantasy of destruction—experienced as a sense of power —and the image of the self as prophetic visionary, able to glimpse and record in advance an approaching historical catastrophe. But what happens to the everyday self that lives in and is bounded by a uniquely troubled phase of historical reality? It is, I think, for the moment abandoned, or its claims considerably muted, and plays little or no part in the affective state I have described as participation in a sense of power. But this essential part of the self can hardly be abandoned completely, for a long time, in the total relationship one develops with the poem and the history the poem addresses. The awesome view of history presented by the poem becomes implicated in our response to it, but through a part of our response that can be isolated from our participation in its power.

Early in this essay I suggested that a distinction must be made between the imaginative engagement generated by a fully felt reading of " The Second Coming " and the range of meaning the poem claims for itself as we place it in our experience. In order to place the poem in the context of our own confrontation with history, we must dissolve " the fusion or merger of self and book " that Norman Holland sees at the heart of literary experience (*Dynamics,* p. 67). We move from an imaginative fusion of self and poem toward a still intense subject/object relationship of self to poem. As we do so, our thoughtful response to the poem is focused primarily in terms of our regard for the poem as aesthetic object and our place in history as defined by the poem. But the inner dynamics of these concerns extend psychological trends initiated by the prior immersion of self within poem. The awe we feel for the poem—which we express as admiration for the extraordinary technical mastery it embodies—conveys in part our gratitude for the sense of power that the poem has let us share. The distress we feel in so far as we grant that the poem has presented a significant image of historical possibility is in part the price we pay for having shared in the fantasy of destructive power.

The prophetic insistence on historical helplessness becomes a part of our experience of the poem as we relinquish our identification with the poem's destructive fantasy, and are confronted by the image of destructive omnipotence as external historical force directed against us. But this sense of helplessness before history is itself influenced by our unconscious response to the poem. Through its disguises, the poem gives generous sway to repressed destructive wishes. But as we give up our identification with the power of the beast, we re-experience the infantile conflict that develops when the wish to destroy an intolerably frustrating world confronts the recognition that we only exist in and through that world, which is the same world that provides love and security. In this sense, the sphinx-image, consciously understood as alien historical force, finds a third unconscious context. It is the expression of feared retaliation—of anger and aggression turned back upon the ego as guilt—projected onto historical fate. As our involvement with the poem moves away from an experience of participation in inhuman power toward a personal orientation in terms of historical force, the unconscious meaning of the sphinx-image blends into the unconscious situation that lies behind the earlier image of the blood-dimmed tide. Infantile helplessness before the force of one's own projected rage is generalized into the powerlessness of a whole culture before the force of destiny.

My purpose has been to account psychoanalytically for the impact of "The Second Coming" in terms of both the strange sense of power that it generates in a fully felt reading and its capacity to "persuade us of our powerlessness." The split that Bloom sees between "exultation on the speaker's part" (*Yeats*, p. 321) and powerlessness on the part of the reader I have described as two parts of a total process initiated by the poem and experienced by the reader. Certainly this process does not proceed with such mechanical neatness that in any one person's reading and thinking about this poem the two parts are kept completely separate. But however blurred they may be in the complexities of literary response, I think it is important to distinguish them analytically as component parts of the larger process that moves in the direction I have indicated.

This process, which culminates in a sense of powerlessness, is not, however, an adequate presentation of the poem's psychological range. It describes only one strand of meaning influenced by the poem's unconscious content. The fantasy of helplessness overcome by rage is primary to our experience of the poem's power, but the resolution of this fantasy into a sense of powerlessness before history is only one possible psychological outcome. In closing this discussion I would like to point to two further dimensions of response to the poem that bear on its unconscious strategies. Each of them describes a pattern which builds on the expression of rage released by the poem, but each serves a purpose significantly different from the transformation of that rage into a sense of powerlessness.

In the conclusion of his study of Yeats, Bloom regrets that Yeats made his visionary power serve a conception of history that is controlled by fate rather than by human freedom. He applies to Yeats Martin Buber's criticism of "'the dogma of gradual process,' by which the quasi-historical thought of our time has worked ' to establish a more tenacious and oppressive belief in fate than has ever before existed'" (p. 470). Such a presentation of history as fate serves a defensive purpose in "The Second Coming." The powerlessness that the poem conveys is justified by its place in an historical cycle that makes it necessary. The very experience of individual powerlessness provides, paradoxically, an avenue to a larger power, understood as fate. The threat of separation and psychic disintegration presented in the first section of the poem resolves into a parody of lost "omnipotent oneness." The helpless individual and the imperiled culture are merged with and participate in the larger controlling flow of historical necessity. An order of meaning is restored in which the agonies of "anarchy" find their necessary place. To the extent that Yeats and his readers embrace the beast image of inevitable historical force, the poem employs a form of the defense known as identification with the aggressor.

In affective terms, this identification is related to the force of infantile rage discussed above, although it presents a controlling position taken toward experience by the ego rather than an emotional release. It also serves similar defensive purposes: it places the self, as merged with historical necessity, within the larger context of an active, aggressive relationship to a frustrating world; and it defends against the defense of schizoid flight from the world—a defense that poses dangers greater than the situation that called it into service. But there is reason to isolate this identification analytically from the defenses discussed thus far, since it is more closely tied to the immediate experience of the specific historical situation of violence, disorder, and disillusionment that Yeats shared with his contemporaries, a situation that still touches our lives. This identification is more closely linked to the sense of mastery conveyed by the poem's prophetic voice than to the forces that the prophecy discloses. Through that voice, as it becomes the voice of history, the identification is made. It should be noted, however, that identification with the aggressor includes in this context creation of the aggressor with whom the identification is made, since Yeats discovers the shape of his private historical mythology in an experience of world wide catastrophe which for many destroyed the very grounds of the idea of transcendent historical purpose.

The final psychic purpose I would point to in " The Second Coming " is simply a purgative one. The poem releases rage in a context that at least partially frees this release from the cycle which doubles back on the self as guilt. The venting of anger and hatred may lead to a kind of peace—indeed, for an infant, may lead beyond frustration back to fulfilling participation in the mother's goodness that was lost in the conditions leading to rage. In the poem that follows " The Second Coming " in Yeats's own ordering of his poetry, and which is clearly conceived with the terrible vision of " The Second Coming " in mind,[17] Yeats imagines a condition that may follow the driving out of rage. Yeats offers in " A Prayer for My Daughter " a vision of " radical innocence "—not a " ceremony of innocence " which is drowned, but a condition of the soul which may be recovered. This recovery is achieved through the discovery that the soul's " own sweet Will " is identical with " Heaven's will," a discovery which forms an enduring base of self-contained

[17] Ellman provides these dates of composition: "The Second Coming," Jan. 1919; "A Prayer for My Daughter," Feb. 19—June 1919, *The Identity of Yeats*, p. 290.

strength that can absorb the hazards of a life lived in troubled times:

> Considering that, all hatred driven hence,
> The soul recovers radical innocence
> And learns at last that it is self-delighting,
> Self-appeasing, self-affrighting,
> And that its own sweet will is Heaven's will;
> She can, though every face should scowl
> And every windy quarter howl
> Or every bellows burst, be happy still.

I think this vision of individual will fused with a higher, beneficent will is made possible, in large part, by a purgative logic of released rage presented in "The Second Coming," and completes one important strand of a rhythmic experience of frustration and fulfillment begun in the earlier poem.

Bernard Levine has suggested, in a very different critical context, that "The Second Coming" should "be read as proof of the speaker's journey toward psychological equanimity."[18] I think that such a "journey" is one trend that the poem develops. This reading of "The Second Coming" as a movement toward self-affirmation within a higher order understood as "Heaven's will" seems clearly to contradict my earlier attempts to show that the poem may lead to the experience of powerlessness or to participation in the reassuring power of fate. But all three possibilities are valid. They are also, in an important sense, out of the poem's control. Whether, for any reader, the deep reservoir of rage that the poem taps is turned back against the self as the image of historical catastrophe, or whether he gives himself over to that rage as it is bound to a vision of historical inevitability, or whether the release of that rage clears the mind for the recovery of "radical innocence," will depend on the reader and the psychological circumstances he brings to his reading. Each possibility is there, and each is grounded in the core situation of infantile helplessness and separation overcome by a fantasy of omnipotent rage.

---

[18] *The Dissolving Image* (Detroit: Wayne State University Press, 1970), p. 99.

LeRoi Jones's *Dutchman*: Inter-racial Ritual of Sexual Violence

Dianne H. Weisgram

I

The artist and the political activist are one. They are both shapers of the future reality. Both understand and manipulate the collective myths of the race. Both are warriors, priests, lovers and destroyers. For the first violence will be internal—the destruction of a weak spiritual self for a more perfect self. But it will be a necessary violence. It is the only thing that will destroy the double-consciousness—the tension that is in the souls of the black folk.

—Larry Neal, *Black Fire*

As Larry Neal has said, both the artist and the political activist are manipulators of collective myths; and they are both destroyers whose violence turns first inward in a suicidal destruction of psychic doubleness, and then outward to a reshaping of the external world.[1] The career of LeRoi Jones, from author of the *Preface to a Twenty Volume Suicide Note*[2] to political

---

[1] Larry Neal, "An Afterward," *Black Fire*, ed. LeRoi Jones and Larry Neal (New York: William Morrow & Co., Inc., 1968), p. 656.

[2] The last poem in this first collection (written between 1957 and 1961) expresses Jones's sense of the double-faced psychic alienation inherent in the black schizoid condition:

NOTES FOR A SPEECH

African blues
does not know me. Their steps, in sands
of their own
land. A country
in black & white, newspapers
blown down pavements
of the world. Does
not feel
what I am.
            Strength
in a dream, an oblique
suckling of nerve, the wind

activist, and finally to psychic metamorphosis as Imamu Amiri
Baraka, is a model of the black artist described by Larry Neal.
Jones's early play, *Dutchman* (1964), stages the first step in this
metamorphic process.

The setting of *Dutchman* is " the subway heaped in modern
myth." [3] This myth involves an archetypal American nightmare: the miscegenated primal scene and consequent ritual
revenge lynching. But Jones has given it another twist by
projecting the woman as a maternal night visitor who invites
her son to join in the primal scene and then revenges herself
for his violation. Jones's vision of this ritual of seduction and
violence casts Clay, a twenty-year-old Negro, as the victim; and
Lula, a thirty-year-old white woman, as his temptress and victimizer. The climax of the play is Clay's murder as the train
tears through the underbelly of the city.

There is something uncanny about Lula's presence, especially about her way of claiming to know all about Clay. One

(Note 2, *cont.*)   throws up sand, eyes
are something locked in
hate, of hate, of hate, to
walk abroad, they conduct
their deaths apart
from my own. Those
heads, I call
my " people."
                (And who are they. People. To concern
myself, ugly man. Who
you, to concern
the white flat stomachs
of maidens, inside houses
dying. Black. Peeled moon
light on my fingers
move under
her clothes. Where
is her husband. Black
words throw up sand
to eyes, fingers of
their private dead. Whose
soul, eyes, in sand. My color
is not theirs. Lighter, white man
talk. They shy away. My own
dead souls, my, so called
people. Africa
is a foreign place. You are
as any other sad man here
american.

[3] LeRoi Jones, *Dutchman and The Slave* (New York: William Morrow & Co,
Inc., 1964), p. 3. All quotations are from the Apollo edition.

might say that she has the three faces of Eve—mother, lover, and death itself.[4] In terms of the matrix of religious allusions woven through the play, Clay is Adam, whose origin was clay; and Lula is a composite Eve-Lilith, the original evil woman.[5] As Adam and Eve, Clay and Lula are the primordial parents fused in a violent sexual encounter; and in keeping with the fluid identifications of primal scene fantasies, they are also mother and son. Clay's expulsion from the car at the end of their struggle suggests an image of violent birth, as though Lula and Clay had come together to murder him in preparation for the recreation of Black identity. Lula refers to Clay as her " Christ," an avatar about to be sacrificed and resurrected.[6]

Lula is the bringer of Destiny. She rides time after time through the underground seeking out victims for her ritual drama of love and death. Her voice is both coarse and gentle, a " sidewalk throb." Her hand is "dry as ashes." Her hair is turning gray " a gray hair for each year and type " of man she has destroyed. Luring Clay to his fate, she says, " It's always gentle when it starts." And she warns him in advance, " You look like death eating a soda cracker." Lula is the forbidden woman, not only from the perspective of the racial taboos on sex, but also from the perspective of the taboo on the original incestuous object. Incest is mentioned specifically once in the play—Lula accuses Clay of trying to make it with his sister when he was ten, and notes that although he failed, she herself succeeded two weeks ago. " Ten years " is the difference between their ages, so it is as if they were discussing by displacement an unconscious incestuous union in which Lula, not Clay, is the phallic partner.

The title " Dutchman " is over-determined: first, as the name of the original slave ship between Africa and America; second, as an ironic name for Negro—the Dutch were the original settlers of Harlem; and third, as an allusion to the legend of *The Flying Dutchman*, a spectral ship of disaster unable to

---

[4] For a discussion of the triple-goddess, see Sigmund Freud, "The Theme of the Three Caskets" (1913), *Collected Papers* IV.

[5] For a discussion of the Eden Myth in *Dutchman*, see John Gassner and Bernard F. Dukore, *A Treasury of the Theatre*, II, 4th ed. (New York, 1970), p. 1247; and George R. Adams, "Black Militant Drama," *American Imago*, 28, 2 (Summer 1971), 118.

[6] Cf. Adams, "Black Militant Drama," 118–119.

make port and perpetually haunting the seas around the Cape of Good Hope. As a condemned man on his death ride, Clay belongs to the legend; as the roaming spectre, Lula embodies it.

The rhythm of the play may be described as turning on and turning off, and then repetition, as if in a ritual cycle. A pattern of attraction across boundaries is established between the two main characters at the outset. Clay sits inside the subway car looking out vacantly. Lula smiles premeditatedly through the window at him; he reciprocates. After a brief flirtation, she confronts him inside the car, challenging, "Weren't you staring at me?" "What do you think you're doing?" "You think I want to pick you up, get you to take me somewhere and screw me, huh?" Lula's style is to tempt her victim to interact with her and then to slam a barrier in his face. She instructs him to ask her to a party; like a playwright-director, she even gives him his lines. When he does ask her, she refuses:

Lula:

> Now you say to me, "Lula, Lula, why don't you go to this party with me tonight?" It's your turn, and let those be your lines.

Clay:

> Lula, why don't you go to this party with me tonight, Huh?

Lula:

> Say my name twice before you ask, and no huh's.

Clay:

> Lula, Lula, why don't you go to this party with me tonight?

Lula:

> I'd like to go, Clay, but how can you ask me to go when you barely know me?
>
> . . . . .

Clay:

> Are you going to the party with me, Lula?

Lula:

> (Bored and not even looking)
> I don't even know you.

The family model for this kind of exchange is the dominating mother who instructs a child's speech and behavior, and then rejects his attempts to establish contact.

Not only does Lula impose a role to play and words to speak and then ignore Clay's presence as a human being, she gives him a name and a history, telling him he is a well-known type. He is such a cliché, she tells him that he should be on television. She demands: " Who do you think you are now? " When he replies, " Well, in college I thought I was Baudelaire," she challenges, " I bet you never once thought you were a black nigger." And then she reveals his true latent identity: " You're a murderer, Clay, and you know it." As the play continues, she says: " And we'll pretend the people cannot see you. That is, the citizens. And that you are free of your own history. And I am free of my history. We'll pretend that we are both anonymous beauties smashing along through the city's entrails." But as the play demonstrates, one is not free of history, for the past imposes an identity, and to be free of it is to die.

Lula manipulates Clay with perfection. She ridicules his middle-class conformity, and finally, she provokes his aggression: " Clay, you liver-lipped white man. You would-be Christian. You ain't no nigger, you're just a dirty white man . . . shaking that wildroot cream-oil on your knotty head, jackets buttoning up to your chin, so full of white man's words. Get up and scream at these people. Clay, you got to break out. Don't sit there dying the way they want you to die. Get up." When Clay does get up and scream, Lula's verbal " knifelike cynicism " becomes an actual knife thrust.

Clay, the conformist, buttoned-up behind white conventions to keep from wreaking vengeance, and Lula, his beautiful seductress, are, as Jones makes unmistakably clear, emblems of Black and White America. The Whites premeditatedly tantalize the Blacks in order to arouse Black aggression and justify White violence.

This political theme is expressed in pervasive body imagery. The " underbelly of the city " is linked to the drama between Lula and Clay when she invites him to " rub bellies," to do " the navel scratcher." He retorts: " Belly rub hates you." In her exhibitionistic come-on, Lula accuses Clay of staring down

in the vicinity of her ass and legs. Clay tells her she rolls her
ass like an elephant. He says that white people don't understand
that Bessie Smith's message is, " Kiss my ass, kiss my black unruly
ass." Similarly, declares Clay, Charlie Parker is saying, " Up
your ass, feeble-minded ofay! "

This polymorphism is continued with references to hands.
Lula grabs Clay's wrist and shakes it so hard he wonders
if she is a lady wrestler. She invites him to imagine her hands
scraping carrots, opening doors, unbuttoning her dress, and letting her skirt fall down. She says: " I know you like the palm of
my hand." And she describes how, at the imagined party, he
will pat her " very lovingly on the flanks "; at her apartment: " I
lead you in, holding your wet hand gently in my hand." Clay
refers to " the pure heart, the pumping black heart "; in contrast, there is the white man's " great missionary heart." In his
long, threatening speech at the turning point of the play, Clay
warns Lula that he could squeeze her throat flat; and in a body-
destruction fantasy culminating the foregoing imagery, he describes how the black people will " cut your throats, and drag
you out to the edge of your cities so the flesh can fall away from
your bones."

Images of penetration envision a violent eruption between
outside and inside and emphasize the theme of sexualized aggression. The train tearing through the subway tunnel inspires
Lula's last words in Act I: " smashing along through the city's
entrails. GROOVE! " Later, there is an imagined climbing of
the stairs to enter Lula's " hovel." And finally, the climactic
stabbing, with its erotic excitement and release made brilliantly
apparent in the sweating glee of Shirley Knight's masterful
performance in the Jihad Films production.

Of all Jones's plays, *Dutchman*, especially in its film form,
has been the most available, popular, and compelling to integrated and predominantly white audiences. It is my purpose
here to offer a psychoanalytic reading of the deeper levels of the
play in order to explain how its activation of fundamental psychological conflicts enhances its political impact. Seeing *Dutchman* is a most upsetting and enraging experience, an experience
not entirely accounted for, I think, in terms of Jones's overriding

secondary process themes. Sociological analysis can say a great deal about the cultural context of the play, but an explication of the internal dynamics of the violent enactment between Clay and Lula and an extrapolation to an analysis of its effect on a theatre audience call for an in-depth psychological reading.

What makes *Dutchman* so powerful and moving? As a parable, the story is built on sharp exaggeration and generalization, on manipulation of collective stereotypes. Jones presents Lula as a symbol of not only white racists and fading Cleaverean belles who want to be attacked by black men,[7] but of *all white people*: racists, belles, liberals, rationalists, missionaries, and educators alike. In the form of a transparent superego trick, the old American ritual of seduction and death has merely assumed a new version: the miscegenated primal scene takes place psycho-politically—white people tease the Negro into asserting his identity, into demanding justice (for Jones, the only justice is genocidal revenge), and then murder him, using his demands as justification. Lula's strategy is: *See, he wants to kill us, you even heard him admit it, let's get him first!* In projecting a paranoid vision [8] of premeditated white malignancy, Jones is mirroring the paranoia he sees around him in American society. This is part of the cultural resonance of the play.

Like all of Jones's works, *Dutchman* is short and immediate —the intention is to shock the audience and move them through astonishment and guilt to revenge. As a mobilization of energy, the play bears a certain similarity to the American proletarian drama of the 1930's. There is little about the form that is " theatrical " in the traditional sense—the staging is not especially arresting, and one has the feeling that the action is pressed very close to the face of the audience, with a minimal degree of distance or diversion. The sexuality, violence, and aggressive speech are like the train—*coming at you*. The play insinuates and imposes itself, and then surprises one in the same way that Lula manipulates Clay. The drama is introjected by the audience, and then erupts toward the outside world. After witnessing

---

[7] See Eldridge Cleaver, *Soul on Ice* (New York: Delta, 1968), pp. 184-185.

[8] As Edgar Friedenberg has said, under certain conditions, paranoid delusions cease to be delusions; reality itself is paranoid, not the people threatened by it. " An R. D. Laing Symposium," *Salmagundi*, 16 (Spring 1971), 139.

Lula's outrageous attack we, like Jones, demand vengeance. As my experience of *Dutchman* merged with life outside the theatre, I analogized Clifford Odets' " Strike! Strike! " except that the words have taken on a more literal meaning in the years since *Waiting for Lefty*.

In psychoanalytic terms, one of the explanations for the successful impact of Jones's manipulation of myth may be found in the resonant connotations of his configurations of imagery, particularly in the underlying themes of oral loss, frustration, and consequent rage. The exaggeration of Jones's vision and his nightmarish characterizations evoke fantasies stemming from the earliest and most intensely affective relationships of human life. As a cultural projection, Lula stimulates in us an image of an evil mother, ambivalent and betraying, who caresses her child-victim, offers to nourish and gratify him, and then pushes him away; she is the eternal frustrator of desire. Clay, as his name suggests, is in a position of passivity and malleability; he is to be imprinted and molded.[9] In their reciprocal arousal, Clay and Lula mirror each other; and at two points in the play, they actually imitate each other—she mimics the way he speaks, and he mimics the way she dances. They are mutual stereotypes merging in conflict. He calls her " Snow White " and " Tallulah Bankhead." She calls him an "escaped nigger," " Ol' Uncle Tom Woolly-Head," "Big Lip," and so on.

Jones is quite definite in specifying the difference between the ages of his two characters and in emphasizing the boundaries between them. Lula's first act is to establish eye-contact and to smile, which Clay reciprocates instinctively, as in the earliest and most fundamental of human relationships.[10] After he has taken her in with his eyes, Lula comes to stand beside him in the car,[11] and Clay looks up into her face with trust as she leans

---

[9] For a discussion of imprinting and identity creation in the earliest stages of mother-child interaction, see Heinz Lichtenstein, " Identity and Sexuality," *Journal of the American Psychoanalytic Association*, IX (1961), especially 206-208.

[10] For a discussion of the smiling response between mother and child, see René A. Spitz, *The First Year of Life* (New York: International Universities Press, 1965), p. 86. Cf. Ernst Kris, *Psychoanalytic Explorations in Art* (New York: Schocken Books, 1964), pp. 227-229.

[11] The developmental model for this is introjection. See Roy Schafer, *Aspects of Internalization* (New York: International Universities Press, 1968).

down from the strap over his seat and encourages him. She eats an apple and gives one to him, saying, " Eating apples together is always the first step." Then she grabs his hand so that he cannot eat; he refuses her next offer of food. Lula says: " You crawled through the wire and made tracks to my side." But Clay replies: " Plantations didn't have any wire "; and he goes on to imagine that in the times of slavery, the plantation was a kind of secure and symbiotic paradise: " Plantations were big open white-washed places like heaven, and everybody on 'em was grooved to be there. Just strummin' and hummin' all day." This is an idyllic, if ironic, rendering of the kind of harmony, reciprocity, and trust Erik Erikson describes as basic to the oral stage of life.[12] Clay's idealization of the plantation past functions in a double way, simultaneously projecting and frustrating with irony a paradisial wish. In terms of the psychosexual significance of paradise as the pre-ambivalent world, the imagined plantation idyll links together with Jones's recurrent imagery of oral association—eyes, lips, teeth, mouths (open, shut, working), throats and breasts—the dominant body foci of our earliest object relationship. As we listen to the play, we hear about licking, kissing, eating, drinking, staring, looking, reading (i.e., taking in through the eyes), talking, whispering, lying—all references to orally oriented modalities.[13] At the point when he is murdered, the focus is on Clay's stupidly working mouth; he has said all his words, and now his mouth is open and empty.

The most dramatic moment of *Dutchman* occurs when Clay throws off or breaks out of his conformist self, his false, white man's self. The theme of the erupting black identity is conceived by Jones in terms of a rage so intense that when Clay's repressed self emerges, he dies in the next instant. The psychic orientation of this fundamental tension in the play between true and false identity is, as we shall see, an orally based schizoid one in which the personality is charged with hatred and disintegrates in a self-destructive defense.[14]

[12] Erik H. Erikson, *Childhood and Society* (New York: W. W. Norton, 1963), p. 247.

[13] See Otto Fenichel, *The Psychoanalytic Theory of Neurosis* (New York: W. W. Norton, 1945), p. 315.

[14] For an analysis of this process, see R. D. Laing, *The Divided Self* (Baltimore: Penguin, 1965), p. 161 and *passim*.

By reviving fantasies of separation, loss, and frustration, Jones evokes a complex revenge response and channels it against all white people as the split-off and evil segment of a self divided from paradise. Lula tells Clay that he is like " all those Jewish poets from Yonkers, who leave their mothers looking for other mothers, or other's mothers, on whose baggy tits they lay their fumbling heads." This bitter and cynical reference to separation and search for restoration has in the context of this play, and in general, a mythic and cosmic resonance; for the cultural and religious myth of the Fall is a universal counterpart of the genetic experience of oral catastrophe, as Erik Erikson has stated so well in his description of the development of ontological boundaries.[15]

This theme is at the heart of the deepest conflict in *Dutchman*: from the idea of an inner saboteur, to the boundary confusion over whether the violence is inside or outside, to the separation rage. Erikson specifies that the feeling of paradise lost is a consequence of the onset of the oral-sadistic stage, when teeth erupt into the mouth; and he analyzes the way in which a child manages oral aggression by means of a black and white splitting of the world into good and evil.[16] To LeRoi Jones, radical splitting is an historical actuality as well as a psychic reality,[17] for the elements of his drama are profoundly over-

---

[15] See Erikson, *Childhood and Society*, *op. cit.*, pp. 78-79.

[16] In the myth of the founding of Thebes, Cadmus sows dragon teeth and raises up an army divided against itself; this is an analogue for the oral aggressive fantasy underlying *Dutchman*.

In Jones's writings, the sense of self that comes with the primordial rupture of oral union is rejected as Western, as belonging to a false value system. In the holistic reality he desires, the true black identity is communal and whole, not individual and split.

[17] Jones is preoccupied with the same psychological issues in *Blues People*, where he describes the cruellest part of black slave trading not as the slavery itself but as the *separation* from Africa, the setting apart of the black man from his anthropological and cultural *Weltanschauung*. He writes, " What a weird and unbelievably cruel destiny for those people who were first brought here. Not just the mere fact of being sold into slavery—that in itself was a common practice among the tribes of West Africa, and the economic system in which these new slaves were to form so integral a part was not so strange either. But to be brought to a country, a culture, a society, that was, and is, in terms of purely philosophical correlatives, the complete antithesis of one's own version of man's life on earth—that is the cruelest aspect of this particular enslavement."—LeRoi Jones, *Blues People* (New York: William Morrow, 1963) , p. 1. In his recent play, *Slave Ship* (1968) , Jones dramatizes the pain of families

determined, condensing issues of psychological and bodily development with the issues of the American socio-political crisis. The evil dividedness in Jones himself and in the culture at large can be healed and the symbiotic matrix restored only through a return to Blackness; and throughout his imaginary projection of this process, Jones's plays fix on the image of a white devil who must kill or be killed, who must be excluded from the world.[18]

The iterative oral imagery and the focus on radical ambivalence in *Dutchman* is the perfect psychological expression of the political call for vengeance that informs the career of LeRoi Jones. The psychoanalysis of Revenge shows that vengeance as a state of mind carries with it an underlying sense of profound oral loss and deprivation, and is connected with pain and rage secondary to frustration.[19] When we, as children, are removed or rejected from the maternal matrix, we experience an overwhelming rage to destroy.[20] In terms of what Erikson says about the form taken by aggressive response to the oral dilemma,

---

separated for the first time; and of course, the song, " Sometimes I feel like a motherless child a long way from home," expresses the same theme of oral loss and maternal separation. Africa clearly resonates as the good black mother for Jones, and he stresses *Umoja* (unity) as the central value for the black family, community, nation, and race; and the second is *Kujichagulia*, self-definition and naming—see *A Black Value System*, by Imamu Amiri Baraka (Jihad Productions, 1970). Whites must be excluded from the body of black people because white radicals are like draculas, " 1930's vampires rerisen to suck black people's blood "—an image of the evil oral mother. Throughout his writings, Jones deplores the post-Renaissance split in Western consciousness and wishes to belong to another world. In *The Slave*, Easley, the white man, says to Walker, the Black revolutionary, " You always used to speak of the Renaissance as an evil time."—*Dutchman and The Slave, op. cit.*, p. 50.

[18] *A Black Mass* (1965), based on the Muslim myth of Yacub the scientist-magician, dramatizes the creation of a white beast who vomits and then eats it to vomit again, and who runs disgustingly through the audience attacking people with horrible kisses and obscene gestures, screaming in parody of Western individualism, " White! White! me! me! me! White! " At the end of the play, the narrator calls upon the audience to rise up and slay the beast. This play is available in *Four Black Revolutionary Plays* (New York: Bobbs-Merrill, 1969). The idea of ritual expulsion of whiteness pervades Jones' later dramatic works—exclusion from the mind and exclusion from the world. *Slave Ship* ends in a rising up of the players and audience in dance, except for white members of the audience, who are barred from the celebration.

[19] Charles W. Socarides, " On Vengeance," *Journal of the American Psychoanalytic Association*, 14 (1966), 356-375.

[20] See Joan Riviere, " Hate, Greed and Aggression," in *Love, Hate and Reparation* (New York: W. W. Norton, 1964), pp. 8-9.

it is crucial to the psycho-dynamics of *Dutchman* that in the
most intense moment of his outburst, Clay says (*through his
teeth*), " I'll rip your lousy breasts off! " But he does not really
hurt Lula at all; instead, he pours out three pages of rhetoric.
In this speech, the oral expression of the blues people—Charlie
Parker on the saxophone, black poetry and song—is described as
a transformation of destructive impulses: "Bird would've played
not a note of music if he just walked up to East Sixty-seventh
Street and killed the first ten white people he saw. . . . Just let
me bleed you, you loud whore, and one poem vanished. . . .
If Bessie Smith had killed some white people she wouldn't
have needed that music." Art is a substitute for murder.

Clay indicates two alternate ways of expressing aggression:
(1) transformation: turning the impulse inward and translating
it into poetry and song, and (2) violent revenge: tearing off
breasts, slitting throats, annihilating the white race. Similarly,
the play itself expresses two alternatives: as a metaphoric enactment within the framed space of a theatre, it illustrates transformation; but as militant propaganda, it inspires a wish for
violence and ultimately recommends acting out. Note that these
alternatives correspond to Erik Erikson's categories of oral defense: the expulsive mode, spitting up and out; as against the intrusive mode, biting into the breast.[21] In Jones's *Dutchman*,
something evil gets inside and must be ejected with violence; an
intrapsychic splitting occurs according to which a female introject kills you from inside unless you can get her outside your
external boundaries: there can be no reconciliation of this basic
split. Hence, for Jones, integration means neurosis and death,
not psychic wholeness. Clay says: " A whole people of neurotics.
. . . And the only thing that would cure the neurosis would be
your murder. Murder. Just murder. Would make us all sane."

Along with the oral and filicidal fantasy at the center of
Dutchman, there are also elements of phallic violence. Lula
keeps telling Clay to get up, but he goes stiff and then limp with
impotence until his verbal outburst. Jones indicates that oral
aggression in expressive language will not defend the black
people so long as real destructive power is in the hands of whites.

[21] Erikson, *Childhood and Society*, p. 74.

Verbal threats are answered with Lula's gleeful knife thrust (in the film, Shirley Knight was all teeth and eyes in a close-up shot as the verbal attack shifted to physical penetration.) [22] And Clay's extended speech suggests the metamorphosis of the oral-submissive Negro into the phallic-aggressive stance now associated with the Militant movement, especially as in the body-phallus equation suggested by the style of the Panthers. Phallic assertion, "manhood," is the psychological direction of the play.[23] Clay envisions a reversal of roles between blacks and whites, with the whites as impotent and passive, and the blacks as aggressive and powerful: "Old bald-headed four-eyed ofays popping their fingers . . . and don't know yet what they're doing. And don't understand that Bessie Smith is saying, 'Kiss my black ass.' And if you don't know that, it's you that's doing the kissing." In a classical revenge movement from passive victimage

[22] Kris suggests that the opening of the mouth in the act of laughter can be an aggressive showing of the teeth—"Laughter as an Expressive Process," *Psychoanalytic Explorations in Art,* p. 233. See Joan Riviere, "Hate, Greed and Aggression," p. 5. The word "retaliation" is rooted in teeth and eyes, as in *lex talionis,* "an eye for an eye and a tooth for a tooth" (Lev. 24: 20). The association of teeth and aggression is a commonplace in psychoanalytic writing; see Fenichel, *The Psychoanalytic Theory of Neurosis,* p. 64 ff.

In general, close-up shots in movies, of which Lula's face during the murder is a terrifying instance, are analogues for the primal mother-child dialogue described by René Spitz in *The First Year of Life, op. cit.*

[23] It is part of the cultural resonance of *Dutchman* that phallic fantasies have been quite consciously and pervasively built into the black power movement: Ossie Davis eulogized Malcolm X as "our manhood, our living, black manhood." And Eldridge Cleaver declared, "We shall have our manhood. We shall have it or the earth will be leveled by our attempts to gain it." The final chapter of *Soul on Ice* is especially unmistakable in its anatomical location of black power.

Among others, Martin Duberman has remarked the similarity between the rhetorical form of black militancy and traditional American values. As Clay says, "those ex-coons will be standup Western men, and they'll murder you. They'll murder you and have very rational explanations." Duberman writes, "When whites descry SNCC's declaration that it is tired of turning the other cheek, that henceforth it will actively resist white brutality, they might do well to remember that they have always considered self-defense acceptable behavior for themselves; our textbooks, for example, view the refusal of the revolutionaries of 1776 to 'sit supinely by' as the very essence of manhood"—Martin Duberman, "Black Power in America," *Partisan Review* (Winter 1967), 45.

Jones seems to have a more skeptical view than some of the other black writers in regard to the efficacy of "manhood" as a solution to the racial dilemma. In the American psychological system, "manhood" means "phallus," or "body-phallus," not membership in the human species. Lula talks a great deal about Clay's manhood, but she responds to his self-assertion as if in self-defense; she uses it as an excuse in the same way that police in Chicago and elsewhere responded to the threat of black militancy, as if in self-defense, the essence of manhood.

to active identification with the aggressor,[24] the blacks will have become the whites in order to destroy them:

> And you tell this to your father. . . . Tell him not to preach so much rationalism and cold logic to these niggers. Don't make the mistake, through some irresponsible surge of Christian charity, of talking too much about the advantages of Western rationalism, of the great intellectual legacy of the white man, or maybe they'll begin to listen. And on that day, as sure as shit, when you really believe you can "accept" them into your fold, as half-white trusties late of the subject peoples . . . all of those ex-coons will be stand-up Western men, with eyes for clean hard useful lives, sober, pious and sane, and they'll murder you. They'll murder you, and have very rational explanations. Very much like your own.

It is noteworthy, in terms of the socio-political context, that the psychological pattern imagined by *Dutchman* saw its historical counterpart in the racial riots in Newark, where Jones was involved, and in other cities just a few years after the play was produced. As Eldridge Cleaver and others have said, whites have denied blacks phallic, masculine, active roles,[25] confining them instead to oral, passive ones. When the reins came off a little in the 1960's, blacks responded with massive retaliation. A great deal of it took oral form—looting; although some of it was phallic—bodies draped with bullets and a rifle in each hand.

II

An especially remarkable feature of *Dutchman* is the presence of the subway passengers, black and white, who observe the final stages of the struggle between Clay and Lula, and on her cue, throw his body out into the subway tunnel. This action may be discussed in terms of the drama of the inner world—a primal scene inside the mind as well as on the stage. (Melanie Klein has noted that a house, a car, a train, or whatever contains

---

[24] Fenichel, *The Psychoanalytic Theory of Neurosis*, pp. 511–512.

[25] See *Soul on Ice* for Cleaver's discussion of the psychodynamics of black and white roles. Cf. Calvin Hernton, *Sex and Racism in America* (New York, 1965).

people, may represent the inner world.[26]) At first, the coach is Clay's domain. Lula comes in to him through his eyes, then she comes inside the coach, and finally she pushes a knife into his body and gets her helpers to eject him entirely. He is being driven out of his head.

Joan Riviere writes, " The projection of persecutory phantasies concerning the inner world has manifestly found its most widespread expression in the myths of frightful and horrible forms of existence, as in nether worlds, notably the Hell of medieval times." [27] Jones specifies that the subway has for him a mythic meaning, and we know from his fiction, *The System of Dante's Hell* (1965), and " A Chase (Alighieri's Dream)," *Tales* (1967), that he associates the city with an infernal nightmare and defines hell as a state of mind.[28] Riviere continues: " Such regions are explicitly of an ' inner ' description, circumscribed and contained; their underground siting links, among other things, with the inner depths of the unconscious and the ' bad ' inner world. Hell is a mythological projection of a personal region within the individual in which all one's own ' bad,' cruel, torturing and destructive impulses are raging against the ' badness ' of others and vice versa." And she notes: " The classical and emotionally most significant example of these unconscious fantasies of inner activities with and by inner objects is that of the primal scene, the parents in intercourse, typically of a monstrous and unutterably terrifying character, inside one." [29]

The primal scene fantasy in *Dutchman* operates by presenting the spectacle of Lula's attractive and outrageous exhibitionism; we are aroused as we watch Clay aroused; and within the primal scene setting of the train tearing through the tunnel, Clay

[26] Melanie Klein, *Contributions to Psycho-Analysis*, p. 303 and p. 333n. Quoted by Joan Riviere in "The Unconscious Phantasy of an Inner World Reflected in Examples from Literature," *New Directions in Psycho-Analysis*, ed. Melanie Klein, Paula Heimann, R. E. Money-Kyrle (New York: Basic Books, 1955), p. 362n.

[27] Riviere, *New Directions in Psychoanalysis*, p. 365.

[28] "Hell in the head. The torture of being the unseen object, and, the constantly observed subject. The flame of social dichotomy. Split open down the center, which is the early legacy of the black man unfocused on blackness. Hell is actual, and people with hell in their heads"—LeRoi Jones, *The System of Dante's Hell* (New York: Grove Press, 1965), pp. 153–154. *Tales* is also available as a Grove Press paperback.

[29] Riviere, *New Directions in Psycho-analysis, op. cit.*, p. 365.

and Lula enact before the passenger-spectators a fantasy of body-phallus mutilation and ejection, while we in the audience introject and elaborate it in our own minds. The riders in the car become, in the course of the action, surrogates for the people in the audience as viewers of the immediate sadosexual encounter, and ultimately as witness-accomplices who first observe and then participate in the primal scene. Thematically, the passengers represent the American public as conspirators in the plot to get the Negro, and we in the audience are trapped into a guilty identification with them. During the course of the drama, we identify in curiosity, and before we realize it, in implied participation as well; but at the end, we dissociate ourselves from their act in outrage and surprise, and the ultimate emotive act is ambivalent complicity. As in the multiple and shifting identifications of primal scene experience,[30] we identify in turn and at once with Lula, Clay, and the on-looking riders as we take in imaginatively a sado-masochistic convergence of aggressive modalities.

To draw my analysis to a conclusion, it may be said that two interlocking modes of violent intercourse define the psychodynamics of *Dutchman,* and oscillation between them shapes the process of the theatric response. Passive internalization is one mode, and active exteriorization is the other: Clay takes Lula in and then spits her out; she enters his life, arouses and receives his verbal aggression, and then reciprocates his threats by killing and ejecting him. In phasic terms, the play condenses oral and phallic fantasies in primal scene confusion of boundaries between races, between inside and outside, and between psychosexual levels. On the oral level, wished for violent revenge is posed against transformation of aggression as art; and on the phallic level, attack as victimizer is posed against reception as victim. These juxtapositionings inform the mechanism behind our changing affective responses to the two main characters as the play progresses.

At first, Lula seems to have most of the good lines; she is the witty, perceptive one. She has more life and motion than Clay, and her criticisms of his conformity seem to be accurate. Bitchi-

[30] Fenichel, *Psychoanalytic Theory of the Neuroses, op. cit.,* p. 408.

ness and ambivalence notwithstanding, one has the impression that Jones sympathizes with her cynicism. After the initial identification, however, our sympathies begin to shift to Clay; and by the turning point, when he erupts, Clay is totally at the center of our response. He is in a position of moral superiority and, for the first time in the play, he has the superior language. In league with his outraged lyricism, we turn against Lula's insensitivity and brutality, and we wish to kill her. This wish is intensified by her verbal insults and sexual teasing, as well as by her characterization as a withholding and phallic-aggressive mother. It is especially during the finale of Lula's come-on that disagreeable maternal allusions proliferate: "Your ol' rag-head mammy," "hump his ol' mama," "You black son of a bitch." But Clay never does what he says he wants to do, he merely speaks his mind; and at the point at which the audience identification with him is complete, he is murdered. So the violence aroused against Lula is displaced in a destruction of our vicarious self embodied by Clay; and having been attacked, we are now put in the position of potential revengers.

Thus, Jones expresses his conscious political and social themes, and at the same time activates the underlying psychic counterparts of racial issues. The violent wish for revenge against the evil female introject is psychically structured to mobilize political activism. As the playwright and projector of an internal world, Jones is both Clay and Lula; and in accord with the principle of multiple-functioning in psychic mechanisms,[31] he gratifies and structures both sides of a son-mother conflict. By identifying Lula as the source and instigator of violence, Jones simultaneously arouses and gratifies primal aggression, effects ego-identification with the role of the black man as victim, and satisfies the superego-watchers in the form of the outrage stimulated in the audience; and he expels a false self in his process of psychic metamorphosis.

The play concludes with the appearance of the train conductor, an old Negro doing a soft shoe and half mumbling a

---

[31] See Robert Waelder, "The Principle of Multiple Function: Observations on Over-Determination," *Psychoanalytic Quarterly*, V (1936), 45–62; and Otto Fenichel, *Psychoanalytic Theory of Neuroses*, p. 467.

song. He greets a young Negro passenger and shuffles on down the aisle, tipping his hat to Lula as he passes out of the car. As a stereotypic image, this conclusion makes an ironic counterpoint. In terms of the internal consistency of the text, the conductor is the return of Clay's grandfather, a night watchman who, we may assume, was passive and deferential, and who survived; while the young Negro in the coach is the next victim on Lula's fatal list. If we analogize *Dutchman* with a nightmare or dream, we can say that the appearance of the conductor outside the frame of the drama proper is like the entrance into a dream of the dreamer himself, as if the play is ending in a self-reflexive gesture and we are about to wake up. The conductor's presence passes briefly like a shadow across the surface of the play, and the effect is as if Jones were to say: " Look, here I am as a playwright writing my words and doing my little dance for you—*I have survived,* but look at the role I have to play."

However, the conductor's train, like LeRoi Jones's *Dutchman,* is flying into blackness.

At Play in the Garden of Ambivalence: Andrew Marvell and the Green World

Jim Swan

In Andrew Marvell's Mower poems, the repeated theme is one of displacement from an original "home" within the nurturing green world. In "The Mower's Song," the original relationship is described as an exact congruence between mind and landscape:

> My mind was once the true survey
> Of all these meadows fresh and gay;
> And in the greenness of the grass
> Did see its hopes as in a glass.[1]

The mind begins as an exact reflection of a green world that simultaneously mirrors the mind's desire. In this poem, though, as in "Damon the Mower" and "The Mower to the Glowworms," this relationship is destroyed, and, in a manner left unexplained, it is a woman, Juliana, who destroys it. Elsewhere,[2] I have attempted to explain in psychoanalytic terms how it is Juliana's tantalizing sexuality (not her rejection of the Mower) that destroys a relationship very much like what D. W. Winnicott calls the "mirror" relationship between mother and nursing infant.[3] In "The

---

[1] "The Mower's Song" (1–4), in *The Selected Poetry of Marvell*, ed. Frank Kermode (New York: Signet, 1967). All quotations are from this edition, which I have preferred for its readable, modernized spelling and omission of italics and most capitals.

[2] "History, Pastoral and Desire: Andrew Marvell's Mower Poems," forthcoming in *International Review of Psycho-Analysis*.

[3] D. W. Winnicott, "Mirror Role of Mother and Family in Child Development" (1967), in *Playing and Reality* (New York: Basic Books, 1971), pp. 111–118. The essays collected in this volume trace Winnicott's development of the concepts of "transitional objects" and "transitional phenomena." For Winnicott, "transition" describes "the place where it can be said that *continuity* is giving place to *contiguity*" (p. 101), where the child is in the process of experiencing a separation out of a state of mother-infant fusion and into a relationship of self and other. The transition extends over a considerable period of time, and the child continues to maintain, symbolically, the original bond with the mother in its play with "transitional objects," like dolls or the proverbial "security blanket." Though I have purposely kept theoretical discussion out of this essay, it does depend a good deal on Winnicott's theories.

Garden," from which Marvell explicitly banishes genital love, he appears to reachieve in recreative fantasy the relationship lost by the Mower. Still, there is a good deal of anxious ambivalence underlying the achievement. In "The Mower's Song," the Mower experiences the loss of his "mirror" relationship with the green world as a catastrophe which drives him into an anxious, suicidal attempt to restore himself to a state of absolute fusion with the body of the world. And yet, in all of the Mower poems, at the level of the poem as a created verbal object, there is clearly an active delight in the play of poetic composition. This is the measure of the distance between Marvell and his poetic mask, a distance that allows him to play out in fantasy the catastrophic potential of his pastoral themes. The use of the Mower as a naive persona means that an implicit dramatic irony maintains the needed distance and control. But then, in a poem where Marvell speaks virtually in his own voice, as in "The Garden," the irony becomes explicit, the tone playful and arch, as the voice keeps its own distance with a kind of urbane *sprezzatura*.

It cannot be overemphasized that it is largely through the ironic play with language and form, which is a manner appropriate to ambivalence, that Marvell maintains control, rather than through the various possibilities of flight into transcendence available from Renaissance syncretism among Christian, Platonic, and Hermetic sources. This is especially true of "The Garden," which has been explained variously as a poem based either on the *Song of Solomon* or the *Enneads* or the *Pimander* or the *Meditations* of Descartes, to name only a few of the intellectual traditions claimed for the poem. Although these claims have developed intriguing and useful suggestions of the intellectual concerns that hover about the poem, they frequently do not touch what is actually said within it, and while attempting to fit the poem within one tradition or another they often do violence to the poem's playful, ironic manner, what Charles Lamb admired long ago as its "witty delicacy."[4] This characteristic failing of approaches based on intellectual history has been well documented by Kermode, Leishman, and, most recently, by Summers.[5] In a comment on the witty

---

[4] *Essays of Elia,* quoted by Pierre Legouis, *Andrew Marvell: Poet, Puritan, Patriot,* 2nd ed. (Oxford: Clarendon Press, 1968), p. 233.

[5] Frank Kermode, "The Argument of Marvell's 'Garden,' " *Essays in Criticism,*

couplet, "Society is all but rude, / To this delicious solitude,"
(15–16) Summers recognizes the ironic contrast between the
speaker's urbanity and his naively extravagant claims for solitary
repose: "Marvell's own phrasing assures us that the speaker must
have received the highest possible polish from society before he
could formulate the couplet; and he (or the author) knows it."[6]
The irony is a fundamental part of the poem's meaning, a control
over the action of retreat into the green world that enables Marvell to keep his balance between motives of complete bodily fusion
and absolute transcendence. The poem, though, has already been
so variously and repeatedly interpreted that the following analysis
will concentrate almost entirely on the three stanzas, V through
VII, that describe the speaker's experience within the garden.
Taken for granted are the jokes and paradoxes of the first four
stanzas that elevate solitary repose in the garden over all striving
in society for public fame or sexual conquest.

At least since William Empson's reading of the poem in the
1930's, the crucial passage has been stanza V, with its evocation of
an aggressive vegetable world urging its fruits on the passive
speaker:

> What wond'rous life is this I lead!
> Ripe apples drop about my head;
> The luscious clusters of the vine
> Upon my mouth do crush their wine;
> The nectarine, and curious peach,
> Into my hands themselves do reach;
> Stumbling on melons, as I pass,
> Ensnared with flowers, I fall on grass.

Readers have been divided in seeing the action of the plants as
menacing or benign, sexual or "innocent." Empson himself saw it
as a "forceful generosity" and a "triumph of the attempt to impose a sexual interest upon nature." Kermode disagreed that the
sensuous appeal of the garden is sexual, while he found Marvell's
allusion to the Fall more ironic than Empson did, a sign of the

2 (1952), 225–241; J.B. Leishman, *The Art of Marvell's Poetry* (New York: Funk &
Wagnalls, 1968), pp. 292–318; Joseph H. Summers, "Reading Marvell's 'Garden,' "
Centennial Review, 13 (1969), 18–37.
   [6] Summers, "Marvell's 'Garden,' " 27–28.

innocence of *this* garden's apples. Milton Klonsky, however, spoke of the "ripe round feminine forms" of the fruit, suggesting a steadily rising sensuality that is "climactically discharged." Harold W. Smith, adding oral engulfment to genital climax, discovered "a sort of giant fleshy orchid . . . which closes around the man and devours him." Such Freudian sport aroused the amused disdain of Pierre Legouis, although it is difficult to tell if his parody refutes or confirms the presence of a "sexual interest" in the stanza: "Indeed I wonder why nobody has yet (to my knowledge) given a psychoanalytic explanation of these 'melons': in Greek they are apples, Mr. Empson reminds us, and in French 'pommes' is sometimes applied, in a very informal style, to those globular charms that have made Marilyn Monroe and Gina Lollabrigida famous in our time." Legouis, in fact, unintentionally invokes the developmental perspective that makes sense of the poem's sexuality.[7] After all, it is not a question if there is any sexuality in stanza V, but what kind of sexuality it is. Stanzas III and IV explicitly—and jokingly—banish aggressive, genital sexuality, and it is clearly a passive oral sexuality being celebrated in the garden. Only, the "wond'rous life" of oral pleasure is experienced ambivalently. It is not even necessary to read back the revaluation of it in stanza VI as a lesser pleasure. There is enough menace in the way the fruits drop, reach, and crush themselves upon the passive speaker, ensnaring him and tripping him up, to arouse the reader's doubt and, perhaps, anxiety about the pleasure depicted. This has been asserted and denied so often in the poem's recent critical history that it is only reasonable to conclude that the poem has succeeded in communicating its ambivalence to its readers.

For instance, Ruth Wallerstein, upon turning her attention to stanza V, remarks how "with startling suddenness *we are absorbed in nature herself.*" And, then, a few paragraphs further on, she claims that in spite of the humorous tone, "there is something of violence in the stanza," as if sensuous delight has "taken possession of Marvell." Kermode, on the other hand, denies any menace: the garden is "not a trap for virtue but a paradise of perfect

[7] William Empson, *Some Versions of Pastoral* (London: Chatto & Windus, 1935), p. 132; Kermode, "Argument," 235; Milton Klonsky, "A Guide Through the Garden," *Sewanee Review*, 57 (1950), 21; Harold W. Smith, "Cowley, Marvell and the Second Temple," *Scrutiny*, 19 (1953), 190; Pierre Legouis, "Marvell and the New Critics," RES, N.S. 8 (1957), 384.

innocence," and he seems to be directly contradicting the language of the stanza ("ensnared"), as if trying to banish with just a wave of the scholar's hand any uneasiness about the experience. In Klonsky's account, orgasm leads to guilt and death—his reading of the withdrawal of mind from body—since the pleasure apparently requires punishment, a view firmly rejected by Pierre Legouis. Stanley Stewart sees the trees aggressively "thrust themselves upon a passive speaker." Similarly, Geoffrey Hartman speaks of "aggressive fruits" answering the speaker's love with "alarming intensity": in stanza V nature "hunts man into one body with it." Then Summers, answering Hartman, denies anything alarming or sexual about "pleasurably aggressive fruits" bestowing on the speaker "a truly 'wond'rous' ecstatic fulfillment of the body."[8] And so on.

These contrary responses arise, apparently, from a trick of style characteristic of Marvell, the use of violent or menacing verbs in otherwise pleasant and usually pastoral contexts. Two famous instances occur when Damon the Mower swings his scythe, "Depopulating all the ground," and when mowers at Appleton House, "With whistling scythe and elbow strong,/ . . . massacre the grass along." Marvell is the poetic master of double perspectives, simultaneous desire and fear, pleasure and terror. Thus Klonsky's account of pleasure followed by guilt and punish-

---

[8] Ruth Wallerstein, *Studies in Seventeenth-Century Poetic* (Madison: University of Wisconsin Press, 1950), pp. 325 (my italics), 328; Kermode "Argument," 235–236; Klonsky, "Guide," 22–23; Legouis, "New Critics," 384; Stanley N. Stewart, *The Enclosed Garden* (Madison: University of Wisconsin Press, 1966), p. 159; Geoffrey H. Hartman, "Marvell, St. Paul, and the Body of Hope," ELH, 31 (1964), 175, 180, 183; Summers, "Marvell's 'Garden,' " 31. Ann E. Berthoff, *The Resolved Soul: A Study of Marvell's Major Poems* (Princeton: Princeton University Press, 1970), pp. 147–148, says the body is "brought low by a surfeit of delight," and the poet's senses are "stupefied." Berthoff reads the stanza as comic personification, cautioning against construing it as "the bearer of dark and complex significance," lest the garden's innocence and solitude are rendered "meaningless." See also Rosalie L. Colie, *"My Ecchoing Song": Marvell's Poetry of Criticism* (Princeton: Princeton University Press, 1970); Colie's fine appreciation of the poem's anamorphic quality— "altering with altered angles of vision" (p. 152)—apparently does not extend to the doubleness of pleasure and terror in stanza V. Of course, the "stern" meanings of the Fall are irrelevant here, but the stanza's language vibrates between lush sensuality and violent or menacing action. Significantly, in her analysis of the stanza, (pp. 161–163) Colie never mentions the word "crush." A possible source for the language of the stanza, which I have not seen mentioned before, occurs as Guyon approaches Acrasia's Bower (*F. Q.* II. xii, 54): " . . . an embracing vine,/Whose bounches hanging downe seemd to entice / All passers by to taste their luscious wine, / And did them selves into their hands incline."

ment is wrong, if for no other reason, because pleasure and terror
occur *simultaneously* in the stanza. Like the garden/battlefield mata-
phors in "Upon Appleton House," its effect is a disturbing ambivalence, an uncertainty about point of view which readers have,
understandably, tried to resolve one way or the other. At one
level, the level identified by Summers as the poet's wit and polish,
there are strong controls over the experience, but at the level of
the speaker's own perceptions the double perspective of pleasure
and terror leaves the reader uncertain about even the possibility
of control, especially since the speaker seems to be so helplessly
passive. Like the lamb in the midst of Herrick's pastoral dream, in
"A Country Life,"[9] the speaker here is wooed to come and be
nourished, in an apparent reversal or denial of his own urgent
desire: rather than seeking nourishment, he finds it seeking him.
Only, unlike the lamb, Marvell's speaker has no Faunus watching
over his communion with the green world, no protective father
standing guard against ravening wolves. In the absence of any
such defense, the scene in the garden fills simultaneously with
pleasure and terror. Consequently, relief is gained only by the
mind's withdrawal, which is actually not one but two withdrawals,
in the next stanza.

Stanza VI, with its famous, vexing couplet about annihilation
and greenness, has probably occasioned more commentary during
the past fifty years than any other stanza in all of English Renaissance poetry:

> Meanwhile the mind, from pleasure less,
> Withdraws into its happiness:
> The mind, that ocean where each kind
> Does straight its own resemblance find:
> Yet it creates, transcending these,
> Far other worlds, and other seas;
> Annihilating all that's made
> To a green thought in a green shade.

---

[9] Robert Herrick, "A Country Life: To his Brother, Master *Thomas Herrick*," in
The Complete Poetry of Robert Herrick, ed. J. Max Patrick (New York: New York
University Press, 1963), ll. 49–52:
> Then dream, ye heare the Lamb by many a bleat
> Woo'd to come suck the milkie Teat:
> While *Faunus* in the Vision comes to keep,
> From rav'ning wolves, the fleecie sheep.

Without reviewing the many interpretations already made, I would prefer to suggest briefly how this stanza functions between stanzas V and VII in the light of what has been said already about stanza V. Right away, in the first line, the pleasures of the body are devalued as lesser pleasure, as if the anxiety they excite is of no consequence once the mind withdraws into itself and leaves them at a safe distance. And yet, once withdrawn, the mind is still in a passive attitude, one in which each "kind," each species of object in the world, immediately ("straight") and actively "finds" its "resemblance" within the mind. Marvell appears to be invoking a quasi-platonic theory of forms preexisting in the mind but remaining passively at rest until "found" by active sense-impressions impinging from outside. This is the mind's version of the body's passivity in stanza V.[10]

But then there is another withdrawal, one in which the mind transcends whatever "these" are. There is a problem of uncertain reference here, but the plural pronoun appears to mean both an implied world *and* the mind ("that ocean"), both each "kind" and its "resemblance." That is, the entire relationship between a passive mind and an active object of perception is transcended. Discovering its own activity, the mind creates other "seas" as well as other "worlds," that is, other forms of mind as well as other worlds. This is an important point: readers have tended to take the undialectical view that Marvell is invoking here only the mind's power to create other worlds, without itself being changed in the process. Instead, by an act of transcendence, the mind *re-creates* itself as well as the world, thus creating a new relationship between mind and world. But the syntax of the stanza still produces uncertainties. Is "annihilating" in apposition to

---

[10] See Daniel Stempl's interesting though contrary interpretation, *"The Garden: Marvell's Cartesian Ecstasy,"* JHI, 28 (1967), 108–109: "Marvell's sharp distinction between that Ocean, the mind, and the solid continental mass of the physical world is Cartesian, not Platonic. . . . Although the two realms are separate, they confront each other in the human brain; the code of the material world, transmitted through the senses as a mixture of noise and information, is *immediately,* but not simultaneously (the occasionalist theory), translated into a mental analogue which is part of an already existent parallel language. This, then, is how each kind finds its own resemblance." See, also, Colie's comment (*Ecchoing Song,* p. 164): " 'Each kind' must actively find 'its own resemblance' in the mind. As soon as that passivity is established by the syntax, the mind's activity is at once counterpoised; this mind can create into spatial and temporal infinity. . . . "

"creates," or is it a parallel construction with "transcending"? It may well be both. That is, the mind's act of transcending the world destroys it, annihilates it, and similarly the mind's creation of other worlds means destroying this one. Marvell is close to the view that thought "negates" the empirically perceived world, though he is more of a platonist than a materialist. Still, the important point is that the mind in stanza VI realizes itself, not in passive reflection, but in recreative activity, a qualitatively different relationship between world and mind from the one described in the first four lines.

But what is "a green thought in a green shade"? I want to attempt a simple answer, but one that does not have simple consequences. At one level, "A green thought in a green shade" is a beautifully succinct portrayal of the same relationship between mind and world already described as each kind finding its resemblance in a passive mind. That is, what exists already created in the material world appears to the transcendent mind as no more than a green thought in a green shade: it is a given, unchangeable object that can evoke no other relationship with the viewer than to summon a simple copy in the mind, a green thought in response to the green world. The transcendent mind, when it discovers its own recreative activity, looks back on its former relationship to the world as producing only a green thought in a green shade, a form of thought passively dependent on the actual presence of its object—hardly thought at all. And yet, uncertain syntax is again a problem, this time concerning the word "to." That is, alternatively, the mind perceives the created world as nothing *compared to* a green thought in a green shade, which Kermode glosses as "what can be imagined by a retired contemplative."[11] In this version, the passive relationship of the mind to the world represents, paradoxically, not the mode of thought transcended and destroyed but the mode *achieved*. In this case, too, it is a mistake to try to resolve this ambiguity one way or the other. The stanza asserts both the mind's transcendence *and* its regression to passive fusion with the world. The stanza's last line actually returns again to the passive condition of a mind, like the body in stanza V, flooded by the green world.

11 Kermode, ed., *Selected Poetry,* p. 109n.

Marvell has, in effect, withdrawn from the anxieties of passive oral pleasure to re-establish that pleasure in another, transcendent mode, "displaced upward" and evidently purged of anxiety. The actual bodily possibilities of a retreat into the green world are fraught with anxiety, but the same possibilities realized in fantasy and *as* fantasy liberate the pleasures of creative play.[12] The speaker in "The Garden" reachieves the mirror-relationship lost by the Mower: "a green thought in a green shade" describes the action of a mind which is the "true survey" of a green world that simultaneously mirrors the mind's desire. "Thought" is the key word, because it denotes an action in the midst of a phrase that literally colors it as passive inaction. Marvell has it both ways: by asserting the creativity of the mind he can then re-assert the pleasure of oral passivity as an *action* of the mind. The sixth stanza, lacking the personal "I" of the fifth and seventh, seems like a theoretical bridge between the two, an interpolation that asserts the mind's activity between the body's absorption within the green world and the soul's transcendence. The poem might conceivably have worked without the sixth stanza, the action moving directly from the body's fall in the midst of aggressive fruits to the shedding of the body at "some fruit-tree's mossy root." But then the poem would have simply repeated the debate between soul and body without discovering the recreative action of the mind, the level of consciousness that usually appears only through irony in Marvell's poems, but manifests itself here as the creative agency of the poem *in* the poem.

Then, having firmly located fantasy in relation to the body, Marvell's speaker can temporarily forget the body and allow his fantasy the freedom to play—although, as it happens, the play continues working out the ambivalence occasioned by the body's passive relation to the green world. The soul, shedding the body and gliding like a bird into the boughs of the trees, repeats the mind's double action of withdrawal and return. There it perches, halfway between the body and the ultimate withdrawal of a

---

[12] Cf. Harry Berger, Jr., "Marvell's 'Garden': Still another Interpretation," *MLQ*, 28 (1967), 293: "Poetry allows [Marvell] to withdraw in the image and not in the flesh, in a verbal and not an actual surrender. Since it is the poem which is the garden and green world, he may all the more securely give vent to the pleasure principle."

"longer flight," enjoying the full play of recreative fantasy. Marvell's silver-winged bird, waving the "various light" in its plumes, virtually overcomes the pain of the Mower's displacement by a paradoxical recovery of his "home" in the green world through an initial withdrawal from it. It is as if the Mower were to recover something like the nightingale's location in the landscape, although the bird in "The Garden" does not study, but engages effortlessly in recreative play. A better figure for comparison than the Mower, though, is the narrator in "Upon Appleton House."

The movement from stanza V to stanza VIII in "The Garden" parallels a similar movement from stanza LXXVII to stanza LXXXII in the longer poem. In "The Garden" the speaker moves from passive body to recreative mind, to the soul at play, perched securely in transitional space, and then in stanza VIII he emphasizes—with typically humorous extravagance—the necessary solitude, the "happy Garden-state" of Adam without Eve. Similarly, in "Upon Appleton House," the speaker moves from urging the green world to chain, fetter, even nail him in place, to a river surface that, mirror-like, makes everything "doubt / If they be in it or without," then to a moment of secure mediation while fishing, which is suddenly interrupted, exactly contrary to what happens in "The Garden," by the arrival of Maria and the speaker's shamefaced hurry to hide his "slight" pleasures from her. The parallel makes each poem a gloss on the other and reinforces the sense of how Marvell's solitary recreation is as much a troubled withdrawal from woman and the body as it is an achievement of creative fantasy. Repeatedly in Marvell's poems, a dangerous Juliana breaks into his solitude, or else his solitude is realized precisely as a retreat or defense against her.

But there is a remarkably close parallel between stanza VII in "The Garden" and stanza LXXXI in the longer poem. In both stanzas a figure perches in the branches or boughs, and in both stanzas occurs the phrase, "sliding foot," and the rhyme of foot and root. In "Upon Appleton House," the moment of fishing enjoyed by the narrator, suspended in branches above the river and dropping his lines to the fish below, is a moment when he achieves a brief, secure mediation between himself and the green world appearing in its regenerative form of a flood that has lately receded. Hanging in the trees above the water, and connected with it by his fishing lines, the narrator resolves the potentially anxious question whether he be "in it or without." He is in fact neither one nor the other, but still connected at a safe distance. The words describing his perch in the branches are particularly significant. What a pleasure it is, he says, "to suspend my sliding foot / On the osier's undermined root, / And in its branches tough to hang, / While at my lines the fishes twang." The perch is doubly precarious: a sliding foot on an undermined root. With the repeated uncertainty, the rhyme appears to equate foot and root as means of support and connection with the earth, while both the connection and the support seem about to fail. The same rhyme with the same phrase, "sliding foot," appears in stanza V of "The Garden." There the rhyme occurs at exactly the moment when the soul separates from the body.

The equivalence between foot and root is one that Marvell actually dramatizes in "Damon the Mower," where an autochthonous Damon, cutting "Each stroke between the earth and root" (76), slices his own ankle and mows himself down, "the mower mown" (80). The figure is an odd one, since a scythe does not, strictly speaking, cut between earth and root: it cuts grass above the root. Damon's scythe seems paradoxically both to cut the grass and, coming between earth and root, to pull it out of the earth. So, when he cuts his ankle, his wound appears to be both a mutilation and an uprooting, like a birth, from an autochthonous bond with the green world. In fact, the earlier stanzas of "Damon the Mower" suggest just such a bond which, in a variation on the Mower theme, he himself destroys.

From the Mower, then, comes a range of meaning for the equivalence implied by the rhyme between foot and root. In "Upon Appleton House," it is an equivalence of uncertainty over one's relationship to the green world: either rooted or uprooted, either standing or slipping and falling down. In "The Garden" it suggests a similar uncertainty at just the moment when the soul parts from the body and thus from a passive fusion with the green world. Only, in "The Garden," the soul does not withdraw altogether. But, like the narrator in the longer poem as he fishes from the osier's branches, the soul perches in transitional space, neither in nor altogether out of the green world. And there, enacting still another transitional figure, it does not passively reflect but meets with the movement of its wings a light made various in their waving.[13] The internal rhyme of "waves" and " various" blends their meanings together, so that it is uncertain whether the light is various to begin with or becomes various in the waving of the soul's silver plumes. As with "a green thought in a green shade," it is both, while this figure is much more active in a wider freedom of recreative play.

Stanza VIII returns to the ironic wit of the opening stanzas and, as remarked before, underscores the solitary character of the soul's play. In Eden before the creation of Eve, Adam enjoyed a perfect garden of solitary repose: "After a place so pure, and sweet, / What other help could yet be meet!" What is intriguing about the couplet is the explicit comparison of the place with the woman. Much of the puzzling quality of "The Garden" arises from the rejection of women simultaneously with the clearly erotic relation to a place. As Lawrence Hyman asked, "What kind of a garden is this where all the pleasures of passion can be enjoyed among trees and flowers, where plants are sexual and man is not?"[14] Again, the poem needs to be read in a developmental perspective. The place symbolizes, psychoanalytically speaking, the pre-genital but nonetheless erotic mutuality of a mother with her infant who is in the process of discovering his own active creativity. Marvell's play on "mate" and "meet" is exactly appropriate. In the happy solitude of the garden no mate could be a helpmeet: another's presence would not be "meet" (fitting) because it would spoil the *meeting* of the solitary wanderer with the garden in mutual play. But, then, this perfection existed securely only in the prelapsarian past:

> But 'twas beyond a mortal's share
> To wander solitary there:
> Two paradises 'twere in one
> To live in paradise alone. (61–4)

Now, in history, it can be found only in a retreat inward where, in

---

[13] Colie, *Ecchoing Song*, 166n, notes how Marvell reverses the expected syntax: "the bird 'Waves *in its Plumes* the various light' instead of waving its plumes in the light."
[14] Lawrence W. Hyman, "Marvell's *Garden*," *ELH*,, 25 (1958), 13.

fantasy, one momentarily recovers a perfect meeting of self and other in recreative play.[15]

Then, after this reminder of historical time, the last stanza carries the recreational impulse forward into the present as an experience of "sweet and wholesome hours" amidst a sundial of flowers and herbs. Here, the perfect meeting of mind and place is translated into the dimension of time, as the "industrious bee / Computes its time as well as we" (69–70). There is perhaps a hint of the lover's extravagant desire for himself and his Coy Mistress, if not to make the sun stand still, then to make him run. "Computing" time is gentler, not nearly so aggressive, but like the activity of a green thought, and of waving plumes, it means neither existing passively "in" time nor fleeing out of it into transcendence, but actively meeting and reckoning it with all the deliberation of a "skillful gard'ner" who lays out a sundial with herbs and flowers.

[15] Those who infer a Hermetic, prelapsarian androgyne in stanza VIII appear to have overlooked the contradiction in speaking of an "androgynous Adam" or "hermaphrodite man." (See the discussion by Harold E. Toliver, *Marvell's Ironic Vision* [New Haven: Yale University Press, 1965], pp. 141–142.) The logic of androgyny, strictly speaking, ought to work both ways, but where do we ever find any mention of an androgynous *Eve*? That we do not find any probably results from the same *andro*centric viewpoint implicit in Genesis, 2: "man" is created first and woman afterwards out of his side, in an apparent reversal of the man's experience of being born of woman. It may well be that "The Garden" reflects an acquaintance with Hermetic teachings shared by Fairfax and Marvell, but then both the poem and the *hermetica* are open to the same general interpretation, namely that the androgynous condition of "man" before the Fall is intelligible in a developmental perspective as an androcentric fantasy of mother-infant symbiosis. For the fullest account of the *hermetica* as a key to "The Garden," see Maren-Sophie Røstvig's essay, newly revised and expanded for a casebook on the poem, "Andrew Marvell's 'The Garden': A Hermetic Poem," in *Andrew Marvell: "The Garden,"* ed. T. O. Calhoun and J. M. Potter (Columbus, Ohio: Charles E. Merrill, 1970), pp. 75–90. Earlier versions of her essay appear in *English Studies*, 40 (1959), 65–76, and in *The Happy Man: Studies in the Metamorphoses of a Classical Ideal*, 2nd ed., I (Oslo: Norwegian University Press, 1962), pp. 154–172.

Leontes' Jealousy in *The Winter's Tale*

Murray M. Schwartz

Fatum est in partibus illis quas sinus abscondit.

Juvenal

Criticism of *The Winter's Tale* discloses an almost uniform denial of significant motivation in the representation of Leontes' jealousy. Norman Holland (in his pre-psychoanalytic criticism) writes: " In fact, [Shakespeare] is really quite perfunctory about the source of trouble; he doesn't even bother to motivate Leontes' jealousy." [1] Frank Kermode thinks that " Shakespeare removes Leontes' motives for jealousy." [2] G. W. Knight, committed to theological notions of Shakespeare's divine inspiration, says " His evil is self-born and unmotivated." [3] A. D. Nutall, to my mind the play's most responsive critic, courts " Freudian " suggestions in the text but tactfully avoids a psychoanalytic reading of Leontes' delusions.[4] J. H. P. Pafford, the editor of the Arden edition, states flatly: " Causes of the jealousy are no concern of ours." [5] D. A. Traversi speaks only of "The evil impulse which comes to the surface...." [6] Implicit in this dominant attitude toward Leontes' jealousy is the proposition that its *specific* expressions lack coherent psychological significance. Leontes simply goes mad without cause. In the language of the French psychoanalyst J. Lacan, we can say that these critics refuse to take Shakespeare's metaphors seriously as " significant." [7]

Of course, these critics are responding to one aspect of the play's dramatic reality. There is no *external* explanation of

---

[1] *The Shakespearean Imagination* (Bloomington, 1964), p. 284.
[2] *Shakespeare: The Final Plays* (London, 1963), p. 30.
[3] *The Crown of Life* (London, 1947), p. 84.
[4] *Shakespeare: The Winter's Tale* (London, 1966), p. 22.
[5] "Introduction," *The Winter's Tale* (London, 1965). Arden edition, p. lxxii.
[6] *Shakespeare: The Last Phase* (London, 1955), p. 112.
[7] "The Insistence of the Letter in the Unconscious," in *Structuralism*, ed. J. Ehrmann (New York, 1970). In Lacan's terminology, Leontes' metaphors "signify" or represent unconscious traumas.

Leontes' behavior provided for us. What the critics call lack of motivation is lack of rationalization. Yet, even if there were external motivation, a critical response that denies unconscious motives would impoverish the power of Shakespeare's over-determined language.[8] In psychoanalytic terms, we can say that the literary creation is always an attempt to synthesize private and unconscious motives with public forms of comprehending the meanings of experience. Such a synthesis is what we mean by symbolic discourse.[9] *The Winter's Tale*, then, can be understood to dramatize not "motiveless" jealousy, but jealousy whose motivation is embodied in the structure of linguistic and personal relationships acted out on the stage (and in our minds). The function of criticism is to locate the stylistic terms of its expression and the unconscious significance of those terms.

Three psychoanalytically informed critics have preceded me in the analysis of Leontes' jealousy.

J. I. M. Stewart was the first to recognize that Leontes' jealousy can be partially explained by applying Freud's formula to the play: " I do not love him; she does." [10] In this explanation, Leontes converts the sexual motive of his tie to Polixenes into a perverse relationship between his wife and his friend. Hermione replaces Leontes and, in his fantasy, acts out the prohibited homosexual role Leontes repudiates in himself. This seems plausible, although Stewart reaches far for justification when he accepts Dover Wilson's suggestion that Leontes confesses actual " immoralities " to Camillo, his " priest-like " vehicle of purification. No actual homosexual event need precede the onset of such jealousy as Leontes', and the play gives us at best only unspecified suggestions of boyhood events, as when Leontes, facing Florizel in Act V, says:

> Were I but twenty-one,
> Your father's image is so hit in you,
> His very air, that I should call you brother,

[8] See Robert Waelder's paper, "The Principle of Multiple Function," *Psychoanalytic Quarterly*, V (1936), pp. 45–62.

[9] See Marion Milner, "Psycho-Analysis and Art," in *Psychoanalysis and Contemporary Thought*, ed. John D. Sutherland (New York, 1959), pp. 77–101.

[10] *Character and Motive in Shakespeare* (London, 1949), pp. 30–39.

> As I did him, and speak of something wildly
> By us performed before.   (V.i.125-29) [11]

Besides, even if we hypothesize some actual homosexual violation, a procedure which seems to me itself to violate the boundary between the play as a work of art and the play as a transcript
of life, we gain little, for the focus of Leontes' rage cannot be
accounted for if we assume that Hermione is merely a surrogate
for himself in relation to Polixenes. Freud's formula, taken in
itself and without consideration of the whole dynamics of
Leontes' " disease," has little heuristic value. It closes off rather
than opens up a consideration of jealousy in the play as a
whole.[12]

C. L. Barber, in his sensitive essay on the play, accepts
Stewart's application of Freud but goes on to suggest a deeper
fabric of motives:

> I have found Stewart's application of Freud convincing,
> and I think one can make the case even stronger by close
> analysis of the opening scene. Beneath this level of psycho-
> logical extrapolation there is another, still less directly
> demonstrable, that relates Leontes' jealousy to very early
> levels of infancy, when the child, though he communicates
> richly with the maternal side of the mother, fears and
> hates the father's power to possess her sexually. The pro-
> jective jealousy can put the rival in the position of the
> archaic father. An accepted and accepting relation to the
> father is a condition of positive relationships to other men,
> so the onset of jealousy means as important a loss of rela-
> tion to the crucial man as to the crucial woman, crucial
> in the sense that they are those in whom is invested the
> core of love which has its root in childhood and is the

[11] Quotations from *The Winter's Tale* follow the Arden edition (London,
1965).

[12] Contemporary analysts do not regard paranoia simply as a defense against
homosexuality. See David Shapiro, *Neurotic Styles* (New York, 1965), Chapter
3 on " Paranoid Style." Charles Rycroft writes, " Contemporary analysts tend
to reverse the relationship and regard homosexuality as a defensive technique
for dealing with paranoid fears by submission." Quoted by Vincent Brome,
Freud and His Early Circle (New York, 1969), p. 129. This defensive technique
is precisely how Posthumus resolves his paranoia in *Cymbeline*.

ground of piety toward the larger powers of life which we
encounter first through the parents.[13]

Leontes in his jealousy, then, loses contact with the benevolent aspects of both parents and, in the concluding scenes,
regains access to the maternal Hermione after first reconciling
himself to Polixenes through his intercession on behalf of the
magical pair of children, Florizel and Perdita. The psychology of this loss and recovery is immensely complex in the play,
as Professor Barber realizes, and I believe that his suggestion,
that we need a closer analysis of the first scenes to see how this
complex projective process develops, can be followed fruitfully.
Let me suggest here that the maternity of the mother is not
wholly benevolent; we may find that deeper determining
motives than those involved in the split between mother and
father inform the unconscious logic of the play.

The most extensive discussion of Leontes' jealousy is
Stephen Reid's hypothetical reconstruction of the Oedipal dynamics which must underlie so extensive a breakdown of the
capacity for reciprocal relations with others. Shakespeare, Reid
argues, presents us with a pathological condition involving the
following determinants: (1) an original incestuous wish toward
the mother; (2) a subsequent placating attitude toward the
father which activates the very fear of castration it was intended
to ward off; (3) a final turning toward the protective strength
of the mother as a defense against the original wish and subsequent fear. In the departure scene (I.ii), Leontes turns
toward the protective strength of Hermione only to fantasize
that she has betrayed him by reviving the homosexual attraction he has been covertly striving to control. Reid believes that
Leontes' delusional jealousy centers ultimately in his inability
to accept his "feminine self," and that the rest of the play is
designed to recover, by a mixture of mimetic drama and allegory, the original bond between the men by embodying the
fulfillment of homosexual attraction in the love of Florizel and
Perdita. " Perdita is Leontes' feminine self; Florizel is Polixenes'

[13] " 'Thou that begett'st him that did thee beget': Transformation in *Pericles*
and *The Winter's Tale*," *Shakespeare Survey*, 22, p. 75.

masculine self. Their union is the fulfillment of Leontes' homosexual wish." [14]

Professors Barber and Reid seem to agree that the crucial relationship restored symbolically and actually is the friendship between Leontes and Polixenes, whatever name we choose to give it. Yet, neither dwells on the actual nature of their bond as it is expressed in the text of the play. I believe, however, that the manifest and unconscious features of that bond reveal a special kind of relationship which Leontes, even in his jealousy, and the play as a whole, strive to reconstitute.

In the opening scenes of *The Winter's Tale*, before the shock of Leontes' jealousy ruptures the intricate web of aggressive playfulness and formality that characterizes courtly dialogue, Shakespeare offers us two descriptions of the childhood affection between Leontes and Polixenes. The first is spoken by Camillo, and it recalls the image of the tree made whole at the end of *Cymbeline:* [15]

> Sicilia cannot show himself over-kind to Bohemia. They were trained together in their childhoods, and there rooted betwixt them then such an affection which cannot choose but branch now. Since their more mature dignities and royal necessities made separation of their society, their encounters, though not personal, have been royally attorneyed with interchange of gifts, letters, loving embassies, that they have seemed to be together, though absent; shook hands, as over a vast; and embraced, as it were, from the ends of opposed winds. The heavens continue their loves!   (I.1.21-32)

The more we read *The Winter's Tale,* the more this speech becomes a metaphor of the whole. Variations of many words (and the evocation of ideal relationships in words) recur,

[14] " 'The Winter's Tale,'" *American Imago*, XXVII (1970), pp. 263–267. Reid builds his analysis in agreement with W. H. Auden's conviction that "Leontes is a classic case of paranoid sexual jealousy due to repressed homosexual feelings." "The Alienated City: Reflections on 'Othello,' " *Encounter*, 1961, p. 11.
[15] See *Cymbeline*, Act V, scene v, ll. 436–443.

gathering significance as their meaning and suggestiveness meta-morphoses in new contexts. The hands, for example, here metonymic images of union, will shortly become the sign of the bond between Leontes and Hermione ("And clap thyself my love"). Then, as Leontes becomes immersed in a fantasy of betrayal, the hands become a symbol of boundary violation, " paddling palms, and pinching fingers," " virginalling/Upon his palm." The image of " a vast," an immense space (usually ominous in Shakespeare) suggests, in its temporal dimension, the " wide gap of time " to which Leontes refers in the play's last lines. Just as here the " vast" is bridged by symbolic gestures which would undo the " necessities " of separation in space and absence in time, at the end, language, social discourse, fills the gap of time " since first/We were dissever'd." The story is filled in, and time, like a container, filled up. In the world of romance and in dreams, space and time are interchangeable categories.

Interchangeable categories also function to provide the illusion of presence in *The Winter's Tale*. The artifice of culture, " gifts, letters, loving embassies," substitutes for personal encounters. Interchange of symbols represents interchange of physical actions, a shaking of hands, an embrace. In the face of separation and distance, it is the work of art to mediate between " then " and "now," to express symbolic continuity. Symbolic action, then, counters the real divisions of " mature dignities and royal necessities." In the extent of their exchanges, we see the depth of their bond and the need for union that manifestly informs it.

Yet, for all of Camillo's emphasis on the efficacy of symbolic exchange, he is aware that his metaphors are not identical with reality. The embrace, after all, is only " as it were," and they only " seemed to be together, though absent." Separation *is* real, and they *have* been absent. As he praises the art of their exchanges, he also makes us aware of the realities which generate the need for and the limits of that very art. In art, they show themselves the way they want to seem and to be seen; they take and give symbols and metaphors.

Why? Camillo has an answer for us, if we take the art of his metaphor seriously. The answer is that they want to preserve by symbolic means a childhood bond, an affective union at the root of the whole artifice of their culture. It is the symbiotic nature of this bond that his metaphor expresses, and even the subtle ambiguity of " branch " (it suggests both separation and growth) retains the idea of a common root. The process of growth and separation is here imagined in terms of dual unity.[16] Leontes and Polixenes shared a communion, rooted deeper than their conscious wills; it " cannot choose but branch now."

Dual unity is a psychoanalytic paradox in which two equals one, as in " The Phoenix and the Turtle ":

> Hearts remote, yet not asunder;
> Distance and no space was seen
> 'Twixt this Turtle and his queen:
> But in them it were a wonder.   (29-32)

But the turtle here is at one with his queen, not his boyhood friend. The rooted affection of Leontes and Polixenes is itself rooted ontogenetically in the mother-child relationship, as we shall see. The myth of childhood affection, I am suggesting, preserves in masculine form a narcissistic and idealized version of the mother's dual unity with the son. Notice how in Camillo's speech there is no differentiation of one king from the other, either in image or in action. The speech implicitly denies any difference between the two. Indeed, the deepest function of their exchanges is to deny or undo change itself. The denial of difference (spatial) and the denial of change (temporal) leaves us with the fantasy of perfect mutuality. *The Winter's Tale* is a play about how this fantasy of perfect mutuality can be made to survive the impact of " great difference " (I.i.3) and yet remain itself; or, in psychoanalytic terms, how Shakespeare seeks to realize the wish for oral perfection without the denial of social and sexual differences either through violence or through individual infantile regression.

The second description of childhood affection bears out the implications of Camillo's metaphor, but its dramatic con-

---

[16]See Géza Roheim, *Magic and Schizophrenia* (New York, 1955). The fullest expression of dual unity in Shakespearean language occurs in *A Midsummer Night's Dream*, Act III, scene ii, ll. 201–211.

text extends the consequences of the wish for dual unity. After being convinced (should we say " seduced "?) by the power of Hermione's words ("a lady's Verily's/As potent as a lord's " [I.ii.50-51]) to remain in Sicily longer, Polixenes responds to Hermione's probing of his and Leontes' boyhoods with a denial of difference and an assertion of innocence:

> *Her.*   Was not my lord
>   The verier wag o' th' two?
>
> *Pol.* We were as twinn'd lambs that did frisk i' th' sun,
>   And bleat the one at th' other: what we chang'd
>   Was innocence for innocence; we knew not
>   The doctrine of ill-doing, not dream'd
>   That any did.   (I.ii.65-71)

He insists on identity, mutuality, a time prior to the frustrations of time and the vicissitudes of socially categorized guilt. A few lines later he explicitly dissociates that time from the " hereditary " guilt of original sin:

>   Had we pursu'd that life,
>   And our weak spirits ne'er been higher rear'd
>   With stronger blood, we should have answer'd heaven
>   Boldly ' not guilty,' the imposition clear'd
>   Hereditary ours.   (71-75)

Polixenes' language suggests that the fall into post-edenic guilt involves the " imposition " of phallic desire (" The expense of spirit in a waste of shame ") , with a consequent splitting of their masculine egos:

>   O my most sacred lady,
>   Temptations have since then been born to's; for
>   In those unfledg'd days was my wife a girl,
>   Your precious self had then not cross'd the eyes
>   Of my young playfellow.   (76-80)

His repeated " then " expresses the tension adhering to this developmental fantasy. Now, in the immediate relationship with Hermione, he would preserve her as an idol (" sacred," " precious ") even as he imagines her to be the source of sexual temptations. In her sacredness Hermione embodies for men the antidote to separation inherent in all religious structures, and this attribute of herself remains in precarious contact with its opposite, as she points out when she says, " Of this make no conclusion, lest you say/Your queen and I are devils " (81-82) . The sacred is the realm of infantile desire raised to the level of collective ideal identities beyond change, but the devil is a shape-shifter in the minds of men; hence the play's obsession with forms of constancy, fixity, with oaths and vows. Polixenes' metaphor of birth (" born to's ") suggests both that the men themselves are the source of " temptations " and that they identify with the woman as a mother. (There is even a hint, in " cross'd the eyes," of the visual intoxication that will be brought to full expression in the final scene and reiterated throughout when sacred boundaries are confirmed or jeopardized.) [17]

Hermione probes Polixenes' idealization, puts the myth in perspective, so that we recognize the wish simultaneously with the actuality of the present. They are not innocent, and the heritage of the myth is the ambivalence it denies. The realm of the sacred is inseparable from the realm of guilt; the obverse of the wish for communion with a narcissistic version of oneself is a defensive splitting of the ego. The myth of " twinn'd lambs " is a retrospective idealization of boyhood in the interest of clinging to a paradisal version of pre-Oedipal existence when confronted by the temptation toward sexual contact. Michael Balint points out that " a truly narcissistic man or woman is in fact a pretense only. They are desperately dependent on their environment, and their narcissism can be preserved only on the condition that their environment is willing, or can be forced, to look after them." [18] In their attempt to arrest time, the men of the play are forced to seek the image of the past in every present gesture. This explains why Polixenes so readily acquiesces to Hermione's verbal manipulations. He will not risk the loss of her as a " kind hostess " (I.i.60) . His constancy consists in the capacity to change in ways that preserve her sacred status, or, to put it negatively, to change in ways that express his ambivalence while preserving him from its consequences.

---

[17] See Weston La Barre, *The Ghost Dance: Origins of Religion* (New York, 1970) , Chapter III, " The First World."
[18] *The Basic Fault: Therapeutic Aspects of Regression* (London, 1968) , p. 55.

Leontes and Polixenes may be manifest opposites in Act I, but latently they remain as identical as twins, each a mirror image of the other. Great difference, on one level, is no difference at all. Each is absolutely dependent on external sources of narcissistic supplies, each projects a split image of woman (the maternal nourisher becoming a malevolent seductress when they feel deprived of signs of love), each succumbs to change in the interest of validating the identifications and values he believes he shares with the other. Polixenes avoids contact with Leontes' jealousy in a way which affirms the system of internalized controls that Leontes sexualizes: [19]

> This jealousy
> Is for a precious creature: as she's rare,
> Must it be great; and, as his person's mighty,
> Must it be violent; and as he does conceive
> He is dishonour'd by a man which ever
> Profess'd to him; why, his revenges must
> In that be made more bitter.   (I.ii.451-57)

From the perspective of the internalized taboo, Leontes *must* become violent and seek the restoration of purity through vengeance. Within the structure of the sacred myth he acts out a psychologically appropriate pathology. He contains the disease which corresponds to the religious therapy the play as a whole acts out.

In respect to narcissistic self-definition and the split conception of woman, Polixenes, Leontes, Antigonus and Camillo are doubles of one another. Each reflects a specific orientation toward the taboo on sexualized touch which is an integral part of the Platonized conception of woman. Camillo " cannot/ Believe this crack to be in my dread mistress/ (So sovereignly being honourable) " (I.ii.321-23). And Antigonus offers us a version of masculine pathology second in its primary process logic only to Leontes' confusions:

---

[19] Later Polixenes makes Camillo, in effect, into a maternal support from whom separation is equivalent to death. " I pray thee, good Camillo, be no more importunate: 'tis a sickness denying thee anything; a death to grant this " (IV.ii.1-3). And a few lines later, ". . . the need I have of thee, thine own goodness hath made; better not to have had thee than thus to want thee" (IV.ii.11-13). This is the language of symbiotic relations.

> Be she honour-flaw'd,
> I have three daughters: the eldest is eleven;
> The second and the third, nine and some five:
> If this prove true, they'll pay for 't. By mine honour
> I'll geld 'em all; fourteen they shall not see
> To bring false generations: they are co-heirs,
> And I had rather glib myself, than they
> Should not produce fair issue.[20]   (II.i.143-50)

In this confusion of his own potency with feminine loyalty, in the view of women as the guarantors of masculine honor, and in his insistence on the economics of moral debt, Antigonus duplicates the dynamics of the disease he manifestly repudiates. He becomes, therefore, the surrogate for his master and the carrier of Paulina's curse (II.ii.76-79), the vehicle for Shakespeare's displaced exorcism of Leontes' jealousy.

In his paranoid delusions of betrayal, Leontes acts out the whole range of pathological boundary violations that define the lower half of the circle of grace. Unlike his double, who avoids conflict until Act IV and who, significantly, never actually has the wife he mentions (even at the end when three other pairs are created), Leontes becomes the play's vehicle for the release of the repressed. Shakespeare condenses in him the fragmented components of the de-differentiated psyche symbolically represented in *Cymbeline* by a whole range of characters— Cloten, Iachimo, Posthumus, and Cymbeline. In his jealousy, we see the great difference between accommodation of oneself to the myths of ideal mutuality and feminine sacredness and the precariously contained psychic realities that give rise to those myths. In *The Winter's Tale*, jealousy and the sacred are dialectical terms; each implies the other, as separation implies union or winter spring.

In the departure scene (I.ii), Leontes is reticent until he erupts (at line 108), and he seems less than determined to reciprocate Polixenes' rich compliments. After Hermione succeeds

---

[20] Gelding daughters means destroying their genitals. *Oxford English Dictionary* under *geld* l.b. says, "To extirpate the ovaries of (a female), to spay." In 1557 Tusser first used the word in this sense, referring, of course, to animals. Antigonus' fondness for viewing women as horse-like carries on a strand of imagery first articulated by Hermione (I.ii.94–96).

in retaining Polixenes, he seems defeated in comparison to her.
In lines that seem manifestly designed to compliment her, he
evokes the sense of his deprivation:

> Why, that was when
> Three crabbed months had sour'd themselves to death,
> Ere I could make thee open thy white hand,
> And clap thyself my love; then didst thou utter
> ' I am yours forever.'   (I.ii.101-105)

He seems to be analogizing past and present: now, by the
power of her words, she has kept Polixenes' presence, just as
then she vowed her own presence. But the lines are obliquely
accusative, as if to say, " Then you vowed to be mine forever,
but now you have violated that vow in giving yourself to my
rival. Then I felt as deprived of love as a child abandoned by
a mother (soured to death) and now I feel just as excluded." [21]
Almost immediately after he speaks Hermione gives her hand
to Polixenes, and Leontes is instantly jealous.[22]

> [*Aside*] Too hot, too hot!
> To mingle friendship far is mingling bloods.
> I have *tremor cordis* on me: my heart dances,
> But not for joy—not joy. This entertainment
> May a free face put on, derive a liberty
> From heartiness, from bounty, fertile bosom,
> And well become the agent: 't may, I grant:
> But to be paddling palms, and pinching fingers . . .
>
> (I.ii.108-115)

As Professor Barber points out,[23] "mingling friendship far" is
as appropriate to his relationship to Polixenes as it is a distortion of present reality. Beneath the myth of ideal masculine
correspondence there lies a deeper set of fantasies in which the

[21] Reid recognizes the importance of these lines in the course of his own
analysis of this scene. In " Mourning and Melancholia," Freud lends support
to my argument: " The loss of a love-object constitutes an excellent opportunity
for the ambivalence in love-relationships to make itself affective and come to
the open." *Standard Edition*, XIV, pp. 250-251.

[22] The Stage Direction at 1.108, " *Giving her hand to Polixenes*," is not in
the Folio, but it seems perfectly appropriate at that point, since it concretizes
the growing suggestiveness of the play's language.

[23] *Op. cit.*, p. 76.

brothers are rivals for maternal love, the "fertile bosom" Leontes imagines violated by sexualized contact. Leontes fantasizes the loss of the boundary between sublimated forms of erotic involvement and usurped gratification in defiance of the superego. As his disease develops, we see a massive projection of the contents of a psyche, an attempt simultaneously to relieve himself of an inner burden of guilt and to seek punishment for his forbidden wishes.

Paranoia is a form of psychic imprisonment in which the loss of ego boundaries makes the external world *nothing but* a confluence of symbols, selected according to subjective and ambivalent wishes and fears. For the paranoid, others become what D. W. Winnicott has called "subjective objects," embodiments of psychic realities that exist only in relation to the subject.[24] Others lose their otherness. In this sense, paranoia can be seen as a radical denial of separation, a perversion of the mutuality of the boyhood myth which shares with it a crucial element. In his delusions Leontes identifies with both Hermione and Polixenes and tries desperately to exclude himself from the fantasies he projects on to them.

Leontes surrenders to Polixenes and Hermione the impulses and identifications he harbors in himself. We can find all of the components previous critics have identified, but this does not seem to get at the unconscious strategies of his disease. Polixenes does become the archaic image of the father Leontes fears, the "harlot king" (II.iii.4) of childhood fantasy.

> Fie, fie! no thought of him:
> The very thought of my revenges that way
> Recoil upon me: in himself too mighty,
> And in his parties, his alliance; let him be
> Until a time may serve.   (II.iii.18-22)

And Hermione is transformed in his perception into a container of disease, at once infected by genital penetration and possessed as a narcissistic ornament by the intrusive other, Polixenes, "he that wears her like her medal, hanging about

---

[24] "Communicating and Not Communicating Leading to a Study of Certain Opposites" (1963), in *The Maturational Process and the Facilitating Environment* (New York, 1965), pp. 179-192.

his neck . . ." (I.ii.307-308). In his psychic decomposition
Leontes descends, " o'er head and ears a fork'd one " (I.ii.186),
into a nightmare world where the fluid boundary " twixt his
and mine " (I.ii.134) threatens him with the psychotic loss of
the distinction between perception and hallucination, even to
the point of somatic enactment of the punishments he dreads:

> You smell this business with a sense as cold
> As is a dead man's nose: but I do see't and feel't,
> As you feel doing thus; and see withal
> The instruments that feel.[25]   (II.i.151-154)

His ego devolves to the condition of bodily responsiveness;
he cannot choose but branch the horns of the cuckold, nor deny
by projection the identifications within him. Like Posthumus
in *Cymbeline,* Leontes can only expand the circle of contamination in his effort to rid the borders of his consciousness of the
internalized parents he imagines his wife and friend to be.
Paranoia is a defense which fails at the moment of its enactment,
for to externalize what is internally intolerable is to find it
everywhere, and to risk the emptying of the self in the effort to
restore inner and outer purity. It corresponds to the effort of
the infant who projects aggressive wishes on to the source of
nourishment only to " discover " outside the transformation
repudiated by the ego.[26] Once projected, the inner wishes and

---

[25] " The instruments that feel " are, according to the Arden note, " pre-
sumably Leontes' fingers," but the line also carries genital significance, as the
hands frequently do in Shakespeare. Compare *Cymbeline,* I.vii. 99-112. See
Eric Partridge, *Shakespeare's Bawdy* (New York, 1960), entries under " instrument " and " finger."

[26] See Marion Milner, *On Not Being Able to Paint* (New York, 1957), p.
40. In one of her " free " drawings, she made the shape of a baby's bottle which,
instead of a nipple, has a mouth held up in a pleading posture. " And here
I suddenly became aware of a reversal," she says, " for the bottle was demanding
from the baby, not the baby from the bottle." This, in a kind of " original "
crystalization, is a central strategy of Leontes' paranoia. See also Harold Searles,
" The Sources of the Anxiety in Paranoid Schizophrenia " (1961), in *Collected
Papers on Schizophrenia and Related Subjects* (New York, 1965), pp. 465-486.
On p. 466 Searles writes against the view that paranoia simply defends against
repressed homosexual desires. " It seems to me a more adequate explanation to
think of the persecutory figure as emerging into the forefront of the patient's
concern, not primarily because of repressed homosexual interest on the latter's
part, but rather because the persecutory figure is that one . . . who most readily
lends himself to reflecting or personifying those qualities which the patient is
having most vigorously to repudiate in himself and project on to the outer
world."

objects seem utterly alien to the ego, and yet Leontes clings
to his fantasy as if his life depended on it:

> is this nothing?
> Why then the world, and all that's in't, is nothing,
> The covering sky is nothing, Bohemia nothing,
> My wife is nothing, and nothing have these nothings,
> If this be nothing.   (I.ii.292-296)

Love recoils to its opposite when confronted with what seems to
be a challenge to its totality. The fantasy is globalized; on its
truth depends the ontological status of the whole world, as if
to lose the bond, however painful, with the externalized embodiments of himself were to lose himself entirely. Paranoia
is better than nothing, even if it hinges the universe on the
contingency of a hypothesis. If his delusion is not real, then
the world is empty of identities. And if it is real, then he is
excluded from the world of others, like a child who suddenly
perceives that parental intimacy is not just *for him,* but has an
autonomy of its own.

In his progression from the sudden flooding of his ego in
scene ii to the apparently catastrophic loss of his wife and
children in the clamor of Act III, Leontes grasps simultaneously
for external validation of his condition and for means of annihilating the monstrous conception at its source. It is as if his
disease acts out a grotesque parody of creation itself, a mockery
of the larger fertility Hermione's generativity symbolizes. " Go,
play, boy, play: thy mother plays, and I/Play too; but so dis-
grac'd a part, whose issue/Will hiss me to my grave " (I.ii.187-
89). Imagining himself deprived of nurturant relatedness,
hating the violations he fantasizes, yet terrified of losing contact
with symbolic others, Leontes " gives birth " in an abstract
version of the primal scene, the intercourse of something and
nothing:

> Affection! thy intention stabs the center:
> Thou dost make possible things not so held,
> Communicat'st with dreams;—how can this be?—
> With what's unreal thou coactive art,
> And fellow'st nothing: then 'tis very credent
> Thou may'st co-join with something; and thou dost,

(And that beyond commission) and I find it,
(And that to the infection of my brains
And hard'ning of my brows).   (I.ii.138-146)

The disease happens to him; in effect, Leontes watches himself get lost and then finds himself in the fantasy to which he himself has metaphorically given birth. We witness his regression *in process*.[27] Camillo and Polixenes confirm the nature of this process even as they avoid its issue:

Pol.   How should this grow?

Cam. I know not: but I am sure 'tis safer to
        Avoid what's grown than question how 'tis born.
                                        (I.ii.431-433)

Fantasizing the loss of " some province, and a region/Lov'd as he loves himself " (I.ii.369-370), Leontes fills the vacuum with pathologically conceived violations of the sacred space Hermione occupies in the minds of the others at the court. The opposite of symbiotic relatedness is the narcissistic confusion of self and other by the generation of a pseudo-universe, an autarchic assumption of omnipotence. Even if he plays a dis-graced part, he writes the play himself.[28]

But only to a degree, for Shakespeare does not risk degree in this play, but keeps Leontes bounded by others' refusal of collusion in his delusions, and by structural and linguistic ironies that reveal in instance after instance that his projections are self-descriptions and that his assumption of autonomy is based on a sequence of dependency relationships. As he moves closer toward the attempt to annihilate his fears he also moves toward cloture with the parental authorities who will subdue his violence by the counter-violence of the sacred the play is designed to validate. Paulina, and above her, Apollo, reassert the ontological status of the identities Leontes contaminates.

His jealousy saturates Leontes' language with overdeter-

---

[27] In the initial stages of his paranoia, Leontes retains the capacity for what Roy Schafer calls "reflexive self representation." Only later, and especially in the court scene (III.ii), does he merge completely with his fantasy. See Schafer's *Aspects of Internalization* (New York, 1968), pp. 85–97.

[28] Northrop Frye has recognized this pattern. See his "Recognition in *The Winter's Tale*," in *Shakespeare: The Winter's Tale: A Casebook*, ed. Kenneth Muir (London, 1968), p. 194.

mined meanings and condensed fantasies. Metaphors of violent punishment intrude upon his effort at self-vindication, making his articulation of imaginary betrayal into a confession of anxiety related to all psychosexual levels. For example, he says to Camillo:

> Dost think I am so muddy, so unsettled,
> To appoint myself in this vexation; sully
> The purity and whiteness of my sheets,
> (Which to preserve is sleep, which being spotted
> Is goads, thorns, nettles, tails of wasps)
> Give scandal to the blood o' th' prince, my son,
> (Who I do think is mine and love as mine)
> Without ripe moving to 't? Would I do this?
> Could man so blench?   (I.ii.325-333)

His effort at rhetorical negation of the fantasy succeeds only in elaborating the ambivalence he would deny. Anal contamination is denied and expressed, castration anxiety accompanies the thought of contaminated purity, superego anxiety leads him to externalize mockery, and doubt of his paternal role is triggered by the fear of losing possession of the pure woman. On one level, Leontes fantasizes himself replaced by Polixenes:

> Go to, go to!
> How she holds up the neb, the bill to him!
> And arms her with the boldness of a wife
> To her allowing husband!   (I.ii.182-185)

Here Polixenes is virtually invited to usurp oral gratification. A few lines later Hermione becomes his property, the imagery becomes genital, and there is a clear implication that Leontes identifies with the woman:

> And many a man there is (even at this present,
> Now, while I speak this) holds his wife by th' arm,
> That little thinks she has been sluic'd in's absence
> And his pond fish'd by his next neighbour, by
> Sir Smile, his neighbor: nay, there's comfort in't,
> Whiles other men have gates, and those gates open'd
> As mine, against their will.   (I.ii.192-198)

The genital violation of the woman-as-property is equivalent to homosexual assault. He is not differentiated from her, nor is his own psychic activity (for he is "angling now" [I.ii.180]) differentiated from the fantasized activity of others. Neither are Hermione and Polixenes differentiated from one another:

> Is whispering nothing?
> Is leaning cheek to cheek? is meeting noses?
> Kissing with inside lip? stopping the career
> Of laughter with a sigh (a note infallible
> Of breaking honesty) ? horsing foot on foot?   (I.ii.284-288)

Yes, Freud's formula applies, "I do not love him, she does." But it is only one of the operative variables. Leontes' imagery also signifies, "I do not love her in this perverse and taboo way, he does." And, "I do not identify with her and her with myself, he does." He substitutes identifications for identities, assimilating social differentiation of roles to a private system of unstable, vivid impositions. Finally what Leontes cannot abide is the fact that the sacred institution of marriage actually requires sexual contact between different sexes to propogate the human race. At the deepest level of his psyche (which is the potentially psychotic level of Shakespeare's psyche) , bodily contact itself is dreaded whenever it is imagined outside the boundaries of institutionalized legitimacy. Outside those boundaries, mutuality becomes the loss distinction itself in both its moral and psychological senses.

The extent of Leontes' psychic decomposition forces us to seek an explanation of his pathology not so much in a variation of the Oedipus complex, although there are Oedipal anxieties involved, nor even in an earlier dread of retaliation for forbidden wishes, but at the deepest level of oral anxieties. At that level the infant craves love as nourishment and dreads the possibility of maternal malevolence. Identifying well-being with mother, he finds himself in the reflections of his surroundings. It is no accident that Leontes shifts craving confirmation of his manhood from his son to an attempt to elicit Camillo's service in the poisoning of his double, Polixenes, to the violence of infanticide and to aggression directed at Hermione herself. He plays out, symbolically, a regression that leads to the source

of nurturance, and he would destroy that source in the delusion
that the woman and not himself contains the contamination he
dreads.

First he turns to his son. Identifying with Mamillius as a
symbol of phallic integrity, Leontes seeks to find himself externalized in the image of his offspring: " Why that's my baw-
cock. What! hast smutch'd thy nose?/They say it is a copy out of
mine " (I.ii.121-122). But as Mamillius' name implies, Leontes'
masculine image of himself is maternally fixated. Seeking
"comfort" (I.ii.209) in the identity of father and son is a false
therapy for him, since the identity fails to ward off a deeper
ambivalence he harbors. Shortly, Leontes turns to Camillo in
his desperation to restore the correspondence of inner desires
and outer actualities. His wish for " servants true about me,
that bare eyes/To see alike mine honour as their profits "
(I.ii.309-310), bespeaks his growing obsession with converting
the outside world into the form of his fantasy.

To find a dependency he can trust involves for Leontes
the murder of the external embodiment of himself by oral
means. He turns to poison. Camillo, to prove his oneness with
Leontes, must become the instrument of oral violation, " bespice
a cup,/To give mine enemy a lasting wink;/Which draught to
me were cordial " (I.ii.316-318). Polixenes' death is Leontes'
oral gratification. Through Camillo, Leontes would act out an
identification with an orally catastrophic mother; he would
become actively the figure at whose hands he dreads to suffer
passively. This strategy fails also, as Polixenes, " one condemned
by the king's own mouth " (I.ii.445), flees the court under the
paternal guidance of Camillo, leaving Leontes to confront
mother and child.

In Act II, scene i, Hermione becomes the object of Leontes'
obstinate substitution of projection for perception. The scene
is richly symbolic even before he enters, for Shakespeare enacts
in miniature a version of the mother-child relationship Leontes
has unconsciously failed to integrate. Hermione first rejects
Mamillius:

> *Her.*   Take the boy to you: he so troubles me,
>   'Tis past enduring.   (II.i.1-2)

Soon after, rejection is followed by intimate, seductive acceptance:

> *Mam.* A sad tale's best for winter: I have one
> Of sprites and goblins.
>
> *Her.*   Let's have that, good sir.
> Come on, sit down, come on, and do your best
> To fright me with your sprites: you're powerful at it.
>
> *Mam.* There was a man—
>
> *Her.*   Nay, come sit down: then on.
>
> *Mam.* Dwelt by a churchyard: I will tell it softly,
> Yond crickets shall not hear it.
>
> *Her.*   Come on then,
> And giv't me in mine ear.   (II.i.25-32)

The pattern of rejection and return duplicates in the play's
reality precisely that rhythm which Leontes cannot tolerate in
his jealousy.[29] When he storms in, the son is whispering in his
mother's ear (" Is whispering nothing? " he had asked Camillo
[I.ii.284]). Mamillius exists in a symbiotic relationship with
his mother, as his later incorporation of her " shame " shows.
Like the Queen-Cloten dyad in *Cymbeline,* mother and son exhibit reciprocal dependencies (but here the import of the relationship is positive rather than destructive). Leontes comes
to rupture this mother-child intimacy. Symbolically, he wishes
to destroy the symbiosis at the center of his own identity. In a
crucial passage he articulates the deepest ambivalence in the
play: [30]

> There may be in the cup
> A spider steep'd, and one may drink, depart,
> And yet partake no venom (for his knowledge
> Is not infected) ; but if one present

[29] Philip E. Slater, in *The Glory of Hera: Greek Mythology and the Greek Family*
(Boston, 1968), finds this same configuration reflected in Greek drama. "The
rejection of and dependence upon women mirror the mother's own ambivalence"
(p. 44).

[30] The spider passage has no counterpart in Greene's *Pandosto,* and it can be
removed from its context in Leontes' speech without losing any information.
Shakespeare has converted a conventional superstition into a means of symbolizing
the deepest motives he is dramatizing. The fact that this passage reads almost like
a summary parable emphasizes its significance.

Th' abhorr'd ingredient to his eye, make known
How he hath drunk, he cracks his gorge, his sides,
With violent hefts. I have drunk, and seen the spider.
                                                    (II.i.39-45)

The great difference between trust and oral violence is here
condensed. Equating knowledge and visual awareness, Leontes
is saying that the *consciousness* of the spider (what it symbolizes) breaks the boundaries of the body itself, and utterly
inverts the expectation of nourishment, like the spider in
Donne's "Twickenham Garden":

But oh, self-traitor, I do bring
The spider love, which transubstantiates all,
       And can convert manna to gall;
And that this place may thoroughly be thought
       True Paradise, I have the serpent brought.

Lacking Donne's irony, Leontes would violently eject the incorporated object. The spider symbolizes a fundamental threat
to his existence, and its visual-oral context locates this threat
unconsciously in the infantile nursing situation. Mistrust,
helplessness, and the certainty of conspiracy accompany this
image. What vision, then, leads Leontes to divorce the son
from the mother with the line, "I am glad you did not nurse
him " (II.i.56)? What does the spider signify?

Psychoanalysis has shown that the spider, like the serpent,
is an over-determined symbol. On one level, it represents the
sexually threatening mother, contact with whom signifies incest. On a deeper level, it signifies the horror of maternal
engulfment, frequently confused with the child's own oral-
aggressive impulses. The spider often emerges as a symbol when
an intensely ambivalent person needs to ward off a complete
break with reality. Melitta Sperling writes of patients suffering
from spider phobias:

When the phobic mechanisms as well as the somatic defenses were invalidated by analysis, the split-off pregenital
and potentially psychotic core symbolized by the spider
appeared. The spider was a highly condensed symbol con-

taining the core fantasies and conflicts from various developmental levels. . . . The spider also represented both the patient and the mother in these feared and deeply repressed aspects.[31]

In seventeenth century Apulia, a spider scare led those suffering from the bite of the tarantula to invent songs and rituals designed to cure poisoning. One song goes like this:

It was neither a big nor a small tarantula;
It was the wine from the flask.
Where did it bite you, tell me, beloved,
    where it was.
Oh, if it was your leg, oh mamma!

" The tarantists' egos," writes Howard F. Gloyne, " tried methods other than phobia to defend against anxiety: sexualization of anxiety, intimidation of others, identification with the frightening objects, collection of external reassurances."[32] The list of attempted therapies reads like a description of Leontes' paranoid strategies.

Shakespeare knew nothing of this outbreak of tarantism, but the conflicts embodied in Leontes parallel the tarantists' disease. We need not go to Apulia, however, to confirm the maternal significance of the spider in Shakespeare. Richard II, returning to his motherland after his journey to Ireland kneels to the earth and says:

Dear earth, I do salute thee with my hand,
Though rebels wound thee with their horses' hoofs.
As a long-parted mother with her child
Plays fondly with her tears and smiles in meeting,

---

[31] "Spider Phobias and Spider Fantasies," *Journal of the American Psychoanalytic Association*, XIX (1971), p. 491. See also Richard Sterba, "On Spiders, Hanging and Oral Sadism," *American Imago*, VII (1950), pp. 21–28 and Ralph B. Little, "Oral Aggression in Spider Legends," *American Imago* XXIII (1966), pp. 170–176. Sterba writes: "Both of these [the spider and the vampire] are symbols to us of the oral destructive danger of being loved and represent the endangered object as a victim of oral aggression." In Renaissance emblems, the spider is associated with the sense of touch. Some emblems bear the legend, "*Sed aranea (nos superat) tactu.*" See Guy de Tervarent, *Attributs et Symboles Dans L'Art 1450–1600* (Geneva, 1958). The fear of sexual contact is thus associated with the deepest infantile fears of the mother.

[32] "Tarantism," *American Imago*, VII (1950), pp. 29–42.

So weeping, smiling, greet I thee, my earth,
And do thee favours with my royal hands;
Feed not thy sovereign's foe, my gentle earth,
Nor with thy sweets comfort his ravenous sense,
But let thy spiders that suck up thy venom
And heavy-gaited toads lie in their way,
Doing annoyance to the treacherous feet,
Which with usurping steps do trample thee. . . (III.ii.6-17)

Like Leontes, Richard confuses mother and child in himself,
and he would split the catastrophic mother from her nourishing
counterpart. Leontes' final strategy, one which leads to Mamillius' death and his own separation from Hermione, consists in
his attempt to sacrifice the catastrophic mother he tragically
confuses with his child-bearing wife. In vengeance he would
fuse destruction and the re-creation of his bond with her.

> . . . *she*
> *I can hook to me:* say that she were gone,
> Given to the fire, a moiety of my rest
> Might come to me again.   (II.iii.6-9; italics added)

Finally, the aim of Leontes' paranoia is to reclaim his bond with
the mother by means of the private magic which is his disease.
He would sacrifice Hermione, paradoxically, to recreate the
image of his sacred ideal, and to reclaim his own repose.[33]
   In the terrible irony of the court scene (III.ii) this strategy,

---

[33] Of jealousy, Fenichel writes: " It is a striving to avoid the very situation
which is longed for unconsciously. Where this attempt at avoidance originates
from is clear. Like all infantile instinctual defenses, it comes from the anxiety
which opposes the idea of instinctual action—in our case, from a fear of retribu-
tion for the patient's oral sadism." " A Contribution to the Psychology of
Jealousy," in *The Collected Papers of Otto Fenichel, First Series* (New York,
1954), p. 359. Jealousy, vengeance, and deification share a common root. They
are all extreme responses to deprivation, real or fantasized. See also Charles W.
Socarides, " On Vengeance: the Desire to 'Get Even'," *Journal of the American
Psychoanalytic Association*, XIV (1966), pp. 356-375. On p. 357 Socarides writes:
" The originally deprived patient can no longer tolerate further deprivation; the
originally satisfied (satiated) one is intolerant of any severe deprivation in
adulthood." The re-creative function of sacrifice is supported by Levi-Strauss:
" Sacrifice seeks to establish a desired connection between two initially separate
domains [the Human and the Divine]." *The Savage Mind* (Chicago, 1962),
p. 255. Leontes' fishing imagery, in addition to its phallic symbolism, is a
magical attempt to deny separation from Hermione. See D. W. Winnicott,
" String: A Technique of Communication," *op. cit.*, pp. 153-157.

too, breaks down, as Leontes moves from the wish for vengeance
to his vow of ritualized reparation. His confusion of self and
other is absolute: " Your actions are my dreams " (III.ii.82).
Attempting public vindication, he stages his own trial, articulates his own guilt, and, finally, accepts his sentence, *to live*
without lineage (his " immortality " and his potency) in utter
separation from the " sweet'st, dear'st creature " (III.ii.201)
he could not separate from his infantile fears of her power. Like
a child made submissive and ashamed of his aggression, Leontes
exits from the world of the play under the guidance of Paulina,
the representative of Hermione who embodies both her feared
and ethically essential aspects. Mother and son are to be re-
united in death, and Leontes' rebirth, his " recreation " (III.ii.
240), consists in his mourning for that lost bond.

Leontes' jealousy is far from motiveless. Shakespeare has
articulated through his character precisely those aspects of his
psyche—and, in a larger sense, of the collective idealizing imagination of Renaissance dramatists—that threaten the structure
of sacred identities. In a sense, we can say that Leontes *does*
possess a crucial knowledge, the knowledge of maternal malevolence. But his is a knowledge, like much knowledge we call
paranoid, directed at the wrong people, in the wrong language,
at the wrong time. What Freud said of Schreber applies to
Leontes: *" The delusional formation, which we take to be the
pathological product, is in reality an attempt at recovery, a
process of reconstruction."* [34] That process of recovery is the
focus of Shakespeare's theatrical magic in the sacred personalities of the second part of *The Winter's Tale.*

[34] *Standard Edition*, XII, p. 71.

Melville's Lost Self: *Bartleby*

Christopher Bollas

Herman Melville's short novel *Bartleby* is a tale about a " pallidly neat, pitiably respectable, incurably forlorn "[1] (p. 10) young man who answers an advertisement for a position as a scrivener. He is accepted for employment, disrupts the routine of his new environment when he " prefers not to " engage in certain assigned tasks, forces the employer to feel a resourcelessness that compels him to move his office. It ends in Bartleby's pathetic death after he has been hustled off to prison.

I believe that Bartleby's arrival at the office and his subsequent breakdown into negativity is a mimetic representation[2] of a need to find a nurturant space where he can regress toward the healing of a " basic fault "[3] in the self. I want to focus on *Bartleby* as a transitional moment in Melville's fiction when his central heroic type (Ahab, Ishmael, Taji, Pierre) shifts from searching to being found, where Bartleby's search for the employer becomes a move toward discovery, his existential ambience that of throwing out a deeply dissociated self state. *Bartleby* provides us with an opportunity to study a subject's expression of his autism,[4] where relinquishing of the self's executant ego[5] functions becomes a lingual invitation to the other to fill the absence of function with the nurture of

---

[1] All references to *Bartleby* are from Herman Melville, *Four Short Novels* (New York, 1963).

[2] See Christopher Bollas, "Character: The Language of Self," to be published in *The International Journal of Psychoanalytic Psychotherapy*. I argue that character is the language of self and is realized in part in a paralingual style, the mimetic evocation of the repressed. That is, the subject speaks himself through mime, and mime evokes ego states that could not be spoken in language proper.

[3] See Michael Balint, *The Basic Fault* (London, 1968).

[4] I use autism in a broad sense following Tustin's formulation that there is a normal specific period of autism in the development of the child. See Frances Tustin, *Autism and Childhood Psychosis* (London, 1972).

[5] Masud Khan, personal communication. Khan believes that the term "executant self" is less open to distortion than Winnicott's idea of the "false self" which should be reserved for more pathological conditions (i.e., the "as if" or "schizoid" character).

care, to cradle in supporting arms the dissolving self in its unintegrated muteness, as the other is induced, without words, to create the ambience desired by a self dying in order to be reborn. *Bartleby* is uniquely suited for study of several central concerns in contemporary psychoanalysis[6] because it can provide the literary critic with an appreciation of the contribution current psychoanalytic studies of the self can make to literary studies.

The narrator begins the story by describing himself as a "rather elderly man, . . . a man who, from his youth upwards has been filled with a profound conviction that the easiest way of life is the best" (p. 3) and his life is made easier by "the cool tranquility of a snug retreat" where he does a "snug business among rich men's bonds, and mortgages and titledeeds." " All who know me," he tells us, " consider me an eminently *safe* man " (p. 4). Indeed, it is lucky for his employees, Turkey, Nippurs, and Ginger Nut, that he is such a gentle man. For in the " snug retreat " of their office space, these workers—whose names have been mutually conferred as embodying their characteristics —regularly complement one another in the dripping of ink, knocking over of chairs, spilling of sandboxes, breaking of pens, and hoarding of food. In their kaleidoscopic world, these workers incarnate the instincts: oral; in their food names, their teeth grinding, hoarding and spilling of food; anal, in the spilling of ink, of sand, and waste of food remains; phallic, in the comic erections of self (i. e. when Turkey is up, Nippurs is down). Despite the kindergarten atmosphere, the narrator values each of his helpers, and by dividing his space from theirs by a folding glass door, he indicates a distance between their embodiment of instinct and his own function as the executant self.

[6] Several psychoanalysts in England (Balint, Khan, James, Winnicott) and in America (Giovacchini, Kernberg, Modell) have written about patients who come to therapy with deep character illnesses, "basic faults," "blank selves," schisms between "true and false selves." Their attendance to these patients—previously thought to be unanalyzable—has brought to psychoanalytic theory a new understanding of the person suffering from a dissociated internal emptiness and despair. See Peter L. Giovacchini, *Tactics and Techniques in Psychoanalytic Therapy* (London, 1972); Michael Balint, *The Basic Fault* (London, 1968); D. W. Winnicott, *The Maturational Process and the Facilitating Environment* (London, 1965); Masud Khan, *The Privacy of the Self* (London, 1974).

Then Bartleby arrives. The employer-narrator hires him
and provides him with a special space on his side of the sliding
doors, facing a wall some three feet away. " Still further to a
satisfactory arrangement," he says " I procured a high green
folding screen, which might entirely isolate Bartleby from my
sight, though not remove him from my voice. And thus, in a
manner, privacy and society were conjoined " (pp. 10-11).
In setting up this "necessary arrangement," the narrator
continues his function as the facilitating agent in providing
for others, his arranged space for Turkey, Nippurs, and Ginger
Nut already termed a " good natural arrangement, under the
circumstances " (p. 9).

Readers of Melville's novel *Pierre* [7], which preceded this
short novel by less than a year, may note the similarity between
Bartleby's arranged space and Pierre's closet, where the latter
lapsed into reverential time before a portrait of his idealized
dead father. Pierre's ritual withdrawal to his closet is vital to
our knowledge of Bartleby and to the *meconnaisance* between
the narrator and his curious employee. Disillusioned by the
shattering news of his father's illegitimate siring of a daughter,
Pierre rips his father's portrait from the wall of his closet.
This collapse in the *image* of the idealized father precipitates a
violent and more troubling rift with his mother, who casts him
out of her home. Pierre flees to New York with his new wife,
none other than his illegitimate sister. Above all, it seems to
me, *Pierre* is a novel about the collapse of illusion—metaphorically stated, in the mimesis of Pierre's removal of his
father's portrait—and in a youth's incapacity to rescue himself
from catastrophic disillusion. As Pierre wanders through an
art gallery not long before his violent death, he muses: " All
the walls of the world seemed thickly hung with the empty and
impotent scope of pictures, grandly outlined, but miserably
filled " (p. 392). Walls no longer hold ideal images on their
surface; and in Melville's fiction, I believe, this signifies the
absence of generative illusion,[8] so that Bartleby's disfunctional

---

[7] Herman Melville, *Pierre* (New York, 1964).

[8] Illusion that sponsors the growth of the self. Winnicott argues that a
mother must provide the infant with an illusion of his omnipotence. See D. W.
Winnicott, *The Maturational Process and the Facilitating Environment* (London,
1965).

autism is a psychosomatic communication, a use of the self as signifier[9] where the signified, broadly, represents the loss of generative illusion, and specifically, the loss of the paternal and maternal imagos. As we learn at the end of the story, Bartleby has come to this work after being fired from his post in the Dead Letter Office at Washington, a job that compels the narrator to reflect aptly: " Dead Letters! does it not sound like dead men? " " On errands of life," he ponders, " these letters speed to death," (p. 41) and Bartleby's former work signifies, I think, his retreat after his failure to find a voice in the Word to speak his pain, dead letters signifying the death of the Word.

The narrator senses Bartleby's needs by providing him with a private space, alongside of a protective other. " At first, Bartleby did an extraordinary quantity of writing. As if long famishing for something to copy, he semed to gorge himself on my documents." But the feeding fails to nurture the novice scrivener, who writes "silently, palely, mechanically" (p. 11), his craft pointing to the absence of any internal creative potential. A man who has sorted dead letters now writes in a dead manner, his copying an empty gesture marking the absence of language. Copying of the Word leads not to an identification with the other (as a child's learning of language sponsors an identification with his parents), but to a truncated isolation from the fruits of grasping the Word. Embryonic in his enclosed space, the young scrivener resorts to the Word—spoken in neutral and economic tones—only to ward off the other. When asked to join in the varied routines of collective tasks, he refuses:

"I would prefer not to," he said. I looked at him steadfastly. His face was leanly composed; his grey eyes dimly calm.

---

[9] See Roland Barthes, "Elements of Semiology" in *Writing Degree Zero and Elements of Semiology* (Boston, 1964). Ferdinand de Saussure founded a lingual theory based on a sign system that distinguishes between a signifier (some sign) and the signified (what the signifier points toward). I view Bartleby's ambience, particularly his "dead wall reveries" as signifying a specific event—Pierre's disillusion with his father—which, of course, occurred in *Pierre*. What is absent in *Bartleby*, therefore, is the signified and I take *Bartleby* to be a signifier pointing back to *Pierre*, who is the signified.

Not a wrinkle of agitation rippled him. Had there been
the least uneasiness, anger, impatience or impertinence
in his manner; in other words, had there been anything
ordinarily human about him, doubtless I should have
violently dismissed him from the premises. But as it was,
I should have as soon thought of turning my pale plaster-of-
paris bust of Cicero out of doors. (P. 12)

At first outraged and perplexed by Bartleby's uncommon
reply, the narrator shifts his response when he grasps that his
new employee's resistance is unintended as rebellion, indeed,
he feels himself drawn into " a bond of common humanity "
with his strange office fellow. So, when he learns that Bartleby
lives in the office, the narrator is plunged into sharing a sense
of Bartleby's homelessness: " It is evident enough that Bartleby
has been making his home here, keeping bachelor's hall all by
himself. Immediately then the thought came sweeping across
me, what miserable friendlessness and loneliness are here
revealed! His poverty is great; but his solitude, how horrible! "
(p. 20). He reflects on his new employee's habit of gazing in
perfect solitude on " the dead brick wall," a phenomenon he
describes as " dead-wall reveries " (p. 21). Feeling the new
scrivener to be a " victim of an innate and incurable disorder,"
he says: " I might give alms to his body; but his body did not
pain him; it was his soul that suffered, and his soul I could not
reach " (p. 22). With the others he has found viable interplay
between his function as director (executant ego) and their
rhythmic expression of instinct; but Bartleby brings to him a
deep absence in the self, a subject prior to the reflexive experience of instincts. This vacant quality in the new employee
threatens the narrator's moderately compulsive defenses and
leaves him with the uncertain feeling that he is incapable of
doing anything for Bartleby.

Matters worsen. As if sensing the narator's recognition of
his own helplessness, Bartleby gives up working altogether.
The employer tries unsuccessfully to fire him, but fails because
Bartleby remains unresponsive to demand. Once again,
Bartleby's presence creates an alien feeling in the narrator: " I
might enter my office in a great hurry, and pretending not to

see Bartleby at all, walk straight against him as if he were air " (p. 29). Again he accommodates, in fact, finds solace simply in Bartleby's presence. " I never feel so private as when I know you are here," he muses and adds humorously, " my mission in this world, Bartleby, is to furnish you with office-room for such period as you may see fit to remain " (p. 31). He considers acting as if his existence were to serve his strange companion, but this reflection is never actualized because his colleagues' reaction to his eccentric employee compels him to acknowledge reality. Unable to budge Bartleby, the narrator goes to the extreme of moving his office—"Strange to say—I tore myself from him whom I had so longed to be rid of" (p. 34)— but is later called upon by the legal counsel of the building's new occupant—who is faced with the same dilemma—to remove this strangely unresponsive character who now says: " I like to be stationary " (p. 36).

As the story comes to its enigmatically tragic end, Bartleby is hustled off to the Tombs by an irate crowd and a furious landlord. After a while, the narrator comes to visit him in the prison and discovers that because of Bartleby's serenity and apparent harmlessness, the prison authorities have allowed him to freely wander about the prison. The narrator finds him " standing all alone in the quietest of the yards, his face towards a high wall." As he approaches, Bartleby replies: " I know you ... and I want nothing to say to you " (p. 38). Once again, unable to get through to Bartleby, the narrator takes his leave, but returns several days later to find that he has refused to eat. Told by a guard that Bartleby is asleep, he approaches his friend's space.

> Strangely huddled at the base of the wall, his knees drawn up, and lying on his side, his head touching the cold stones, I saw the wasted Bartleby. But nothing stirred. I paused; then went close up to him; stooped over, and saw that his dim eyes were open; otherwise he seemed pro-foundly sleeping. Something prompted me to touch him. I felt his hand, when a tingling shiver ran up my arm and down my spine to my feet.

The round face of the grub-man peered upon me now.

" His dinner is ready. Won't he dine to-day, either? Or does he live without dining? "

" Lives without dining," said I, and closed the eyes.

(P. 40)

Bartleby, to my mind, is Ahab or Pierre come in out of the cold. The counterphobic search, the manic heroic *quest* is over, the true self finally existentially revealed in its condition of absolute need for the other is Melville's subject, in this, the saddest of his works. In *Bartleby,* the split in Melville's characters (Ahab/Ishmael) is fused temporarily in an isolated figure whose heroic passivity is both an active thrust against the narrator and an evocation of a desire to be provided for, permitting a complete shutting down of the self, willed into, and like Ahab, against existence. Unable to speak, except to use language against itself, Bartleby's loss of a creative use of the Word signifies a final stage in this character's renunciation of culture, begun with Pierre's disillusion with the image of an ideal father. But such withdrawal, like the artist's seclusion from what Heiddegger terms the world of " They," [10] may be a falling into one's privacy in order to intensify the value of " They," to find in one's privacy a way back toward living. Michael Balint [11] terms this a " regression for the sake of progression," a collapse in ego maintenance as the subject falls toward the " basic fault " in the self, in order to constitute a " new beginning." Bartleby falls into the " necessary arrangement " provided by the nurturant narrator, and after an intense satiation of rigid activity, he lapses into dead-wall reveries, in such deep regression that he can no longer work, nor respond to the narrator's exhortations to try.

It seems to me that the narrator, like the reader of this story, waits for something to happen, to materialize like the phoenix from Bartleby's ashen vacancy. Indeed, Bartleby hints at least once that his extraordinary privacy may be temporary when to the narrator's pleas for more information about himself he replies: " At present I prefer to give no answer." (p. 23) . Will he, at some future date, finally tell?

[10] See Martin Heidegger, *Being and Time* (London, 1967).
[11] See Michael Balint, *The Basic Fault* (London, 1968).

Melville's tale suggests to me an answer. In the culture of the 1850's, there is no generative space or time to permit a shutting down of the executant function of the self. Bartleby's only hope is to find some capacity to use the Word. The narrator's placement of his new employee, secluded in private, yet joined to a facilitating other, sequestered before the Word that he must copy if he is to live, is an instinctive and " necessary arrangement " for Bartleby's survival. The first step in this new beginning will be imitation (copying), like the child's imitating his mother's tongue, a preliminary to the child's creative use of his own Word. But Bartleby's copying of the Word does not revivify the dead letters, and failing to find a transformational grammar, he can only repeat an empty phrase that signifies his incapacity to symbolize his needs. In the America of the 1850's, there is no space but a prison for someone so desperately ill.

On one level, as I have argued, Bartleby's *presence* sponsors a series of actions by the narrator, responses to an *absence* in Bartleby, that in the dialectical rhythm of presence of the subject, signifying an absence in the subject eliciting a presence in the other, mimetically recreates the need of the lonely scrivener to have his pain held by the other. This mimesis— sponsored by the dialectical interplay of presence/absence/ presence—is Bartleby's language, his way of in-forming the other's response. With scant information about Bartleby through verbal language, the narrator comes to know his new friend by allowing himself to be manipulated (used as Bartleby's object), and by sensing the other through internal psychic and affective presences in himself. Like the narrator, we discover Bartleby as he exists inside the narrator. Indeed, Melville's story is primarily concerned with how Bartleby sponsors affective states in the narrator who feels compassionate, nur- turant, helpless, resourceless, anxious, dispossesed, enraged, humiliated, abused, playful, pleaful, and guilty, and who tries to defend himself by compliance, compulsive boundary setting, avoidance, denial, exorcism, and finally flight. This phenomen- ology of affect and defense is a phantom reflection of the silent scrivener, an affect language not spoken to the narrator, but thrown into and then lived out by him.

It seems to me, after some reflection, that Bartleby embodies an absence in the self of this blithely cheerful narrator, a psychic double who represents the dramatic and aggravating presence of a repudiated true self: the internal other in the personality that is a collage of psychically, familially, and culturally disowned instincts and ego states that are never realized in the active life of the subject. Never actualized because they are sequestered through repression or splitting from being lived out, they are known to the executant self by the energy and style of the defenses organized against this true self. Ironically then, the presence of the true self is known primarily by the defenses that signify its absence. Bartleby, however, assaults the narrator's defensive style, forcing the narrator to feel the pain of the true self, to meet its needs, and to acknowledge its absence as a horrid personal loss. Gradually, the force of the true self threatens the executant self as the latter (personalized in the narrator) feels itself merging with the true self (personalized in Bartleby).

> Somehow, of late, I had got into the way of involuntarily using this word "prefer" upon all sorts of not exactly suitable occasions. And I trembled to think that my contact with the scrivener had already and seriously affected me in a mental way. And what further and deeper aberration might it not yet produce? This apprehension had not been without efficacy in determining me to summary measures. (P. 24)

It is when the narrator begins to merge with Bartleby—by adopting his habit of mind—that he is prompted by his anxiety to dissociate himself from Bartleby, the latter's state of being compelling the former toward a series of actions (doing) designed to protect the executant self (the doing self) against the true self (in Melville the self in inert being). Indeed, the more the narrator is compelled toward doing, the more isolated is the being of Bartleby, until finally action becomes a psychic repudiation of being that leads to ultimate social dissociation (prison) and death.

Bartleby mimes the insistent presence of the unknowable and unspeakable. (Since the ultimate dissociation is separation from the Word, then the true self's vital dependency on the executant self's capacity to speak from it is lost). But this is not a story about the repudiation of a troubling and troubled presence as in *Moby Dick* (perhaps, a final exorcism of Ahab), for the narrator is made to mourn the loss of Bartleby. "For the first time in my life," he says "a feeling of overpowering stinging melancholy seized me. Before, I had never experienced aught but a not unpleasing sadness." The overpowering melancholy draws him toward his friend even after he has been removed from him: "the bond of a common humanity now drew me irresistibily to gloom. A fraternal melancholy" (p. 20). So Bartleby does make the heretofore smooth running executant self feel the pain of grief for the first time in his life, a sadness sponsored by the unmet needs and desperate isolation of a double, a figure "out there" who embodies an internal absence. When this internal vacant self confronts the blithely cheerful narrator in his old age, he tries to provide for it, nurture it in his own way toward a lively integration with the natural order of things: the culture of his office. All his efforts fail to vitalize an absence in his being. For Bartleby is, finally, like the damaged true self, an internal presence that is *unconsolable*.[12] All that is left to the grieving narrator is a profound recognition and sense that something terribly needy, horribly isolated, "incurably forlorn" is lost forever.

All of Melville's heroes feel this internal haunting other in themselves, whether it is the mysterious stranger that lives inside Babbalanja or the gnawing presence in Ahab. Sometimes, the other is projected outside, writ large upon the landscape and encountered by the executant self as with Ahab and the whale. I believe this aggravated and mysterious other is also in the author of all these stories, an absent presence in Melville who tries in his fiction to throw it out into imaginary characters, but whose novels signify its mysterious isolation. Failing to exorcize this other in *Moby Dick,* to marry it in *Pierre,* or to revivify it in *Bartleby,* Melville turns in *The Confidence Man* to an apparently bitter expostulation of the sorcery—the compensatory cleverness—of the false self (the executant self

---

[12] Masud Khan, personal communication.

uninformed by the true self). In the *Confidence Man*, illusion manipulation becomes the tool of the con man who metamorphoses himself into multiple false selves, and Melville signifies in this novel the end of his effort to give voice to the unknown interior self by fashioning an illusionist who, like the artist, can obscure the existence of an interior presence by sheer artifice. If the *Confidence Man* is born of despair and failure, if it is a magical evocation of the art of deceit, it is still a curious celebration of Melville's talent for fashioning illusion, a sweet bitterness before the long years of silence and absence.

Myth and Mystery in Steinbeck's "The Snake": A Jungian View

Charles E. May

John Steinbeck's short story about a woman who buys a rattle-snake and then pays to watch it eat a white rat has been a mystery to readers since it was published in *The Long Valley* in 1938.[1] Accord-ing to Steinbeck, it was a mystery to him as well, one of the mysteries that were constant at the laboratory of his friend Ed Ricketts. "I wrote it just as it happened. I don't know what it means and do not even answer the letters asking what its philosophic intent is. It just happened." Summarizing the actual incident, Steinbeck says that the frightening thing was that as the snake unhinged its jaws before swallowing the rat, "the woman, who watched the process closely, moved her jaws and stretched her mouth as the snake was doing. After the rat was swallowed, she paid for a year's supply of rats and said she would come back. But she never did come back. Whether the woman was driven by a sexual, a religious, a zoophilic, or a gustatory impulse we never could figure."[2]

The few readers who have commented in passing on the story seem satisfied that the mystery stems from the psychological problems of the woman. Most of them agree that the story is a tale of sex perversion about a neurotic woman who intrudes into a zoological garden of Eden and objectifies her frustration by watching a male rattlesnake eat a white rat.[3] Edmund Wilson has

[1] Peter Lisca tells us that Steinbeck tried several times without success to get the story published. Finally he had it printed in *The Monterey Beacon* in 1936, a small magazine run in conjunction with a stable. Steinbeck's payment for the story was six month's use of a big bay horse. The following year when Steinbeck tried to get the story published again, it was rejected by both *Atlantic Monthly* and *Harper's*. "Steinbeck: A Literary Biography," in *Steinbeck and His Critics: A Record of Twenty-Five Years,* eds. Ernest W. Tedlock, Jr., and C. V. Wicker (Albuquerque: University of New Mexico Press, 1957), p. 11.

[2] "About Ed Ricketts," *The Log from the Sea of Cortez* (New York: Viking Press, 1951), pp. xxiii–xxiv.

[3] See Peter Lisca, *The Wide World of John Steinbeck* (New Brunswick, N.J.: Rutgers University Press, 1958), p. 95; Joseph Fontenrose, *John Steinbeck: An Intro-duction and Interpretation* (New York: Barnes and Noble, Inc., 1963), p. 63; Lincoln R. Gibbs, "John Steinbeck: Moralist," in Tedlock and Wicker, p. 93; Frederick Bracher, "Steinbeck and the Biological View of Man," in Tedlock and Wicker, p. 184.

singled the story out as characteristic of Steinbeck's tendency to present human life in animal terms, not those "aspects of animals that seem most attractive to humans, but rather the processes of life itself." Such a subject is a limited one, Wilson says. "This tendency on Steinbeck's part to animalize humanity is evidently one of the causes of his relative unsuccess at creating individual humans."[4] Only Warren French has suggested that the central focus of the story is not so much the woman as it is "what she allows us to learn about another." Steinbeck's sympathy, French says, "lies not with those who give free rein to irrational drives, but those who seek knowledge of the world they live in."[5] However, French's assumption—that the scientific method is the only way to gain knowledge of the world—is not borne out by the story. In fact, just the opposite is true; the inadequacy of scientific knowledge is the essential subject of "The Snake."

The critics' failure to understand the story is symptomatic of a general failure of readers to understand the short story form itself, to distinguish from the novel the short story's characteristic subject, technique, and aesthetic intent. The basic distinction critics have failed to note (as indicated by their sole concern with what drives the woman to her strange compulsion in "The Snake") is between how we respond to character in the two forms. Edmund Wilson's comments are central, for his criticism of Steinbeck's focus on the "processes of life itself" instead of individual human beings is based on the assumption that fiction must present individualized characters with whom the reader can identify. However, Frank O'Connor has suggested that while such individualizing may be true for the novel, it is not necessarily true for the short story. The novel, O'Connor says, is "bound to a process of identification between the reader and the character. . . . And this process of identification invariably leads to some concept of normality—hostile or friendly—with society as a whole." However, there is usually no character with whom the reader can identify in short fiction and no form of society a character can regard as normal.[6] Northrop Frye makes a similar distinction between the

    [4] "The Boys in the Back Room," in *Classics and Commercials: A Literary Chronicle of the Forties* (New York: Farrar, Straus and Co., 1950), pp. 38, 41.
    [5] *John Steinbeck* (New York: Twayne Publishers, Inc., 1962), p. 82.
    [6] *The Lonely Voice: A Study of the Short Story* (Cleveland, Ohio: World Publishing Co., 1963), p. 17.

novel and the romance which may offer, if not an aesthetic, at least an historical explanation of the difference between the novel and the short story. The generic roots of twentieth-century short fiction are in the nineteenth-century romance, as Frye defines it:

> The romancer does not attempt to create "real people" so much as stylized figures which expand into psychological archetypes. It is in the romance that we find Jung's libido, anima, and shadow reflected in the hero, heroine, and villain respectively. That is why the romance so often radiates a glow of subjective intensity that the novel lacks, and why a suggestion of allegory is constantly creeping in around its fringes.[7]

Once we readjust our generic expectations and see that the woman in Steinbeck's story is a psychological archetype instead of a psychologically abnormal individual, the mystery of the story becomes, not allegorically evident, but mythically significant. Within the short story form, related as it is to the romance, Steinbeck is not bound to create individual human beings. What Edmund Wilson refers to as characteristic of animals in the woman may be better understood as characteristic of her role as anima, that personification of the feminine which Jung says has "'occult' connexions with 'mysteries,' with the world of darkness in general." When in "dreams or other spontaneous manifestation," Jung says, we meet with an ambivalent, unknown female figure, "it is advisable to let her keep her independence and not reduce her arbitrarily to something known. . . . In all [such] accounts the anima . . . is a being that belongs to a different order of things."[8]

And because the woman belongs to a different order of things, so does the story embody a different level of activity than either the practical or the theoretical. It embodies rather that lower substratum, which Ernst Cassirer says we are prone to forget, that lies beneath them both—the level of mythical activity. In fact, the mysterious incident recounted in "The Snake" is a reac-

[7] *Anatomy of Criticism* (New York: Atheneum, 1957), p. 304.
[8] "The Psychological Aspects of the Kore," in G. C. Jung and C. Kerenyi, *Essays on the Science of Mythology,* Bollingen Series, XXII (New York: Pantheon Books, 1949), pp. 150–151.

tion of the mythic world against the efforts of science to obliterate it. The anima force embodied in the woman rises out of the primeval sea, disrupts the doctor's methodical scientific process, upsets his calm and ordered existence, and then goes back to her sea home never to be seen by him again. Critics have failed to respond to the story because they have failed to distinguish between the theoretical world and properties and the mythical world which Cassirer says is more fluid and fluctuating.

> In order to grasp and to describe this difference we may say that what myth primarily perceives are not objective but *physiognomic* characters. . . . The world of myth is a dramatic world—a world of actions, of forces, of conflicting powers. In every phenomenon of nature it sees the collision of these powers. Mythical perception is always impregnated with these emotional qualities. Whatever is seen or felt is surrounded by a specific atmosphere—an atmosphere of joy or grief, or anguish, of excitement, of exultation or depression.[9]

For various complex historical and aesthetic reasons (which I intend to examine in detail at another time) such physiognomic characters and emotional qualities have always played a more important role in short fiction than they have in the novel. Several fiction writers have suggested but failed to explore or substantiate this characteristic of the form. Elizabeth Bowen has said that the short story must have the emotion and spontaneity of the lyric; Alberto Moravia says it is the product of lyrical institutions rather than philosophic ideas as the novel is; and Joyce Carol Oates recently suggested that the short story is a "dream verbalized" and that its most interesting characteristic is its mystery.[10] Eudora Welty, in an article that predates Oates's observation by over twenty years, has also said that the first thing we notice about a story is its mystery. The cause of this mystery, as she describes it, sounds quite similar to the emotional qualities of myth that

---

[9] *An Essay on Man* (New Haven, Conn.: Yale University Press, 1944), p. 76.
[10] Elizabeth Bowen, "The Faber Book of Modern Short Stories," in *Collected Impressions* (New York: Alred A. Knopf, Inc., 1950), p. 43; Alberto Moravia, "The Short Story and the Novel," in *Man as End: A Defense of Humanism,* trans. Bernard Wall (New York: Farrar, Straus and Giroux, Inc., 1969), p. 182; Joyce Carol Oates, "The Short Story," *Southern Humanities Review,* 5 (Summer 1971), 214.

Cassirer notes. "The first thing we notice about our story is that we can't really see the solid outlines of it—it seems bathed in something of its own. It is wrapped in an atmosphere."[11] Finally, we need only to turn to one more great story teller, Joseph Conrad, to grasp the relationship between Oates's suggestion that the story is a dream verbalized and Welty's idea that it is wrapped in an atmosphere. For Marlowe, Conrad's story-telling surrogate, the meaning of an episode is a mythic, not a theoretical one, to be found "not inside like a kernel, but outside enveloping the tale which brought it out only as a glow brings out a haze." In his attempt to convey to his listeners the significance of the story of Kurtz, Marlowe understands the difficulty of verbalizing those physiognomic characters which inhabit the heart of darkness. "Do you see the story? Do you see anything? It seems to me I am trying to tell you a dream—making a vain attempt, because no relation of a dream can convey the dream sensation, that commingling of absurdity, surprise, and bewilderment in a tremor of struggling revolt, that notion of being captured by the incredible which is the very essence of dreams. . . . "

In the following discussion I hope to show that "The Snake" is a paradigmatic example of this quality of short fiction; for in describing a thing that "just happened," Steinbeck conveys that very commingling of absurdity, surprise, and bewilderment of the young Dr. Phillips being captured by the incredible forces of the mythic realm. And because the story is an account of dream reality rather than phenomenal reality, its meaning is not to be found in a kernel within but in the atmosphere which surrounds it, in the emotional qualities which impregnate it.

The forces which oppose each other in the story are suggested in the first paragraph by the juxtaposition of the laboratory and the tide pool: the one a "tight little building" closed off from nature yet built for the purpose of observing nature, the other the primal source of life itself where the mysteries of nature truly take place.[12] The action that opens the story—Dr. Phillips' leaving the

---

[11] "The Reading and Writing of Short Stories," *Atlantic Monthly*, 83 (February 1949), 56.

[12] In *Classics and Commercials*, Edmund Wilson says that the laboratory is one of the key images in all of Steinbeck's fiction. Stanley Edgar Hyman suggests that it is the tide pool which is the central metaphor of *The Sea of Cortez* and perhaps much of Steinbeck's fiction as well. "Some Notes on John Steinbeck," in Tedlock and Wicker, p. 184.

tide pool for the laboratory—creates an atmosphere that echoes
with ominousness. We need only think of the pervasive stereotype
of the misguided scientist—Hawthorne's Rappaccini and Mary
Shelley's Dr. Frankenstein come immediately to mind—to recognize this first scene. In the growing darkness the doctor swings a
sack over his shoulder, squashes through the street until he enters
a laboratory where rats scamper in their cages and captive cats
mew for milk; he turns on a light over a dissection table, dumps
his clammy sack on the floor, and goes over to glass cages where
rattlesnakes "recognize" him and pull in their forked tongues.

Even when we discover that the clammy sack is filled only with
common starfish and that the dissection table is used for small
animals, we are still apprehensive that something is not "natural"
about the laboratory or the young doctor who has the "preoccupied
eyes of one who looks through a microscope a great deal" and
whose bedroom is a book-lined cell containing an army cot, a reading light and an uncomfortable chair." The imagery is too much
that of one who, having withdrawn from life, is content merely to
look on, of one who does not live life but experiments with it.

A central and recurring element of the conflict between the
laboratory and the sea, one that reminds us that the doctor may
not be completely safe in his "tight little building," is the sound of
the waves that wash quietly about the piles underneath. For the
laboratory, as might be expected in a story that deals with the
conflict between primal reality and everyday reality, stands "partly
on piers over the bay water and partly on the land." Until the
woman enters and symbolically embodies the sound of the sea, the
washing of the waves are counterpointed against the homey,
everyday hum of the doctor's kettle boiling water for his dinner.
This sound then establishes another juxtaposition of the doctor's
normal activity of preparing and eating his meal with the instruments of his "abnormal" scientific experiments. He lifts the can of
beans out of the boiling water with a pair of forceps and eats his
meal out of one of the specimen watch-glasses. "While he ate he
watched the starfish on the table. From between the rays little
drops of milky fluid were exuding." With the same disinterested-
ness he takes a cat out of a cage, strokes her for a moment, and
then places her in "the killing chamber" and turns on the gas.
"While the short soft struggle went on in the black box he filled

the saucers with milk." The short soft struggle of the cat echoes the sound of the waves which become "little sighs" as the doctor begins his work on the starfish and hears "quick steps on the wooden stairs and a strong knocking at the door."

Most of the description of the woman clearly and simply establishes her physical identity with the snake. Tall and lean, dressed in a severe dark suit, she has straight black hair growing low on a flat forehead. "He noted how short her chin was between lower lip and point." Her dark eyes, "veiled with dust," look at him without seeming to see him. As she waits to talk to him, she seems completely at rest. "Her eyes were bright but the rest of her was almost in a state of suspended animation. He thought, 'Low metabolic rate, almost as low as a frog's, from the looks.'" However, other details and actions of the woman are not so clearly related to the snake. She does not want to look into the microscope although the doctor thinks, "People always wanted to look through the glass." Her eyes do not center on him; "rather they covered him and seemed to see in a big circle around him." When the doctor goes over to the rattlesnake cage, he turns to find her standing beside him. "He had not heard her get up from the chair. He had heard only the splash of water among the piles and the scampering of rats on the wire screen." Later, when the doctor puts the rat into the snake cage, the room becomes very silent. "Dr. Phillips did not know whether the water sighed among the piles or whether the woman sighed." Finally, when the woman leaves, the doctor hears her footsteps on the stairs but "could not hear her walk away on the pavement." These details do not identify the woman with the snake so much as they identify her with the sea itself. The yoking of the sounds she makes with the sound of the waves underneath the laboratory make this clear. The doctor does not hear her walk away on the pavement because she does not walk away; she goes back to the tide pool that she came from, back to the "deep pool of consciousness" out of which she awakens when the doctor is ready to talk to her.

She does not wish to look in to the microscope because, being a mythic creature, an embodiment of mana, her vision is a mythical one that sees not narrowly but in a large circle that is all-encompassing. These images which identify her with the sea as well as those that identify her with the snake, such as swaying as it sways and opening her mouth when it does, are, of course, the primary ones. Since both these identifications are inherently related, the mythic significance of the snake and the sea and their connection with the mysterious anima force deserve more detailed exploration.

We can certainly believe Steinbeck when he says that he wrote "The Snake" just as it happened, that he was conscious of no philosophical intent. The very success of the story is proof of this just as the failure of *Of Mice and Men* is proof of his deliberate manipulation there. Although, as Harry Thornton Moore tells us, apropos of *The Long Valley,* that Steinbeck had been for a long time working out a theory of subconscious symbolism, "by which certain elements of the rhythm and certain hidden symbols prepare the reader's unconsciousness for the ultimate effect of the story," we can see that the rhythm and symbols of "The Snake" are too integrated to have been the result of Steinbeck's conscious aesthetic theories.[13] More helpful in understanding the nature and origin of the woman in the story are Steinbeck's tentative notions of a racial unconscious developed by analogy to biology and the sea in *The Log From the Sea of Cortez*. This account of his scientific expedition with Ed Ricketts has been rightfully termed as important to Steinbeck's art and thought as *Death in the Afternoon* is to Hemingway's.[14]

In his account of the Old Man of the Sea, a phenomenon seen by many people in Monterey, Steinbeck says he hopes it is never photographed, for if it turns out to be a great malformed Sea-lion, "a lot of people would feel a sharp personal loss—a Santa Claus loss. And the ocean would be none the better for it. For the ocean, deep and black in the depths, is like the low dark levels of our minds in which the dream symbols incubate and sometimes rise up to sight like the Old Man of the Sea. And even if the symbol vision be horrible, it is there and it is ours."[15] Developing the analogy between the sea as primal source of man and source of the dream symbols of man's unconsciousness even further, Steinbeck gives us a basis for understanding that the strange

[13] *The Novels of John Steinbeck: A First Critical Study* (Chicago: Normandie House, 1939), p. 52.

[14] Freeman Champney, "John Steinbeck, Californian," in Tedlock and Wicker, p. 146.

[15] *The Log from the Sea of Cortez*, p. 21.

woman in "The Snake" comes from the tide pool of the sea at the same time that she comes from the unconscious of the young doctor and all men:

> And we have thought how the human fetus has, at one stage of its development, vestigial gill-slits. If the gills are a component of the developing human, it is not unreasonable to suppose a parrallel or concurrent mind or psyche development. If there be a life-memory strong enough to leave its symbol in vestigial gills, the preponderantly aquatic symbols in the individual unconscious might well be indications of a group psyche-memory which is the foundation of the whole unconscious. And what things must be there, what monsters, what enemies, what fears of dark and pressure, and of prey![16]

Surely the woman is one of these monsters—an entity from the mythic realm which persists always in dreams.

Since Steinbeck's formulations here are so similar to Jung's theories of the Collective Unconscious, we might better understand what kind of dream symbol the woman is and why she rises out of the doctor's unconscious to confront him if we turn to Jung's compilation of such archetypes in *Symbols of Transformation*.[17] Jung says that in dreams and fantasies, the snake is an excellent symbol to express the sudden and unexpected manifestations of the unconscious, "its painful and dangerous interventions in our affairs, and its frightening aspects" (p. 374). According to Jung, the snake is a representation of the world of instinct. "Snake dreams always indicate a discrepancy between the attitude of the conscious mind and instinct, the snake being a personification of the threatening aspect of that conflict" (p. 396). To understand why the snake-woman or instinctual force has rise abruptly from the doctor's unconscious to confront him, we do not have to try to understand the "personal" contents of his unconscious any more than we have to try to understand or postulate a particular sexual neurosis for the woman. Indeed, the story

[16] *Ibid.*, p. 32.
[17] Carl G. Jung. *Symbols of Transformation: An Analysis of the Prelude to a Case of Schizophrenia*, trans. R. F. C. Hull, Bollingen Series, XX (New York: Pantheon Books, 1956). All subsequent references to Jung are from this edition of *Symbols of Transformation*. Page numbers follow the citation in the text.

gives us no basis for trying to understand either as individual characters. The doctor, embodying as he does a scientific and therefore detached existence, is simply intolerable in his one-sidedness. As Jung might say, he is one who has rejected the unconscious to such an extent that the instinctual forces rise up in opposition (p. 294). The woman is a threatening force to the doctor because he refuses to recognize and integrate the archetypal contents of his unconscious which she embodies.

The chthonic message the woman brings the doctor is the essential message of the mythic world. By her very existence she challenges the doctor's scientific realm of being and his Cartesian mode of knowing, both of which separate him from life and make him an observer only. Accustomed to dividing life into the two spheres of practical and theoretical activity, the doctor, like most men, has forgotten that primitive substratum which underlies them both. As Ernst Cassirer says, primitive man's feelings are still embedded in this lower substratum.

> His view of nature is neither merely theoretical nor merely practical; it is *sympathetic*. . . . Primitive man by no means lacks the ability to grasp the empirical differences of things. But in his conception of nature and life all these differences are obliterated by a stronger feeling: the deep conviction of a fundamental and indelible *solidarity of life* that bridges over the multiplicity and variety of single forms.[18]

And just as the woman challenges the doctor's level of being in the world, she also challenges his mode of apprehending the world. Warren French is right when he says that Steinbeck's sympathy is with those who seek knowledge of the world they live in, but he is surely mistaken when he assumes that Steinbeck's sympathy is with scientific knowledge in this story. Steinbeck affirms a deeper level of being and knowing in *The Log from the Sea of Cortez*:

> The whole is necessarily everything, the whole world of fact and fancy, body and psyche, physical fact and spiritual truth, individual and collective, life and death, macrocosm and microcosm (the greatest quanta here, the greatest synapse be-

[18] *An Essay on Man*, p. 82.

tween these two), conscious and unconscious, subject and object. The whole picture is portrayed by *is,* the deepest word of deep ultimate reality, not shallow or partial as reasons are, but deeper and participating, possibly encompassing the Oriental concept of *being.*[19]

The doctor's sense of reality, based on reason and science, is determined by what Jung calls "directed thinking"; he has no concern with "fantasy thinking" or what Cassirer calls mythic or sympathetic perception. This mode of thought, often called "poetic" or "religious," has always been associated in myth with woman's connections with the mysterious source of life. Karl Stern has suggested that it stems from woman's biological connections with the life processes:

> One of the reasons why we associate all praeter-rational thinking with womanhood is that the knowledge by connaturality originates in the child-mother relationship. All *knowledge by union*; all knowledge by incorporation (incorporating or being incorporated); and all knowledge through love has its natural fundament in our primary bond with the mother. The skeptic warns the believer not to "swallow" things and not "to be taken in." And from his point of view he is right. Faith, the most sublime form of nonscientific knowledge, is a form of swallowing or of being taken in.[20]

Stern's metaphor of swallowing also helps us understand the imagery in Steinbeck's story of the snake's unhinging its jaws to swallow the rat and the woman's identification with this act as well as her general identification with the snake. The centrality of this action (it is the action which originally caught Steinbeck's imagination in the actual incident) in the story is obvious: the climax of the story, it is so intense and frightening the doctor cannot bring himself to look at it. "Dr. Phillips put his will against his head to keep from turning toward the woman. He thought, 'If she's opening her mouth, I'll be sick. I'll be afraid.' " And because the scene is so central, it explains what the doctor cannot explain even though he says he has read much about phychological sex sym-

[19] *The Log from the Sea of Cortez,* pp. 150–151.
[20] *The Flight from Woman* (New York: Farrar, Straus and Giroux, 1965), p. 54.

bols. If he has done his reading in Freudian psychology and thus associates the snake with the phallus, then perhaps, as he says, "it doesn't seem to explain." Jung, however, does not restrict himself to such allegorical or anatomical explanations; he is often concerned more with the androgynous nature of the symbols in myth and dream he says we must understand not anatomically but psychologically as libido symbols. In the realm of the libido, according to Jung, the fixed meaning of things comes to an end. "We take mythological symbols much too concretely and are puzzled at every turn by the endless contradictions of myths" (p. 222). Moreover, Jung notes that the serpent often has a vaginal as well as a phallic meaning. It symbolizes the "Terrible Mother, the voracious maw, the jaws of death" (p. 251).

The feminine sexuality of the snake/woman parallel now becomes clearer; the archetype here is related to the pervasive and frightening myth of the *vagina dentata,* the vagina with teeth, which often represents man's fear of woman's sexuality. The gaping open of the snake's mouth and the corresponding gaping open of the mouth of the woman represent the female sex as a voracious mouth which threatens to devour the penis. Dr. Phillips realizes that the snake making its kill and eating it has symbolic significance. "I think because it is a subjective rat. The person is the rat. Once you see it the whole matter is objective. The rat is only a rat and the terror is removed." The doctor's confidence that once you see it the terror is removed is shaken in the story just as his other scientific perceptions are. He rejects as simply "sport" those activities which perhaps might give him "poetic" rather than scientific knowledge. When he agrees to feed the snake for the woman he says, "It's better than a bullfight if you look at it one way, and it's simply a snake eating his dinner if you look at it another." But when the doctor says this his tone has become acid, for he hates people "who made sport of natural processes. He was not a sportsman but a biologist. He could kill a thousand animals for knowledge, but not an insect for pleasure. He'd been over this in his mind before." However, the act of killing and swallowing the rat is not only death by devouring; it is representative of life and knowledge by swallowing and being swallowed as well. Suggesting death which is necessary for a deeper level of life, it is the kind of experience which the doctor calls "the most beautiful thing in the world . . . the most terrible thing in the world." Yet the doctor is unable to integrate and accept this necessity into his experience. The only way his conscious mind will allow him to see the process is that of a snake eating its dinner.

The woman who has come to confront the doctor with this conflict and make him aware of mythic being and perception is the universal goddess who has appeared in myth in various guises. Two of her best known embodiments, both of which find echoes in "The Snake," are the Hebrew Lilith and the Greek Lamia. Both these figures, Jung says, are related to the Terrible Mother, for both are personifications of death that precedes rebirth. However, in Steinbeck's story, instead of allowing himself to be drawn into the mythic aura of the woman, the doctor, like the philosopher Appolonius in Keats' "Lamia," exerts his conscious will and refuses. All charms fly at the mere touch of cold science as well as cold philosophy.

The implications of the doctor's refusal to be devoured by the voracious mother, to "die" so that he might be born again, are made clear in the dénouement of the story. After the climactic moment, as the snake begins to engulf the rat with slow peristaltic pulsing, the doctor turns angrily to his work table because he has missed one of the series of starfish germination. Having forgotten the time, having forgotten time altogether in the momentary primal atmosphere of the mysterious woman, his attempt to control the process of gestation has been spoiled.

> He put one of the watch-glasses under a low-power microscope and looked at it, and then angrily he poured the contents of all the dishes into the sink. The waves had fallen so that only a wet whisper came up through the floor. The young man lifted a trapdoor at his feet and dropped the starfish down into the black water. He paused at the cat, crucified in the cradle and grinning comically into the light. Its body was puffed with embalming fluid.

Images of life and death are closely integrated here to fulfill our ominous suspicions about the doctor at the beginning of the story. More importantly, they reveal the implications of his refusal to perform the heroic task of integration by suggesting not death

and consequent rebirth, but rather death in the very process of
birth—the abortion of life. The flushing of the fertilizing sperm
and ova from the bisexual starfish down the drain and the dump-
ing of their bodies down through the trapdoor is the most obvious
such image. The death of life in its very gestation is also reflected
in the grotesque image of the cat's puffed body. Swollen with
embalming fluid, it is literally pregnant with death. However, the
most startling image of death in the very process of life is that of
the cat "crucified in the cradle." In a single phrase it telescopes
the whole history of Christ—that one born in the manger so that
he might die on the cross. That the image reflects neither Christ's
life nor his rebirth suggests the doctor's refusal of both. According to Jung, Christ signifies the "self" psychologically; "he represents the projection of the most important and most central of
archetypes" (p. 368). Moreover, the crucifixion represents the successful establishing of a relationship between the ego and the
unconscious. On the cross, Christ unites himself with the mother
in death so that he might be reborn again (p. 263). That the
Christ image in Steinbeck's story is grotesque and sardonic, stick-
ing its tongue out in derision, however, does not suggest Jung's
heroic Christ, but rather Yeats's "rough beast."

After the woman leaves, the doctor sits in front of the snake
cage and tries to "comb out his thought," but the only explanation
he has, and perhaps the only explanation possible is: "Maybe I'm
too much alone." Indeed, the doctor has been visited by the
mythic force because he is alone. Cut off from life by his sole
attention to the observation of life, cut off from any spiritual
realm by his concern for the scientific, the doctor remains outside
that "solidarity of life" which ultimately is religious. Perhaps realizing this, yet helpless to do anything about it, the doctor admits,
"If I knew—no, I can't pray to anything."

The theoretical scientist mystified by the strange woman
might be seen as a reflection of the critical reader who, although
he may have little difficulty with the novel, finds the short story
often mysterious and strange. The most fundamental feature of
short fiction is perhaps similar to what Ernst Cassirer says is the
fundamental feature of myth. Instead of springing from a special
direction of thought it is "an off-spring of emotion and its emotional background imbues all its productions with its own specific

color."[21] The meaning of short fiction, because it is a product of emotion, because it is the "dream verbalized," is therefore not to be found inside like a kernel, but outside, "enveloping the tale which brought it out only as a glow brings out a haze, in the likeness of one of these misty halos that sometimes are made visible by the spectral illumination of moonshine."

[21] *An Essay on Man,* p. 82.

Reichianism in *Henderson the Rain King*

Eusebio L. Rodrigues

Henderson the Rain King has yet to be recognized as the miracle of creative alchemy that it is, a novel in which Bellow has forged and welded together a wealth of artistic material into a world complete unto itself. This fictional world, a real unreal world into which the reader is transported, has been fashioned from Bellow's studies in anthropology,[1] his profound involvement with William Blake, his propensity to introduce literary and topical allusions, and, above all, his fascination with the ideas and methods of Wilhelm Reich. It is Bellow's imaginative energy, manifest especially in the speed and farcical exuberance of the language used, that has set all these elements spinning together. The axis of this whirling world is the Reichian thrust of Henderson's quest for humanness.

Richard G. Stern was the first to point out that Bellow's interest in Reich is one of the genetic factors of *Henderson the Rain King*.[2] Bellow himself has casually referred to his involvement with Reichianism. In a tribute he paid to his friend, Isaac Rosenfeld, Bellow mentions the fact that Reichianism had absorbed them both for a time.[3] *Seize the Day* (1956), *Henderson the Rain King* (1959), and *Herzog* (1964) are saturated with Reichianism; in *The Victim* (1947) and *Mr. Sammler's Planet* (1970) no significant Reichian elements are in evidence. One can assume that Reich was an important influence on Bellow all through the fifties and the early sixties.

The manner in which the ideas of Reich affected Bellow the novelist needs to be carefully and clearly understood. Bellow did

---

[1] See my article, "Bellow's Africa," *American Literature*, 43 (May 1971), 242–256.

[2] Richard G. Stern, "Henderson's Bellow," *Kenyon Review*, 21 (Autumn 1959), 661: "I know Bellow, and have talked with him about this novel among other things. Indeed, I read an earlier version, and some of my initial reactions to it turned out to be similar to Bellow's as he went over the book, so that changes were made which made me feel—for no good reason—implicated. The point here is that I feel I know what effects were wanted at certain moments; I also feel 'in' on such genetic factors as Bellow's interest in Reich."

[3] Isaac Rosenfeld, *An Age of Enormity*, ed. Theodore Solotaroff, Foreward by Saul Bellow (Cleveland: World Publishing Co., 1962), p. 14.

not immerse himself in Reichianism the way his friend Rosenfeld did. Rosenfeld was apparently a charmingly eccentric Reichian: he would ask people about their sexual habits and calculate how much character armor they wore; he even constructed a home-made orgone box which he used, among other things, to treat the headaches of his friends. Bellow did not allow himself to fall completely under the spell of Reich. His Reichianism was at once more playful and more serious, and his sensibility absorbed what it needed for its creative purposes.

In *Henderson the Rain King* Bellow indulges in a kind of *līlā* (the Indian spirit of divine creative play), enjoying himself hugely as he tosses around and exploits all the wildly comic extravagances of Reichianism, while at the same time exercising a subtle, almost invisible control over its use as a serious form of therapy. The farcical adventures of Henderson take on a meaningful dimension in the light of the ideas and methods of Wilhelm Reich.

Henderson the Rain King tells the story of Henderson's quest for the human, a story which is also a detailed account of his peculiar illness, his frantic running around all through the jungles of America and Africa seeking a cure, and his complete therapeutic transformation after he has been treated by the Reichian King Dahfu of the Wariri. Bellow adopts the fictional strategy of having the patient himself (who insists that the world's wrath has been somehow removed from him, who knows he suffers but doesn't know why, who realizes he has been cured but doesn't really know how) narrate the highlights of his journey to spiritual and physical health. This device enabled Bellow to get away from dry psycho-analytic terminology and psychological jargon, so that the novel is not reduced to a case history. Also, it allowed him to disguise the therapeutic process and dissolve it into fantastic farce. Further, though Henderson has had the experience, he probably missed some of its deeper meaning and it is the reader who has to supply this meaning by aligning his perspective with the Reichian slant of the novel.

Structurally, *Henderson the Rain King* can be divided into three parts that indicate the separate stages of Henderson's struggles towards therapeutic salvation. The first section, set for the most part in America, presents the signs of Henderson's illness in chaotic fashion; in the Arnewi section a preliminary diagnosis is made

but the patient's leap into disastrous action compels him to leave
before treatment; at the end of the Wariri section, which takes up
two-thirds of the novel, we are shown a radiant Henderson in
harmony with himself and with the world around him.

The first four chapters take us into the chaotic state of the
protagonist. His condition does provoke laughter, but to the
reader who knows his Reich it is a case that cries out for treatment. Consider the Gargantua that is Henderson: "Six feet four
inches tall. Two hundred and thirty pounds. An enormous head,
rugged, with hair like Persian lambs' fur. Suspicious eyes, usually
narrowed. Blustering ways. A great nose."[4] Consider, also, his
plight. He is a millionaire, fifty-five, a successful breeder of pigs,
intensely dissatisfied both with himself and with the world he lives
in. He is always a-quarreling: he provokes fights with almost
everyone he comes in contact with. He brawls and curses his way
through life, explodes with sudden anger, and sometimes breaks
into tears, weighed down with suffering and inexplicable misery.
He knows that he "is considered crazy, and with good reason—
moody, rough, tyrannical, and probably mad" (4).

More significant, from the Reichian point of view, than these
obvious tokens of aggression and disorder are the hidden symptoms that erupt without warning or explanation. Death, even the
idea of death, fills him with intense horror: the octopus at Ban-
yules threatens him with death; the death of Mrs. Lennox terrifies
him into thinking of the grave and of the annihilation that awaits
him. Nature, instead of filling him with peace and joy, intensifies
his misery: "The crimson begonias, and the dark green and the
radiant green and the spice that pierces and the sweet gold and
the dead transformed, the brushing of the flowers on my under-
surface are just misery to me" (29). He suffers from a pressure in
his chest. Also, all through the first section, Henderson keeps
referring to and recalling his father: the violin playing is a desperate attempt to reach out to his dead father; when he goes to
France, he lives at Albi where his father had done some research
for a book on the Albigensians; he got his M.A. and he married
his first wife, Frances, merely to please his father. Obviously, the

<hr/>

[4] Saul Bellow, *Henderson the Rain King* (New York: Viking Press, 1965), p. 4.
Hereafter, page numbers will be cited in the text.

relation with his father has something to do with Henderson's restless condition. What the condition is will become apparent later.

Perhaps the most striking of the symptoms of Henderson's illness is the clamorous, insistent voice that arises from the disturbance in his heart. The words that this voice utters, *I want, I want,* have been taken from William Blake,[5] but the voice itself, with its furious energy and its passionate demand, is a comic dramatization of the central premise in Reichian theory, the existence of orgone energy.

As a metaphor for the mysterious life force, orgone energy goes beyond Freud's "id," Aristotle's "entelechy," Bergson's "élan vital," and Kepler's "vis animalis." For Reich, this energy was not a mere concept but *"a visible, measurable and applicable energy of a cosmic nature."*[6] It was an energy that pervaded and permeated all of nature. More significant, it was the living principle in every human being. Reich tells us that he arrived at his discovery of the orgone by a slow process that culminated in 1939. *"The cosmic orgone energy,"* he wrote, *"functions in the living organism as specific biological energy.* As such, it governs the total organism and expresses itself in the emotions as well as the purely biophysical organ movements" (SW, 145). Reich interpreted the word "emotion" not in terms of the psyche but literally as a "moving out" and defined it in terms of sensation and movement as *"an expressive plasmatic motion"* (SW, 146). For Reich, man's psychic apparatus is inextricably linked up with orgone energy, which manifests itself in plasmatic currents and emotions within man and which propels him to expressive movement.

Unfortunately, this living energy in man is dammed up by his muscular structure. Armor blocks in man prevent its natural, spontaneous streaming forth. Reich defines muscular armor as "the sum total of the muscular attitudes (chronic muscular spasms) which an individual develops as a block against the break-

[5] Michael Allen, "Idiomatic Language in Two Novels by Saul Bellow," *Journal of American Studies,* I, 2 (1967), 275–280, and Irving Stock, "The Novels of Saul Bellow," *Southern Review,* N.S. 3 (Winter 1967), 13–42, both refer to this fact.

[6] Wilhelm Reich, *Character Analysis* (Third, enlarged edition, New York: Farrar, Straus and Giroux, 1971), p. 304. Hereafter cited as CA. Other works of Reich mentioned in the text are: *Selected Writings: An Introduction to Orgonomy* (New York: Farrar, Straus and Giroux, 1970), cited as SW; and *The Discovery of the Orgone: The Function of the Orgasm* (New York: Noonday Press, 1970), cited as DO.

through of emotions and organ sensations, in particular anxiety, rage, and sexual excitation" (SW, 10).

One can now just begin to understand the strange plight of Henderson. The surging and searching orgone force imprisoned within his monumental self (somatically speaking, as King Dahfu says) clamors for release. That is the secret of his tremendous but misguided strength. That explains his bursts of uncontrollable rage. That is why he suffers from a pressure in his chest. All these are manifestations of the energy bottled up within Henderson. They are eruptions of the life force that produce strange behavioral distortions. Henderson tries several remedies for his condition: violin playing, pig breeding, violent cursing and yelling. None of these work. The only person who tames the demanding voice for a short while is his second wife, Lily.

Bellow carefully and subtly establishes the importance of Lily, using her as an anchoring reference all through the novel. Henderson goes away from her to Africa, but it is to her that he returns finally. She is in his thoughts all through his strange African safari. Lily is the one who intuitively understands him, who knows he is the only man for her ("You ought to divorce your wife," she tells him at their very first meeting), who, unlike his first wife, is not surprised when Henderson tells her he wants to enter medical school. With her painful teeth, her face with its pure white color which darkens toward the eyes, and the baking odor that arises from her during their love making, Lily is the first person who can assuage the turmoil in Henderson's heart. She is a Reichian without knowing it: " 'Maybe I'm not all there and I don't understand,' she said. 'But when we're together, I *know*' " (18–19). Hers is a knowledge that proceeds from her love. But she cannot help Henderson to wisdom, for she is neither a teacher nor a therapist. She tends to moralize: " 'One can't live for this but has to live for that; not evil but good; not death but life; not illusion but reality' " (16). All these truths Henderson will arrive at in Africa, and perhaps that is why Lily does not object to his going there: " 'Maybe you ought to go,' she said" (40).

The adventures that befall Henderson in Arnewiland are merely a prelude to his soul-shattering experiences among the Wariri. The five Arnewi chapters are important, however, for

Bellow's strategy as a novelist. For one thing, they introduce and accustom the reader to Bellow's Africa and establish its fictional reality. Also, the Arnewi section allows Bellow to elaborate on significant physical symptoms of Henderson's illness and to indicate the armor blocks that prevent the free flow of the orgone energy within him.

The Arnewi section reinforces the fact that Henderson has the build of a gnarled giant. He presents a strange appearance to Queen Willatale. Itelo interprets her reactions thus: " 'You weight maybe a hundred-fifty kilogram; your face have many colors. You are built like a old locomotif. Very strong, yes, I know. Sir, I concede. But so much flesh as a big monument . . . ' " (83). Henderson bewails his physical condition: "But the condition! Oh, my condition! First and last that condition!" (65). The sadness that weighs down on him has made him physically tough and heavy, so that his movements are sluggish and awkward. He refers to the different areas of his body and tells us how they react in times of stress and trouble. His pendulous belly is hard and tough. He butts Itelo with it during their wrestling match and knocks him down. When he is profoundly moved by Queen Willatale's words of wisdom, he feels the hardness of his belly melting and a strange pleasure resulting therefrom. Also, when he broods about his condition, he suffers from a recurring pressure in his chest: "This again smote me straight on the spirit, and I had all the old difficulty, thinking of my condition. A crowd of facts came upon me with accompanying pressure in the chest" (76).

Perhaps the most striking of Henderson's anatomical features is his huge, cartoon face: "My face is like some sort of terminal; it's like Grand Central, I mean—the big horse nose and the wide mouth that opens into the nostrils, and eyes like tunnels" (51). His emotions proclaim themselves on his face: "Whole crowds of them, especially the bad ones, wave to the world from the galleries of my face" (53). In moments of stress and tension his face gets overheated, his great nose (a Jewish Joke, this) puffs out and reddens, and his jaws begin to swell.

Henderson, in Reichian terms, is an armored individual in dire need of orgone therapy. The basic task of such therapy is to destroy muscular armor, to reestablish plasma mobility, and to dissolve the attitude of holding back. In order to grasp the full force of this therapy, one needs to know the emotionally significant organs of the body. Reichian muscular blocks are not the same as individual muscles or nerves. Reichian therapy involves an understanding of the segmental structure of the muscular armor. The human body, according to Reich, can be divided into seven segments (ocular, oral, neck, chest, diaphragmatic, abdominal, and pelvic) separated by armor rings at right angles to the spine. The orgone energy streams longitudinally from the center of the organism along the body axis, but is inhibited by the armor rings that block the orgonotic stream. The orgonotic current flows from the tail end over the back to the head, and then runs backward over the chest and abdomen toward the genitals.

The therapeutic process starts with the progressive dissolution of the upper four armor rings (beginning with the ocular/oral rings) apparent to any observer and even to the patient himself. The lower three armor segments, the diaphragm, the abdomen, and the pelvis, are not readily accessible or obvious and are difficult to dissolve. Therefore, according to Reich, "since the body of the patient is held back and since the goal of orgone therapy is that of reestablishing the plasmatic currents in the pelvis, it is necessary to start the dissolution of the armor in the regions farthest away from the pelvis. Thus, the work begins with the facial expressions" (SW, 158).

Henderson's predicament and his pathologic symptoms now become a little clearer in the light of Reichian physiology. The life force within him has been trapped by segmental armor rings which have transformed his body into "a gross old human trunk" (68), into a "great pine whose roots have crossed and choked one another" (107). The abdominal ring is the cause of the hardness of his belly. His chest armor produces a pressure within him. "In certain patients," Reich writes, "we meet a syndrome stemming from the armoring of the chest which produces a particularly complicated system of difficulties. These patients complain, typically, of a 'knot' in the chest" (SW, 165–166). The face of Henderson, with its various colors, its mobility, its expressiveness, and its distortions, is the biological region where the energy, especially in the form of aggressive rage, manifests itself clearly.

Perhaps the easiest way to grasp the armored plight of Henderson is to contrast his character structure with that of

Queen Willatale. According to Itelo, the queen has risen above ordinary human limitations. In Reichian terms, she has no pathological armor. With her smile, the happy light in her eye, the supple movement of her forehead, the stable harmony of her body, she breathes forth orgone energy: "Good nature emanated from her; it seemed to puff out on her breath as she sat smiling with many small tremors of benevolence and congratulation and welcome" (71). There is no ocular ring segment in her for she can furrow up "her brow in that flexible way peculiar to the Arnewi as a whole, which let the hemisphere of the eye be seen, purely, glistening with human intention" (82). Her heart is not in turmoil: when Henderson's hand is placed between her breasts, as a form of greeting, he feels "on the top of everything else, I mean the radiant heat and the monumental weight which my hand received, there was the calm pulsation of her heart participating in the introduction. This was as regular as the rotation of the earth, and it was a surprise to me; my mouth came open and my eyes grew fixed as if I were touching the secrets of life" (72). Not only is she in harmony with her being as a Bittah, she is also in tune with the universe.

More mysterious and forceful in their impact on Henderson are the heat and power that radiate from Queen Willatale's middle. Henderson gives her a ceremonial kiss on her yielding belly:

> Then I kissed, giving a shiver at the heat I encountered. The knot of the lion's skin was pushed aside by my face which sank inward. I was aware of the old lady's navel and her internal organs as they made sounds of submergence. I felt as though I were riding in a balloon above the Spice Islands, soaring in hot clouds while exotic odors arose from below. My own whiskers pierced me inward, in the lip. . . . I drew back from the significant experience (having made contact with a certain power—unmistakable!—which emanated from the woman's middle). [74]

Twice Henderson experiences this strange power: "A second time my face sank in her belly, that great saffron swelling with the knot of lion skin sinking also, and I felt the power emanating again. I was not mistaken" (77). The power is, of course, orgone energy streaming through the genitals. According to Reich, "*genital excitation* is orgone energy pressing forward at the tail end" (SW, 349). In Henderson the flow of this energy is reversed when he is about to hurl the homemade bomb into the Arnewi water cistern: "And meanwhile all the chemistry of anxious fear, which I know so well and hate so much, was taking place in me—the light wavering before my eyes, the saliva drying, *my parts retracting*, and the cables of my neck hardening" (107, my italics).

The orgone energy of Queen Willatale pours onto Henderson's armored condition. " 'Now please tell the queen for me, friend, that it does wonderful things for me simply to see her. I don't know whether it's her general appearance or the lion skin or what I feel emanating from her—anyway, it puts my soul at rest,' " he tells Itelo (81). Queen Willatale offers Henderson three significant truths: she gives him an insight into his own condition, she makes a statement about human longing, and she presents Henderson with a cryptic message to decipher.

She tells him, first, that he is a man who loves sensations: " 'You heart is barking' " (82). Sensation is a highly significant term in Reichian vocabulary. It is a human antenna, according to Reich, a tester of reality, a tool of natural research. This sensory apparatus has to be kept clean by continuous self-criticism and self-control. Only then can we "feel out, investigate, arrange, and understand ourselves and nature around us" (SW, 292). Henderson is a man of sensations; hence his quest for, among other things, reality. But his tool has become irrationally blurred. That is why he is not really in touch with reality even though he announces he is to Lily: " 'I know more about reality than you'll ever know. I am on damned good terms with reality, and don't you forget it' " (36).

Grun-tu-molani, man wants to live, Queen Willatale tells Henderson. This piece of wisdom, in Reichian terms, is the "life function": the purpose of all life, animal and human, is just to live, to be. The third Willatale truth, "world is strange to a child" (84), is misinterpreted by Henderson, although he does begin with a true insight: " 'All my decay has taken place upon a child' " (84). Henderson goes off at a tangent about the relation between the strangeness of life and death. "I was pretty proud of myself," he tells us, as the Arnewi queen shakes her head softly. "Perhaps admiringly," says Henderson, misreading the import of her gesture. Henderson is a rash person. He destroys the Arnewi cistern and with it his hopes of learning wisdom from Queen Willatale.

The blowing-up of the cistern is a dramatic incident that is also a clever transitional device, a piece of skillful craftsmanship. It enables Bellow to take his protagonist out of the older, simpler Arnewi world to the more complex, more savage, more modern Wariri universe. It also allows Bellow to remove Henderson from the sphere of Queen Willatale's influence in order to suggest that her impact on him is somehow limited. For Henderson's condition is such that words and advice cannot really be effective. According to Reich, word language and concepts cannot penetrate the pathological depth-forms of expression. To understand one's condition intellectually is not enough. What Henderson needs is a more savage and a more dynamic form of therapy. He could not be cured by Lily with her love and her moralizing. Nor does Queen Willatale with her sympathy and her genital power and her grun-tu-molani help him.

It is King Dahfu of the Wariri who treats Henderson, cures him, educates him, and guides him to truth and vision. Dahfu is a magnificent creation, a strange synthesis of King Gelele of Dahomey,[7] of William Blake, and above all, of Wilhelm Reich. One needs to know something about the life and achievements of Reich in order to appreciate the Bellow triumph that is King Dahfu.

What Henderson says about King Dahfu is surely what Bellow thinks of Wilhelm Reich: "And it is possible that he lost his head, and that he was carried away by his ideas. This was because he was no mere dreamer but one of those dreamer-doers, a guy with a program. And when I say that he lost his head, what I mean is not that his judgment abandoned him but that his enthusiasms and visions swept him far out" (235). Reich was a revolutionary thinker and psycho-analyst whose ideas are only now being taken seriously. A brilliant eccentric, he tossed around original concepts and insights almost in the way King Dahfu played, quite seriously, with the skulls of his ancestors during the rainmaking ceremonies.

Reich began as a disciple of Freud but modified and later abandoned Freudian theory to announce new and daring discoveries derived from his psychotherapeutic practice, clinical obser-

[7] See "Bellow's Africa," p. 255.

vation, and scientific explorations. In the nineteen twenties he developed his method of character analysis and set down his technique and his findings in *Character Analysis* (1933). This book, which T. P. Wolfe has hailed as a milestone in psychoanalysis, contains rich psychological material: it defines character as "essentially a narcissistic protection machine" (CA, 158); it sets forth the technique of analysis; it describes the formation of character and the process by which the character armor can be loosened and dissolved; it presents different clinical character types (the hysterical, the compulsive, the phallic-narcissistic, the masochistic character forms); it distinguishes between the genital character and the inhibited neurotic character; and it establishes the therapeutic goal as the liberation of psychic energy and the attainment of orgastic potency.

In the 1930s Reich moved swiftly away from depth psychology and character analysis. Convinced of the inseparability of the psyche and the soma in man, he developed the technique of "vegetotherapy," a method of working simultaneously on the psychic and the somatic apparatus in order to liberate the vegetative energy trapped within the organism by muscular rigidity. But he was not happy with the term "vegetative": it was a correct term in German, he wrote, but made one think of vegetables in English.[8] His difficulties were solved with the discovery in 1939 of orgone energy, the specific life energy that is a physical reality and that flows through both man and nature.

It was the aim of orgone therapy, a term which after 1939 subsumed both character analysis and vegetotherapy, to free this bio-energy from the muscular blocks within man. To achieve this goal, words and language were completely abandoned during the therapeutic process: action was substituted for talking, and there was often dramatic interplay between the patient and his biotherapist. Reich advocated a slow dissolving of the biophysical armor. Massage was frequently used, rigid muscles were stimulated, and breathing exercises, especially expiration, were insisted on. At times Reich would indulge in violent mimicry of a patient's behavior in order to force a response and a breakthrough: "I would

[8] CA, p. 358. Bellow has Henderson refer to this term thus: "He [King Dahfu] kept talking about vegetal functions, some such term, and he lost me every other sentence" (p. 238).

imitate his attitude. I began to use his infantile language. I lay on the floor and kicked and yelled as he did. At first he was surprised, but one day he began to laugh, in an absolutely adult and unneurotic way; a breakthrough, although only temporary, had succeeded" (CA, 225).

Reich's discovery of orgone energy propelled him to Dahfu-like enthusiasms and far-reaching visions. He was fired with an impossible dream, that of transforming man and human society and even the very universe in which man lived. He advocated experimental orgone therapy for the treatment of cancer. In 1940 he invented the orgone energy accumulator, an orgone box to treat people and cure them of psychic and physical disturbances. In the early 1950s he wrote about orgone physics and about cosmic orgone engineering. He performed experiments to show how the inorganic could be transformed into the organic: the forms of transition were known as bions or energy vesicles blue in color. In 1952 he announced in the *Orgone Energy Bulletin* that it "has become possible to *apply the principle of orgonomic potential to the dissolution and formation of clouds" (SW, 433)*, showing that it was possible both to create clouds and to destroy them to produce rain. Perhaps the most sweepingly ambitious of his ideas was one parallel to the concept of Atman equals Brahman of the Upanishadic thinkers: *"THE SAME ENERGY WHICH GOVERNS THE MOVEMENTS OF ANIMALS AND THE GROWTH OF ALL LIVING SUBSTANCE ALSO ACTUALLY MOVES THE HEAVENLY BODIES" (SW, 289).*

Henderson the Rain King, it is apparent, is so completely charged with Reichianism that almost every page, every narrative sequence, every piece of description is full of it. The reader fails to sense it at times because Bellow has transformed and successfully disguised it. One example of such subtle disguise is the Reichian landscape Henderson encounters in Africa. Arnewiland is obviously not a geographical region: "And I believed that there was something between the stones and me. The mountains were naked, and often snakelike in their forms, without trees, and you could see the clouds being born on the slopes. From this rock came vapor, but it was not like ordinary vapor, it cast a brilliant shadow" (46). Despite the aromatic dust and the drouth, there is luster and sparkle all around, a sure sign of the presence of orgone energy. The river boulders look like lumps of gold; the thatched huts give off an inanimate radiance. The people themselves, meek and mild like their cattle, have eyes that are framed with darkness (one is forced to remember Lily's strange eyes) while the palms of their hands have the color of freshly washed granite. "As if, you know, they had played catch with the light and some of it had come off," comments Henderson (50). The air above the village of these children of light is blue: "The air was as still as if it were knotted to the zenith and stuck there, parched and blue, a masterpiece of midday beauty" (57). When Mtalba woos Henderson she dances by a bluish moonlight. For Reich, the color of orgone energy was blue. Arnewiland clearly is permeated with this energy but the Arnewi do not know how to harness it and put it to use.

The Wariri, in contrast, are a warlike people, familiar with death and violence. Their landscape is harsh: "Mesas and hot granites and towers and acropolises held onto the earth; I mean they gripped it and refused to depart with the·clouds which seemed to be trying to absorb them" (113). Henderson smells animal odors in the town. He sees fences of thorn, rocks the size of Pacific man-eating clams, and hot fierce red flowers. He comes across dry, white, calcareous stones: "They were composed of lime and my guess was that they must have originated in a body of water" (116). Water, for Reich, is somehow connected with orgone energy: "Rain clouds, thunder clouds, hurricanes and tornadoes are, seen from the point of orgonomy, different expressions of basically one and the same function, i.e., *combinations of concentrated* OR [gone] *energy streams and water vapors*" (SW, 440). Everything about the Wariri, especially their lack of water, proclaims the fact that their land lacks orgone energy. They require a miracle of cosmic orgone engineering to end the drouth. The miracle-worker—" 'The view of the Bunam is you have been expected. Also you came in time,' " says King Dahfu (190)—will be Henderson, who is fated to help the Wariri and become the Sungo, the rain king, before he himself can be helped and treated by King Dahfu.

Henderson, of course, is bursting with orgone energy. In the Wariri section, Bellow accelerates references to the strange directions this energy takes in Henderson, to familiarize the reader once more with its workings. One begins to recognize the fact that Henderson's face is powerfully affected when he controls the rage that boils within him:

> This face, which sometimes appears to me to be as big as the
> entire body of a child, is always undergoing transformations
> making it as busy, as strange and changeful, as a creature of
> the tropical sea lying under a reef, now the color of carna-
> tions and now the color of a sweet potato, challenging, act-
> ing, harkening, pondering, with all the human passions at
> the point of doubt—I mean the humanity of them lying in
> doubt. A great variety of expressions was thus hurdling my
> nose from eye to eye and twisting my brows. I had good
> cause to hold my temper and try to behave moderately. (131)

Any inhibited aggressive impulse, according to Reich, directs the
energy towards the musculature of the peripheral extremities
where it becomes manifest. Anxiety and fear, however, reverse
the flow of the excitation so that the direction is towards the
center of the organism. One can now understand what happens to
Henderson under the stress of terror. His fever increases, there is
a strain at the back of his neck and in his eyes, and he feels as if
his nose will burst: "Dread and some of the related emotions will
often approach me by way of the nose" (134–135). When he sees
the black corpse in the hut the orgonotic flow in Henderson beats
back in wild fashion: "The entire right side of me grew stiff as if
paralyzed, and I could not even bring my lips together. As if the
strange medicine of fear had been poured down my nose crook-
edly and I began to cough and choke" (134).

On the day of the Wariri rain festival, however, Henderson's
energy gains momentum. He feels "a scratchy sensation in my
bosom, a little like eagerness or longing. In the nerves between
my ribs this was especially noticeable" (145). After Turombo's
failure, the energy asserts its imperatives in bodily signs: "I was
excited to the bursting point. I swelled. I was sick, and my blood
circulated peculiarly through my body—it was turbid and ecstatic
both. It prickled within my face, especially in the nose, as if it
might begin to discharge itself there. And as though a crown of
gas were burning from my head, so I was tormented" (187). Im-
pelled by the powerful stirring within him, Henderson lifts
Mummah, the female power, a wooden Queen Willatale, an abode
of orgone energy, one who "smelled like a living old woman.
Indeed to me she was a living personality, not an idol" (192).

After he lifts her an explosion bursts through Henderson's armor blocks:

> I stood still. There beside Mummah in her new situation I myself was filled with happiness. I was so gladdened by what I had done that my whole body was filled with soft heat, with soft and sacred light. The sensations of illness I had experienced since morning were all converted into their opposites. These same unhappy feelings were changed into warmth and personal luxury. . . . I have also known a stomach complaint to melt from my belly and turn into a delightful heat and go down into the genitals. This is the way I am. And so my fever was transformed into jubilation. My spirit was awake and it welcomed life anew. Damn the whole thing! Life anew! I was still alive and kicking and I had the old grun-tu-molani. (192–193)

Henderson's feat of lifting and carrying Mummah causes clouds to form in the windless sky. This is no African mumbo-jumbo but a direct consequence of cosmic orgone engineering. Bellow's creative magic is in evidence here. The rain-making ceremonies seem to belong to a primitive Africa and may appear to have been derived from Bellow's anthropological reading, but they are in fact a vivid and comic dramatization of the Reichian method of "cloud-busting" and rain making.

"One may create clouds in the cloud-free sky," writes Reich, "in a certain manner, *by disturbing the evenness in the distribution of the atmospheric OR energy*; thus clouds appear upon drawing energy from the air." (SW, 444) Cosmic orgone potential always flows from a weak or low system to a strong or high one. At Orgonon, Reich's home and research laboratory in Rangeley, Maine, he caused long hollow pipes to be aimed at the cloud-free sky in order to draw off OR energy: *"The OR charges are drawn* (not into the ground but) *into* WATER, preferably into *flowing* water of brooks, flowing lakes and rivers. We draw into water since the attraction is greater between water and OR energy than between other elements and OR energy. Water not only attracts OR speedily but it also holds it, as especially in clouds" (SW, 442).

The Reichian principles behind some of the Wariri rain-making rituals, behind priming the pumps of the firmament as

Dahfu puts it, now become clear. It is obvious why Henderson is flung into the cattle pond. He has increased the OR potential of the Wariri region and therefore clouds are drawn toward Wariri-land. Bellow clearly indicates that Henderson is a Reichian "hollow pipe" by making Henderson describe the peculiar shape the rain clouds assume, those "colossal tuberous forms" (200). "And meanwhile the sky was filling with hot, gray, long shadows, rain clouds, but to my eyes of an abnormal form, pressed together like organ pipes or like the ocean ammonites of Paleozoic times" (199). Even more clear now is the magnetic interaction, almost sexual in character, between the cosmic and the individual orgone energies:

> Under the thickened rain clouds, a heated, darkened breeze sprang up. It had a smoky odor. This was something oppressive, insinuating, choky, sultry, icky. Desirous, the air was, and it felt tumescent, heavy. It was very heavy. It yearned for discharge, like a living thing. . . . I felt like Vesuvius, all the upper part flame and the blood banging upward like the pitch or magma. (200)

Henderson's summoning forth of his orgone energy does wonders for the Wariri but does not help him at all. He requires elaborate therapy that only King Dahfu can provide. King Dahfu is a magnificent creation, a powerful figure who threatens to run away with the novel's meaning. Bellow endows him with a great deal of charm, nobility, and vigor. To make him human and to hint at a slightly eccentric Reich, Bellow bestows upon the king a name that has overtones of "daftness."

King Dahfu, unlike Henderson, has orgone energy that flows naturally and easily through his body. He is the greatest of the Reichians in the novel and Bellow, in a suggestive paragraph, brings in the other two to highlight the fact that only Dahfu could be Henderson's doctor-teacher:

> Like all people who have a strong gift of life, he gave off almost an extra shadow—I swear. It was a smoky something, a charge. I used to notice it sometimes with Lily and was aware of it particularly that day of the storm in Danbury when she misdirected me to the water-filled quarry and then telephoned her mother from bed. She had it noticeably then.

It is something brilliant and yet overcast; it is smoky, bluish, trembling, shining like jewel water. It was similar to what I had felt also arising from Willatale on the occasion of kissing her belly. But this King Dahfu was more strongly supplied with it than any person I ever met. (209)

King Dahfu is Bellow's translation into the living, the human, and the concrete of Wilhelm Reich's abstract statement about the genital character: "Purely from the point of view of appearance, sexual charm goes with a relaxed musculature and free-flowing psychic activity. The rhythm of the motions, the *alternation* of muscular tension and relaxation, combines with modulation in speech and general musicality; in such people one also has the feeling of immediate psychic contact" (CA, 348).

The numerous details about King Dahfu now fall into place and gain added significance. His figure is elegant; he is always sumptuously at rest; he breathes deeply and watches events with impervious calm; he moves with powerful grace during the skull-tossing game as he "ran and jumped like a lion, full of power, and he looked magnificent" (114); his voice is hypnotic and reminds Henderson of the hum of a New York power station; above all, Dahfu gives Henderson the impression that they could "approach ultimates together" (156). His face proclaims that he is not an armored individual: it slopes forward, it isn't held back; his eyes are "huge, soft, eccentric" (168), unlike Henderson's tunnel-like eyes, and they gleam with a soft light; there is a continuous smile on his lips which are large, red and tumid; and on his head, says Henderson, hair did not grow, it lived. Henderson immediately senses the difference between his own condition and that of the king: "He seemed all ease, and I was all limitation. He was extended, floating; I was contracted and cramped. The undersides of my knees were sweating. Yes, he was soaring like a spirit while I sank like a stone" (160). It is this regal creature who will transform Henderson into a new man.

The therapeutic process by which Henderson is treated is the climactic core of the novel, the section in which Bellow's creative energy asserts itself triumphantly. The therapy sessions are totally farcical and uproariously funny: Henderson being investigated by the lioness—"I felt her muzzle touch upward first at my armpits, and then between my legs, which naturally made the member there shrink into the shelter of my paunch" (222); Henderson, whose vocal cords "seemed stuck together like strands of over-cooked spaghetti" (266), trying to roar like a lion; Henderson clumping and pounding along trying to imitate Atti's graceful leaps but sinking flat on his hard belly. Bellow allows his imagination to go for broke and indulge in comic horseplay. Reichian technique is turned topsy-turvy. Character-analysis, vegeto-therapy, and orgone therapy jostle against each other as they are put to strange use. Reich's fantastic action therapy is made even more fantastic by having a lioness as therapeutic agent. And the effects of this therapy are wonderfully strange. Beneath the riotous surface of the narrative, however, is Bellow's subtle control over the stages of Henderson's transformation.

The talk sessions between King Dahfu and Henderson serve several important functions. They allow Bellow to project his own ideas (some derived from Blake) about man, his greatness, and his nobility. They also allow Bellow to project Reichian concepts and offer the reader a deeper diagnosis of Henderson's condition.

Reich's clinical character forms are obviously the basis for King Dahfu's catalogue of character types: " 'The agony. The appetite. The obstinate. The immune elephant. The shrewd pig. The fateful hysterical. The death-accepting. The phallic-proud or hollow genital. The fast asleep. The narcissus intoxicated. The mad laughers. The pedantics. The fighting Lazaruses' " (217). Reichian concepts are scrubbed clean of jargon and presented in lay terms: "Disease is a speech of the psyche" (238); "the spirit of the person in a sense is the author of his body" (238). King Dahfu's statement about " 'the flesh influencing the mind, the mind influencing the flesh, back again to the mind, once more to the flesh' " (236), is a free and easy rendering of the Reichian idea of the indissoluble organic unity of the psyche and the soma. Dahfu, of course, takes the idea to a comic, impossible extreme by maintaining that a " 'pimple on a lady's nose may be her own idea, accomplished by a conversion at the solemn command of her psyche' " (237).

The therapy is at once Reichian and homeopathic. Fear is treated by fear as Henderson faces for the first time the stern impersonal countenance of wrath, of death, that he has always avoided. The terror Atti produces in him hurls itself against his armor. An explosion occurs in his chest and he begins to cough. An electric shock passes through him when he is made to touch Atti: "The bones of the hand became incandescent. After this a frightful shock passed right up the arm into the chest" (227).

The loosening of Henderson's armor has begun. According to Reich, resistances exert their pressure as soon as therapy begins. Henderson's whole system resists the dissolution of his protection machine and all the orifices begin to shut: "I stood there half deaf, half blind, with my throat closing and all the sphincters shut" (224). King Dahfu describes in comic detail the anxiety reactions of Henderson: " 'I love when your brows move. They are really ex-traordnary. And your chin gets like a peach stone, and you have a very strangulation color and facial swelling, and your mouth spread very wide. And when you cried! I adored when you began to cry' " (228).

King Dahfu urges Henderson to imitate the rhythmic behavior of Atti, the fluid movements of her supple body: " 'Moreover, observe Atti. Contemplate her. How does she stride, how does she saunter, how does she lie or gaze or rest or breathe? I stress the respiratory part,' he said. 'She do not breath shallow. This freedom of the intercostal muscles and her abdominal flexibility . . . gives the vital continuity between her parts' " (260). This neo-Stanislavski method will establish vital continuity in Henderson's own system, will make him in tune with the universe:

> "Now, sir, will you assume a little more limberness? You appear cast in one piece. The midriff dominates. Can you move the different portions? Minus yourself of some of your heavy reluctance of attitude. Why so sad and so earthen? Now you are a lion. Mentally, conceive of the environment. The sky, the sun, and creatures of the bush. You are related to all. The very gnats are your cousins. The sky is your thoughts. The leaves are your insurance, and you need no other. There is no interruption all night to the speech of the stars." (266)

Only then, suggests King Dahfu, will the change that Henderson desires occur: " 'You could be noble. Some parts may be so long-buried as to be classed dead. Is there any resurrectibility in them? This is where the change comes in' "(261).

The impact of Dahfuian therapy on Henderson assumes strange manifestations. The king consoles him by telling him that " 'sometimes a conditon must worsen before bettering' " (275). Reich states that a breakdown of personality "is inevitable before a new, rational personality structure can develop" (SW, 98). Bellow's strategy, whereby the "shot in the arm from animal nature" (251) uncovers and releases pig elements in Henderson instead of transforming him into a lion, is a stroke of comic genius. Bellow evokes the very last note of farcical laughter from every situation: Henderson emitting suspicious noises that sound more like grunts than roars; Henderson touching his eyelashes surreptitiously wondering whether they have turned into bristles; Henderson stretched out "from the trotters to the helmet," lying on the ground, heaving and groaning and grunting. Perhaps Bellow did pick up a suggestion of this comic transformation from Reich who hints at such a possibility: "The total bodily expression can usually be put into a formula which sooner or later in the course of the character-analytic work appears sponta- neously. Peculiarly enough, such a formula is usually derived from the animal kingdom, like 'fox,' 'pig,' 'snake,' 'worm,' etc." (DO, 269).

Despite such alarming manifestations, a deep upheaval goes on within Henderson, and Bellow gives us many clues to this fact. Black curls begin to sprout on Henderson's head; he becomes strangely sensitive to the clamoring color of flowers; his beard has grown like a broom; he begins involuntarily to spout forth the French he knew as a child. The letter to Lily, a skillful fictional device, allows Henderson to explain directly what has happened to him. He has been called forth *"from non-existence to existence"* (284). He has matured "twenty years in twenty days" (282). Atti's face is now no longer an object of wrath, but a thing of beauty, pure fire like the stars. A Marvellian peace descends upon him at times: *"It is very early in life, and I am out in the grass. The sun flames and swells; the heat it emits is its love, too. I have this self-same vividness in my heart. There are dandelions. I try to gather up this green. I put my love-swollen cheek to the yellow of the dandelions. I try to enter the green"* (283). One notices the strange phrase, "very early in life." One remembers that formerly the beauty of nature was sheer misery to Henderson.

Henderson has changed, but the therapeutic process is not complete. With marvelous fictional tact, Bellow interweaves the final moments of Henderson's therapy with the final moments of King Dahfu's lion day. The reader, in suspense as to what will befall the king, may overlook what happens to Henderson. King Dahfu, eager to capture Gmilo, climbs up to the hopo-platform, all afire with orgone energy: Henderson sees "the smoky, bluish trembling of his extra shadow" (295); and later, "the blue of the atmosphere seemed to condense" about King Dahfu's head (305). As Henderson starts to climb up the ladder, something bubbles out from deep within him: "Illness, strangeness, and danger combined and ganged up on me. Instead of an answer, a sob came out of me. It must have been laid down early in my life, for it was stupendous and rose from me like a great sea bubble from the Atlantic floor" (298). Later, as the King begins to maneuver the net to capture the lion, Henderson feels a "globe" "about the size of a darning egg" (308) rising in his throat. In Reichian terminology, this is a throat spasm and indicates the dissolution of an important block, the chest segment. The armoring of the chest, according to Reich, "was developed at the time of critical conflicts in the life of the child, probably long before the pelvic armor. It is easy to understand, therefore, that the traumatic memories of mistreatments of all kind, of frustrations in love and of *disappointments in parents* (italics mine), appear in the course of dissolving the chest armor" (SW, 167).

Henderson's therapy has ended but the roots of his neurosis have not been uncovered yet. Bellow does not hesitate to use an idea out of early Reich, that "a consistent dissolving of character resistances provides an infallible and immediate avenue of approach to the central infantile conflict" (CA, 48). A footnote, added in 1945, tells us: "In orgone therapy, the pathogenic memories appear *spontaneously* and *without effort* when the somatic emotions break through the muscular armor" (CA, 21).

Henderson is now able to directly recall the origins of his conflict. "Now I understand it," he writes (337). He can now accept and understand his father's disappointment and anger towards him after Dick died. He can now understand that he had violently suppressed his bitterness and his rage against his father (they come out in the form of a sob) on the day of Dick's funeral and expressed them by wrecking old cars and cutting them up with a torch even on the day of the funeral. The reader can now understand the buried logic of Henderson's attempts to please his father and reach out to him on the violin.

Linked up with Henderson's recall of Dick's death and funeral is the memory of Smolak the bear, their roller coaster rides together and their closeness to each other. The comic anxiety about the grunting and the bubbling forth of pig elements is now resolved for Henderson: "So before pigs ever came on my horizon, I received a deep impression from a bear" (338). Smolak the bear probably sprang from Bellow's imagination, but the roller coaster has been imported from the pages of *Character Analysis*, where it is mentioned three times in connection with the fear of falling: "People with inhibited vegetative motility experience them [excitations] as unpleasurable sensations of anxiety or oppression in the solar plexus region. These sensations are very similar to those experienced in fright or with the sudden descent in an elevator or on a roller coaster" (CA, 352). One understands now the reason why Henderson is subject to fits of fainting and to blackouts in elevators (164).

The last pages of *Henderson the Rain King* show us a fully recovered Henderson, who knows now that it is love that makes reality reality, and who is traveling back to Lily, the woman he loves. His spirit's sleep has been broken and he has come to himself. He has recovered his childhood innocence: that is why he speaks oracles and sings nursery and school songs. He now knows how to get along with people without quarreling. He is at peace with himself and sees the world as strange and wonderful, just as Queen Willatale had said it would appear to a child.

Bellow ends his novel with a paragraph that resonates with rich rhythms. " 'Breathe in this air, kid, and get a little color' " (340), says Henderson the Reichian to the orphan, whose eyes reveal the energy within him. Gathering him up in his huge arms, Henderson begins the dance of renewed life, a re-enactment in Newfoundland of the therapeutic dance in the African jungle. But now Henderson is full of flowing orgone energy. No longer is he afraid of death, no longer does he lumber around in awkward fashion; he bounds triumphantly and exultantly like a very lion:

Laps and laps I galloped around the shining and riveted
body of the plane, behind the fuel trucks. Dark faces were
looking from within. The great beautiful propellers were
still, all four of them. I guess I felt it was my turn to move,
and so went running—leaping, leaping, pounding, and tin-
gling over the pure white lining of the gray Arctic silence.
(340–341)

Like orgone energy, Reichianism flows smoothly through
Henderson the Rain King, establishing a vital continuity among the
three sections of the novel. No armor blocks are in evidence, for
Bellow is in absolute control over his fictional material. He can
adapt it, modify it, play with it, poke fun at it, and take it seriously when it suits the needs of his fiction. So complete is Bellow's
creative confidence that he can take up a daring, though apparently exotic, idea of Reich's and introduce it without violating
the surface reality of his narrative. Sitting on the hopo-platform
Henderson sees a strange happening: "The light was finely
grated on the floor. We crouched, waiting under the fibers and
straw. The odor of plants came up on the air-blue heat in gusts,
and because of my fever I had a feeling that I had found, in
midair, a changing point between matter and light. I was watching it being carried from within and thought I saw crying and
writhing outside" (301). What Henderson is witnessing is matter
under-going a process of vesicular disintegration (SW, 201),
breaking into blue bions, forms of transition from inorganic to
organic matter that move with serpentine movements. Bellow has
stripped the Reichian idea clean of technical detail and intro-
duced it quite naturally as a phenomenon that Henderson sees
in the African jungle.

Before one proceeds to criticize and to interpret any novel,
one has to realize how it has been put together. "The integrities
upon which good workmanship depends, and the act of creation
itself, interest critics and scholars very little," complains Bellow.[9]
One cannot, I feel, understand or evaluate *Henderson the Rain
King* without first coming to terms with its Reichianism.

---

[9] "Skepticism and the Depth of Life," *The Arts and the Public,* eds. James E.
Miller and Paul D. Herring (Chicago: University of Chicago Press, 1967), p. 23.

Index

Leonard Tennenhouse is assistant professor of English at Wayne State University. Previously he lectured at the University of Rochester. Mr. Tennenhouse received his B.A. from Wayne State University in 1965 and his doctorate from the University of Rochester in 1969. He has published a number of articles on medieval and Renaissance literature.

The manuscript was prepared for publication by Saundra Blais. The book was designed by Julie Paul. The typeface for the text is Baskerville based upon the original design of John Baskerville in the eighteenth century.

The text is printed on International Bookmark paper and bound in Columbia Mills' Sierra Blanca cottonweave cloth over binders boards. Manufactured in the United States of America.